FLIGHT INTO FEAR

*The stalls were not there, the square deserted,
and loose pillow feathers hung in the air like
snowflakes in the winter. An aged man,
bent in half and carrying a tailor's dummy,
suddenly stood before us.*

"Where is everyone?" asked Mrs. Paizak.

*The old man's eyes slowly widened. "Last
night, in the middle of the night, the Germans
came and took all the Jews away. They
marched them out like a herd of cattle.
There isn't one left."*

*I stared at the man, unable to move or say
anything; then I jumped off the wagon
and began to run . . .*

"The bare bones of this book hold pity and
terror enough"

—NEW YORK TIMES

"Mental and physical sufferings . . . hope
and courage"

—SEATTLE TIMES

CHILD
OF
THE
HOLOCAUST

BY JACK KUPER

CURTIS
BOOKS

MODERN LITERARY EDITIONS PUBLISHING COMPANY
NEW YORK, N.Y.

TO MY WIFE TERRYE,
AND TO MY CHILDREN, ELLEN, MARK, SHAUL, AND SIMCA,
SO THEY WILL KNOW

THE AUTHOR WISHES TO THANK ANTON VAN DALEN,
HARVEY HART AND KURT HELLMER FOR THEIR
ENCOURAGEMENT.

ONE

□ A heavy layer of mist covered the village of Kulik, disclosing a few chimneys and straw rooftops as if they were suspended in the air.

I sat in the back of the wagon clutching the bag of food in my hands and listened to the wheels turning and the horse's trot.

Mrs. Paizak sat in the front holding the reins, her back towards me. "Vio!" she called out to the horse whenever he slowed down, and she would hit him across the back.

The horse, too, could barely be seen, and it seemed as if we were sitting on a cloud, being pulled by some magic force.

Perhaps all this is a dream, I thought. When I wake I'll find Mrs. Paizak and Genia gone.

Every week on market day, Mrs. Paizak would ride into Siedliszcze. She'd sell some produce, buy a dress or pair of shoes, matches, oil, or a spool of thread. Usually Genia would accompany her and I'd be left behind to feed the pigs, the chickens, take care of the cows, and wait impatiently for their return with messages from my mother.

For the first time since leaving home, I was now going to see my mother. There are so many things I want to tell her. How exciting! She'll be so surprised. Probably doesn't even expect me. What will she say when I hand her the bundle and she opens it and discovers a loaf of bread, some potatoes, a small bag of flour, and three eggs?

I pressed this treasure against my body and could see my mother's dark, moist eyes beaming with pride.

The same eyes several weeks earlier had covered my cheeks with tears. "He's only a child, Mrs. Paizak. How can I let him go?"

"I'm not a child anymore," I answered indignantly. "I'm nine."

"You're eight, Jankele," my mother smiled. I lowered my head.

"Well, I'm almost nine, and please, Mommy, don't call me Jankele; my name is Jakob."

The mist settled, and a slow-rising sun appeared in the distance. The countryside now visible was moving away from me. Mud houses with small windows and crooked chimneys from which black smoke rose, were disappearing; here and

9

there a cowherd was taking his flock to pasture; a rooster was waking the village.

In a meadow an old farmer was plowing; on the side of the road an angry dog was barking. Over the roadside hovered a huge dried-out tree, and under it lay a stone on a crudely constructed grave. Buried in the cold ground was my grandfather, but for a moment I now imagined he was running behind our wagon, dressed in his brown leather coat and his hat with earflaps. Icicles hung from his nostrils and beard, and his worn black boots were caked with snow. With one hand he held onto the burlap bag which hung over his right shoulder, while his other hand was outstretched towards me, and he called out, "Jankele wait! I need a ride into town."

Several times Mrs. Paizak turned to look at me, and once she patted the top of my head and winked. I smiled and in a soft voice began to sing a song about an orphaned shepherd boy named Franek:

> Franek takes his cows to pasture,
> And on his flute he plays,
> But what sad, forlorn tones
> Drift, drift across the countryside.

We now crossed a wooden bridge and were soon driving through the winding, narrow streets. It was unusually quiet. Not a soul to be seen except a cat roaming the rooftops. Broken household articles littered the roads, and echoing through the streets was a horrible sound of uncontrollable laughter.

I stared from side to side, then turned to look at Mrs. Paizak. She was staring at me, but quickly turned and faced the horse, lashed him across the back, and called, "Vio!" The horse began to gallop; the wagon jumped and shook along the cobbled road and came to a quick halt in the market square.

The stalls were not there, the square deserted, and loose pillow feathers hung in the air like snowflakes in the winter. Across the street a band of peasants came out of a house carrying a chest of drawers. Another carried a mattress, and a young woman was trying on a coat and circling like a ballerina. An aged man, bent in half and carrying a tailor's dummy, suddenly stood in front of us.

"Where is everyone?" asked Mrs. Paizak.

The old man's eyes slowly widened, he set the dummy down and then answered, "Last night, in the middle of the night, the Germans came and took all the Jews away. They marched them out like a herd of cattle. There isn't one left."

"Dear Jesus!" exclaimed Mrs. Paizak, and made the sign of the cross.

I stared at the man, unable to move or say anything; then suddenly I jumped off the wagon and began to run. My feet pounded the cobbled road and carried me faster than I ever imagined possible. The houses seemed to be removed from their foundations and reclining at different angles; sometimes they appeared to sway from one side to the other and even to turn upside down. Soon they were no more than fast-moving blurs passing in front of my eyes.

Mrs. Paizak, I've left Mrs. Paizak . . . Why am I even thinking about Mrs. Paizak? But what if she needs my assistance? What about Genia? Has she taken the cows to pasture? Why do I persist in thinking about these things?

I finally came to a halt, and now our small, crooked window stood before me. I had hoped to see my little brother Josel's face in it and hear him shout, "Mommy, Mommy, Jankele is home!" But the glass was now shattered and no one looked out from behind it.

Isn't it possible, I began to think, that by some miracle, by some fortunate chance, by an act of God, my family is still inside? Perhaps they hid in the attic, or in the cellar, or under the bed, or maybe the Germans who came to get them took pity and spared them! It's possible, why not?

The door leading to our room now lay broken on the porch, torn from the hinges which once held it. That's only for appearance, I consoled myself, to make it seem that no one lived there. It's possible; in fact, it's very clever.

I entered. A few pots stood on the brick stove. A torn straw mattress lay on the floor, a bed sheet beside it. Several of the floorboards were removed, and in a corner, crumpled and soiled, was a small drawing of Tarzan swinging from a tree.

Uncle Shepsel, I thought. Will I ever see him make drawings of Tarzan again? Will I ever hear his voice keeping me spellbound for hours with tales about cowboys and Indians in a distant, strange land?

"Momma!" I whispered. "Josel, Shepsel . . . don't be afraid, it's safe to come out now."

Under my feet lay two small pieces of fur which I immediately recognized as having once adorned my mother's coat pockets. I picked them up and once more called:

"Josel! Shepsel! Mommy! Please come out, it's Jankele."

I must cry. Why can't I cry? I'll think of onions or the little bird I treasured once, then found dead, its head squeezed between two bars of the cage. I cried then, why can't I cry now? I must cry. What else can I think of? Quickly, something unpleasant has to come to my mind . . .

Suddenly I heard footsteps.

Perhaps it's my mother! It's possible, why not? No, it's probably a German coming to get me. I'll hide . . . but where? No, why hide? I want to be taken with the others. I'll go willingly.

I faced the door. Mrs. Paizak's stocky figure appeared. Her eyes were wet, her head tilted to one side. She made several attempts to say something but nothing came out. She scanned the room, examined the few articles in it, and finally said: "Jakob, we might as well take these." I remained silent. "If we don't, some strangers will grab them," and she gathered the articles in the bed sheet.

She asked about the pieces of fur in my hands, but I refused to part with them and stuffed them into my pocket.

"My mother will be worried about me," I finally said.

"She knows you're in good hands, my child," answered Mrs. Paizak, tying the bed sheet.

"How will I be able to live alone?"

She fell to her knees, held my face in the palms of her hands, and said, "You won't be alone. I'll look after you."

"But there's no one left from my family."

"What about your Uncle Moishe?" she asked. "Isn't he working in some village?"

My Uncle Moishe! How can I find him? Perhaps he was home visiting and was also taken away. How can I find out? Where can I look for him? I have to find him.

My arm was suddenly pulled, and I found myself outside. The looters were now to be seen everywhere, carrying axes and saws, shouting and laughing, and fighting for the spoils.

Outside of town more of them, with empty burlap bags under their arms, were walking briskly towards Siedliszcze, and as they passed us they shouted, "Anything left there, or did you grab everything?"

Again I saw the tree, the grave, the stone, and once more my grandfather Shie Chuen, the shoemaker from Pawia Street in Warsaw, was trudging along the snow-covered road.

Suddenly, a blinding snow storm materialized, and out of it came three German soldiers on horseback, their faces covered in shadow. One German drew his revolver and fired. My grandfather only wavered. The second soldier aimed. A bullet whistled through the air and found its target. The shoemaker groaned, but still stood. The third bullet was the fatal one.

The massive old man in the brown leather coat fell to the ground. The burlap bag flew through the air and out of it fell pieces of bread, frozen potatoes, and shoemaker's tools.

"Have mercy," he whispered, and his lips closed forever.

"Say something, Kubush," I suddenly heard Mrs. Paizak say.

"Kubush? My name isn't Kubush."

"It's the same as Jakob," she answered, "only more fitting for a little boy like you."

I turned my back to her and in choking tones began to sing:

> Kubush takes his cows to pasture,
> And on his flute he plays,
> But what sad, forlorn tones
> Drift, drift across the countryside.
>
> Why such sad melody, poor orphan boy,
> Do you play on your flute?
> Perhaps the world is mistreating you.
> Tell me, tell it to . . .

And then the tears came, and I began to sob.

"Poor boy, poor boy," I heard Mrs. Paizak mutter to herself. The tears filled my eyes and obstructed my vision. The road, the little houses with the straw roofs, seemed to melt.

In the evening, the surrounding neighbors would congregate in Mrs. Paizak's courtyard, and no matter what they began to discuss, it would without fail lead to the Jews.

During my first days at the Paizaks', I had heard them complain about the opportunists, swindlers, connivers, and lice-infested herring merchants who chiseled and swindled them out of their goods and sold them shoes and dresses which fell apart after one outing to church. Now that there was no market in Siedliszcze, no stores, no buyers or sellers, the conversation at the evening gatherings sounded differently.

"You have to travel as far as Lublin now to buy a good dress," one red-faced woman complained.

"Those Jews served a purpose," added another.

Slowly, one by one, they would reminisce, each about his or her favorite Jew who was different from the others.

"Moshek was all right; he sold me a coat twenty years ago and it still looks like the day it was made."

And so it happened that Mrs. Paizak, a Ukrainian, filled the vacuum left by the Jews of Siedliszcze. Equipped with butter, eggs, bread, and other foodstuffs, she traveled to the Warsaw Ghetto, and when she returned several days later, half the village of Kulik would congregate in her small one-room house, with a line stretching from the door to the main road. It was hard to believe that, for the little produce she took with her, she was able to return with so much merchandise: coats, dresses, shoes, underwear, scarves, umbrellas, socks, things made of lace, wool, fine cotton, embroidered pillowcases, pieces of jewelry, fine earrings, and countless other items.

The Jews of Siedliszcze, or for that matter of any town, would have envied her for the brisk business she carried on. The same day she returned, her suitcases would be emptied, and a crowd of angered women would be told that everything was sold, but not to despair, there'd be another batch in two or three days.

I looked at the items being carried out of the house. Articles from the Warsaw Ghetto, bought with a kilogram of butter or a slice of bread, and I would wonder who were the original owners. Perhaps that scarf or that brooch, or maybe this pair of shoes had once belonged to my grandmother, or to one of my aunts, or perhaps even, at one time, to my own mother.

The trips back and forth continued, and now farm women from adjoining villages had heard of Mrs. Paizak, and they too came running, looking for bargains. The lines grew longer, the bartering louder, and I was surprised to see how adept Mrs. Paizak became in her new profession.

She was not the simple, honest farm woman any more, but reminded me of the market women I'd seen on the corner of Pawia and Smocza in Warsaw. If there was a hole in a dress and a prospective customer pointed it out to Mrs. Paizak, she would laugh and say: "That's the style, my dear. It's for ventilation." And the peasant women, who had never worn such fine clothing, took her word for it.

Two gloves of different colors were sold as the latest style in Warsaw; earrings that were costume jewelery were sold as pure gold or silver, or rare diamonds from Africa; and worn-out shoes, faded dresses, and dilapidated coats were gotten rid of for handsome sums by a most unusual method:

"I know it's worn-out, my dear," Mrs. Paizak would say, and then, taking the customer aside, she would whisper confidentially into her ear, "Would you like to guess who this coat belonged to?" The customer would stare in surprise, expecting to hear the world's greatest secret, whereupon Mrs. Paizak would utter a Jewish-sounding name. "Mrs. Blazenblutz herself; of course you've heard of her, my dear." The poor woman had never heard of Mrs. Blazenblutz, and neither had anyone else, but how could she confess her ignorance? In fact she had no time to, for Mrs. Paizak would only give her time enough to take a breath and to say, "Is that a fact!" or "You don't say?" And then add this little gem: "You know of course how rich the Blazenblutzes were! Who knows, maybe something's hidden in this lining, or in the heels of those shoes. I shouldn't really sell it before I have time to examine it myself."

By such methods the item in question was always sold. And even though no one in the village ever found money, gold, or silver in linings, or in the heels of their newly acquired shoes, no one who bought from Mrs. Paizak ever lost hope of becoming rich. Shoes were torn apart and examined; coats were ripped open, searched for treasure, and then resewn.

As time went on, the village had a new look. On Sunday mornings the ladies on their way to church were now attired in high-fashion clothing formerly belonging to the Blazenblutzes, the renowned Tishmans, not to mention the very famous Chuen family, the shoe magnates from Pawia Street.

And so it was with the silk dress. The dress was indeed made of silk, beautiful pale-blue silk, with two delicate narrow straps that held it up at the shoulders. On the left side was embroidered a red rose with a green stem and two green leaves. Mrs. Paizak didn't intend to sell this dress, and had put it aside for Genia. But as it lay there in the corner on the bed, a young girl with long straw-blond braids, about Genia's age, was attracted by it. She wanted it. She had to have it. Was it real silk?

"Yes it is," Mrs. Paizak told her, and then interjected the name of the supposed original owner. But the dress wasn't for sale. She had paid a fantastic price for it, she informed the girl, and added that it was a very rare item, the only one of its kind. The more Mrs. Paizak diverted the girl's attention to other, less attractive dresses, the more the girl fondled her braids; her eyes never really left the silk dress. As a last resort, Mrs. Paizak finally agreed to sell the girl the fine dress, and then quoted her an exorbitant price.

By this time, Genia was put out with her mother for even thinking of selling the dress that was promised her, but Mrs. Paizak soothed her by explaining that it wasn't sold yet, and asking who'd be crazy enough to pay such a price for it.

The girl with the round face and long braids, startled by the price, began to barter. Mrs. Paizak refused to budge one centimeter. The girl picked up the dress, held it in front of her body, and gazed at the oval-shaped mirror on the wall. She put the dress down, sucked her thumb for a moment, meditating, then picked it up again and circled the room several times, holding it close to her bosom. Finally she handed the dress to Mrs. Paizak, commenting that the price was outrageous, and left. Mrs. Paizak winked at Genia as if saying, "I told you so." Genia's beautiful face lit up, but not for long.

A few minutes later the girl re-entered, followed by her mother. The mother examined the dress and said that it was out of the question. The girl cried; she had to have it. The father was summoned. He pounded his feet on the floor and scratched his back on the doorway and then said, "No!"

Genia was crying, the girl was crying, the mother tried to reason with her, the father was shouting at both of them, and Mrs. Paizak was laughing and winking at Genia. There was tumult like in a bazaar, and finally, to Mrs. Paizak's surprise, the mother pulled out a bundle of bills from her bosom and paid the asking price, calling Mrs. Paizak a Ukrainian thief and every other name under the sun. The girl wiped the tears from her face, the father grumbled something, the girl held the dress in front of her and smiled with satisfaction, and Genia, poor Genia sat in the corner crying.

The following Sunday before going to church, the girl with the long blond braids and round face came by to show off her new dress, or perhaps she came only to make Genia jealous. Besides the dress, she wore a large straw hat with a bright blue ribbon and a pair of black-strapped low-heeled shoes. In her hand she clutched a pair of white gloves. From the distance she looked rather smart, and I could see Genia's dark eyes watching her with envy as she approached the courtyard. After greeting us, she pirouetted like a ballerina, then stopped, waiting for our reaction. Mrs. Paizak showered compliments upon her, and even poor Genia had to admit she looked stunning.

"Kubush," Mrs. Paizak addressed me, "tell me, doesn't she look like a Warsaw lady?"

I couldn't recall what a Warsaw lady looked like, but now that my opinion was being asked, I looked closely at the girl and especially at her silk dress. Whose dress was this? I wondered. How can this girl wear it? It's like wearing a dead person's memories. In whose closet did this dress hang once? And who once gazed into a mirror and admired herself in it?

Now I looked even closer at the dress and thought how immodest this girl was. The silk was thin, so transparent that I could see her torn underpants under it, and her bare, firm breasts as well.

I couldn't recall anyone wearing such dresses in Warsaw, and yet the style looked familiar enough. Suddenly I did remember. Yes, my aunts and my mother too wore dresses like that, and as I tried to recall where, and on what occasions I had seen them wearing such dresses, a vivid picture of my mother wearing a similar dress flashed through my mind.

"Yes, Mrs. Paizak," I said, "they do wear such dresses in Warsaw." The girl beamed with satisfaction and departed for church. I could see Genia sticking out her tongue at her as she turned her back to us.

Did Mrs. Paizak know what she had sold this girl, or was she perhaps in the dark as well? Should I tell her or keep silent? I decided to speak up, for no matter what Mrs. Paizak's reaction might be, I felt at least Genia would get some satisfaction.

"Mrs. Paizak," I said, "that dress isn't really a dress."

Mrs. Paizak looked at me inquisitively. "No? What is it then if it's not a dress?"

"I remember my mother wearing one before the war. It's a nightgown."

Mrs. Paizak's face showed surprise, and as if finding it hard to believe, she asked, "For sleeping in? In such fine silk?"

"Yes," I answered.

Genia's face smiled that familiar smile and I too smiled. Gradually her face beamed, and then she laughed, jumping into the air with joy. I too laughed, not so much for the girl's misfortune, but for Genia's happiness. Mrs. Paizak laughed, implying how stupid the girl was not to know the difference between a nightgown and a dress. When she stopped laughing she looked at me for a moment; then, taking me aside, she whispered in my ear.

"Kubush, that isn't a nightgown, understand? That's a dress."

I understood. "It's not a nightgown, Mrs. Paizak, it's a dress."

The summer came. The days were long and hot, and the nights were short and sleepless, for my mind wandered and my body turned restlessly from side to side waiting for day to break.

I slept in the barn on a bed of hay, but on exceptionally

warm nights I made my sleeping place outside the barn on a haystack. I'd lie awake listening to the croaking of the frogs coming from the nearby ponds, and my eyes would gaze at the stars, trying to count them . . . one . . . two . . . three . . . four . . . five . . . Then my thoughts would wander to my mother, Josel, Shepsel, and eventually to Moishe. Where was Moishe? If he's still alive, why hasn't he shown up? He must know where I am. It's been weeks and yet no sign of him.

I thought of Siedliszcze and tried to imagine what the town now looked like. Who occupies our room? I wondered. What does the market square look like now? I could almost hear the town bell striking out the time . . . one . . . two . . . three . . .

Because of my sleepless nights I found it difficult to keep awake during the stifling long days. I would squat down on the ground and slowly my head would drop, my eyes would close. "I must not fall asleep," I told myself, "for who knows where my cows would end up, and then what?" But I wasn't always in control of myself, especially on a day before a rainfall I could feel a weakness overtaking me. . . .

I was in bed back home in Pulawy: clean sheets, a soft quilt, and a pillow of goose feathers. I was flying on clouds, my mother was reading me a bedtime story, "Little Red Riding Hood," no . . . it was "Hansel and Gretel." How were Hansel and Gretel going to find their way back home? I was flying. It was so soft, so sweet, so pleasant, my mother's voice was far away now, I could hardly hear it. The next thing I'd hear would be Mrs. Paizak's voice or feel Genia's soft hand touching my face. My eyes would open and once again I was Kubush the cowherd, far away from home.

When the sun stood directly above me, I eagerly awaited Genia's arrival with my lunch: boiled potatoes with pork gravy, and in another dish, sour milk or cold borsht. If a cow had to be diverted, Genia would say, "Eat in peace, Kubush," and she would jump up and perform the task. She ran briskly with her bare feet, her colorful skirt almost carrying her into the air like a balloon. Genia insisted on bringing me my food and usually stayed longer than was necessary.

In fact, she never left until Mrs. Paizak called her, "Genia, get home, you've got work to do!"

On days when the pasture land was not far from the house, Genia would feel uneasy and usually depart shortly after lunch, but when I was on a piece of grazing land far removed from Mrs. Paizak's voice, Genia was in her glory and almost refused to leave.

Genia was about fourteen or fifteen, with an inner beauty that only enhanced her outward appearance. She had many boyfriends, especially on Sunday. During the week one or two would show up in the evening and take Genia out for a swim or a walk in the village, but on Sunday the whole courtyard was filled with young men in polished shoes and white shirts with ties. She loved fun and had a burning love for life.

When my lunch plates were empty we would converse about something or other; then her eyes would circle the surrounding area, and once satisfied we were alone, she would commence tickling me. The first time this happened I giggled and laughed, and even though I had the urge to tickle her in return, I was a little afraid in case my hand touched her accidentally in a place where it might be embarrassing both for her and for me. But later when she ridiculed me for being so meek and restrained, I tickled her too, always being careful to confine myself to her underarms. We giggled and laughed and chased each other around the field and only stopped when we saw her mother approaching from the distance, infuriated at Genia's long absence, or when a farmer would return to a nearby field after a satisfying lunch.

As the days progressed our tickling game progressed as well. Instead of my armpits, Genia now explored other sensitive parts of my body: my neck, the soles of my feet, my back, my belly button, then my knees, and finally between my legs. The first time this happened, I was sure it was accidental, and pretended not to notice it. But I was wrong. It was no accident. Genia not only repeatedly tickled me there, but eventually confined herself to that area. When I did not fight back by tickling her in her private areas, she taunted and dared me, saying she wasn't ticklish there. I was embarrassed, but then too I wanted to show her that I was a man and would not fail to meet this challenge.

Before long, I forgot the challenge and it became a matter of practice to tickle Genia between her legs and also on her breasts. I'd chase her, catch her, turn her over in the wheat field or grass, and tickle her until she cried from laughter. Then it was her turn. I'd run like a demon but she would always catch me in the end, and almost tear my white cotton pants to shreds. We'd roll on the ground like a wheel down a hill, one moment I on top of her, the next, she on top of me.

I somehow felt that what we were doing wasn't really wrong, but also that it wasn't entirely right. Why, I couldn't tell, and didn't wish to ask. Why spoil it? I thought. Genia seemed to enjoy it, so why deprive her of the pleasure, and I didn't mind it either; in fact as time went on it was something to look forward to at noontime, and these diversions, while they lasted, made me forget bitter memories, and for that I was grateful to Genia.

But when she would depart, a guilt would set in, and I disliked myself for forgetting even for a moment. What kind of a son am I? Imagine rolling in the grass with a Gentile farm girl, laughing and giggling, and even enjoying it, when who knows where my family is at this moment! What would my mother think if she could see me?

One day while sitting on top of me and holding me pinned to the ground. Genia didn't stop at tickling. She undid the only wooden button that held my pants up and proceeded to strip me. I was laughing, but desperately tried to free myself. When I succeeded in throwing her off, she pulled at my pant legs, and had it not been for my firm hold at the top of my trousers, I would have ended up naked. As I tried to do up the button, there was Genia running towards me again. I held on tightly to my pants and ran. She caught me, threw me down and turned me over, then fought to finish what she had set out to do.

I began to plead with her, for my strength wasn't sufficient to hold her back. "Please, Genia, that's enough! . . . No! No!"

"What are you afraid of?" she asked. "I'm not going to cut it off, I just want to look at it, that's all."

I was shocked. "Why?" I trembled.

"Well, I heard that Jews get themselves circumcised."

"So?" I inquired.

"So I want to see what it looks like, that's all."

Now I held my pants tighter than ever. I wasn't going to be put on display for being different. She would probably laugh at me once she saw it, I thought. I must never never let her see it.

At that moment I felt like a cripple; I was different from the others. It was as if when I was born the rabbi had cut off one of my arms or legs, or disfigured my face. How mean, I thought, how unjust to inflict such shame upon an infant and mark him for the rest of his life.

One day she warned me not to tickle her. I was relieved at first and then began to worry. What was the reason for her sudden change? Was she put out with me? Perhaps Mrs. Paizak knew about it and reprimanded her. Even though secretly I had wished many times to end our horseplay for good, now that it was her decision I felt saddened and hurt. I couldn't help inquiring the reason for her new attitude.

My mind was set at ease when Genia explained that it had

nothing to do with me and that it was only temporary, and then she went on to tell me in great detail and with great pleasure that she had become a woman.

Since what she told me seemed so unbelievable, I implied that I was not born on a farm and that I had lived in the big city of Warsaw, and knew something about life, and never heard of such wives' tales.

She immediately pulled up her skirt to demonstrate proof of her story. "Look here and see for yourself, you big nine-year-old from Warsaw who knows so much."

I covered my eyes with my hands. "I believe you, Genia."

"No you don't, don't be shy. I don't mind," she laughed.

"I'm not shy, I just can't stand the sight of human blood." She finally lowered her skirt and, pursuing this line of conversation, she said;

"Jewish girls have it sideways. You know that, don't you, Kubush?"

"No it's not true," I protested. "Their bodies are just like yours."

"It's sideways, Kubush, that's a fact. Ask anyone, they'll tell you." She pointed to the rear of one of the cows. "You see, Kubush, that's the way normal women have it, but not Jewish women." When I continued to protest she finally said, "Why do you argue? Have you ever seen a Jewish girl naked?"

I hadn't, but I wasn't going to let her get away with it. Even if it was true, I had to defend what I felt was a terrible injustice that God inflicted upon Jewish women. For if the cows and the horses and everyone else in the whole world, man and beast alike, had it one way, why did God deem it necessary to set Jewish women apart?

"Sure I've seen it, many times," I said, "and it looks just like yours." Hearing this, she laughed and went on to tell me about all the other terrible things concerning Jews.

"Jews kill Christian children during Passover, and use their blood to bake matzah. That's why the matzah has brown spots on it."

I tried to recall what matzah looked like, and to my sorrow I remembered the brown spots. "Those spots are the burned part of the matzah," I retorted. But she wouldn't accept that reasoning, and told me that she didn't blame me for not knowing the truth. In fact most Jews didn't know about it, only the elders, a very few chosen pious rabbis, the ones who are entrusted to carry out the deed.

Again I couldn't believe her, but then I hadn't believed her about her womanhood and she proved me wrong. Maybe it was true, but how could it be? I remembered my father's father, Reb Shloime, the baker of Pulawy, baking matzah during Passover and I couldn't recall him mixing blood into the dough. It was even harder for me to accept that my grandfather, the baker of Pulawy, would have kneaded dough with human blood in it.

"It's not your fault," she consoled me, "but because of that, and because the Jews killed Christ, the Germans are now repaying you."

How horrible, I thought. If all this is true, then indeed there is reason for our suffering. Why did the Jews kill Christ? This and many other questions plagued me. If only they had not killed Him and all those infants during Passover, then I'd still have my mother and my father and my brother Josel, and we'd all be back in Pulawy. I'd be going to Hebrew school, and every night my mother would tuck me into bed and read me fairy tales. Oh, how I wished that the Jews had not killed Christ.

Even though I wavered within myself, I told Genia that her stories were simply grandmother tales.

"That's a good one," she laughed with satisfaction. "If so, then why can't Jews see the sun?"

What did she mean by that? I wondered. I turned my head in the direction of the sun but had to turn back again, for the rays blinded my eyes. I was sure I could always see the sun ever since I could remember, but was it the sun I had been looking at all my life, or something I only thought was the sun?

"I don't know who filled your head with such silly stories," I said.

"Ask anyone in the village and see if they tell you any differently."

"They're all ignorant," I said defensively.

"All right then, Mr. Educated," she said with a sneer, "let me see you point the sun out to me." I raised my arm and pointed to the sun. "You saw me looking in that direction so you assumed the sun must be there." She took her rose-colored kerchief off her head, tied it tightly around my eyes, then turned me several times to the left, then to the right, then to the left again, and again to the right. I became dizzy, about to fall when she removed the blindfold. "Now point the sun out."

I blinked my eyelids several times, and without hesitation pointed to the sun. She was silent for a moment, looking at the sun and then at me, and finally a smile covered her face. "You're clever Kubush," she said, "you could feel the sun's rays on your face, that's how you are able to tell where the sun is."

Again I protested and tried desperately to convince her I could see the sun, or perhaps I was really trying to convince myself. At any rate she didn't give me a chance, Mrs. Paizak's voice was suddenly heard, heaping all sorts of abuse at Genia for taking so long.

She picked up the empty plates and ran off towards the house saying, "Wait for a cloudy day, my educated cowherd, when there are no warm rays to help you. Wait till then, and we'll see how well you can see the sun."

I waited for such a day, when the clouds moved swiftly, covering one another, and the sun, small in the distance, a circle of golden yellow, like a coin peeking from behind the clouds but yielding no heat. Again I pointed the sun out to Genia, and again I was blindfolded and turned like a merry-go-round, and again I pointed to the sun, each time explaining in detail the sun's exact location, specifying in some cases that it was behind a cloud, or that only part of it was visible. After many tests Genia was finally convinced. She took me in her arms, lifted me off the ground and kissed me, screaming with joy.

"That's fantastic, Kubush, you can actually see the sun!" Again she kissed me and ran off shouting, "Mother, dear mother! Dear Jesus! Kubush can see the sun!"

The night was about to descend. My two cows were resting in the stable from a weary day of grazing and swatting flies with their long tails. Mrs. Paizak and Genia had been out in the field that day weeding the vegetable patch, and now were inside the house preparing the night's supper.

I was outside by the well washing my hands and face, and about to scrub my feet which were caked with dirt and mud, when from the adjoining field of tall golden wheat I heard a rustle. I turned my head and listened, but now it was quiet. It must be my imagination, I thought, and turned back to scrub my feet with a hard brush. Again I heard a movement. Perhaps a dog, a bird, or a field animal, I told myself.

The evening was quiet and warm, and only the frogs could be heard in the distance. All across the village, naphtha lamps were being lit inside the mud houses, and now a faint glow of light appeared in Mrs. Paizak's window.

The rustle in the wheat continued; I tried to ignore it, thinking it would go away, but suddenly I felt I was being watched. I could feel a pair of eyes staring at me from behind the wheat.

What should I do? I wanted to rush into the house and inform Mrs. Paizak, but what if it's only my imagination? Or what if it turns out to be a little bird, or a cat? Then Genia and Mrs. Paizak would laugh at me and call me a city mouse.

I've got to be brave, act like a man, and not run like a child crying for help. I picked up my stick, and though my legs were trembling with fright, I approached the wheat field and said:

"Who's there?"

There was no reply, but now that I was close I could hear the beat of a heart, and the eyes, even though I couldn't see them, were boring right through me. "Who's there?" I asked again, and hoped that a reply would not come. I prayed that it was only my imagination, but moved into the field itself trying to sound brave and confident. I shouted, "Who's there? Come out of there!"

I was about to turn back when suddenly a figure stood up, looking at me with wild, fierce eyes. Facing me was an un-shaven man dressed in the uniform of a train conductor. At a glance I surmised the uniform didn't belong to him; the jacket hung loosely on his shoulders, and the pants were too short.

I wanted to flee, but I feared he might pursue me. I felt I had to ease my way out as one does when confronted by an unfriendly dog. I stood trying to appear as if my finding him there was the most natural thing.

The man's eyes moved swiftly from side to side. He stood for the longest time without uttering a word, but I could see he was trembling. Finally he said something to me. I couldn't understand it. It sounded Ukrainian, and yet it wasn't. He repeated the same words again, but now spoke them very slowly, enunciating every syllable, and gesturing with his hands. I thought he was asking whether there was anyone inside the house.

"My employer and her daughter," I replied.

"No one else?" he asked, looking into my eyes, as if forcing a truthful answer out of me.

"No, I swear," I reassured him. "Do you wish to see my employer?" I asked casually, and began to move towards the courtyard. "I'll go and call her."

I could feel him following me, and when I reached the door of the house, I turned around and caught a glimpse of him at the well, drinking water directly from the pail like a thirsty animal. I rushed into the house, bolted the door behind me, and shouted frantically:

"There's a strange man outside!"

Mrs. Paizak and Genia looked at me in surprise; then Mrs. Paizak unbolted the door and looked out. The man had finished drinking and was now standing by the well looking at us.

I could now see that his feet were bare, and over one of his shoulders hung a pair of black leather boots. Who's this man? I wondered. Certainly not a train conductor.

He's not an escaped Jew either. Then a frightening thought occurred to me: he's a German in disguise, pretending to be a train conductor, and he's here to arrest me. But why does he speak that strange tongue?

"Good evening," Mrs. Paizak finally said to him. He answered her in that strange language. Mrs. Paizak glanced at Genia, and slowly approached the man. They exchanged a few words; then Mrs. Paizak, followed by the stranger, entered the house. His eyes scanned the room suspiciously, and then he sat down on a chair.

Now, by the light of the lamp, I studied his face in detail. He looked like a man of about fifty years of age, almost as old as my grandfather, I thought, and he certainly walked like an old man.

Mrs. Paizak barked orders at Genia to set the table, to mash the potatoes, to cut some bread, to pour the milk.

The stranger just sat there, his eyes taking in the room, and at the slightest noise from the outside, he would quickly jump up like a rabbit about to flee. Mrs. Paizak reassured him at every such instance, and now, to my surprise, she too was speaking that strange language. Some words I understood, but most were unfamiliar.

When the supper was placed on the table, the stranger, without crossing himself, unlike Mrs. Paizak and Genia, commenced to devour the food in front of him. Mrs. Paizak continued to cut slices of bread, and as quickly as she sliced, he ate them up. His glass was refilled with fresh milk time and time again. The pot was emptied to the last potato, and after we had finished eating and sat back, he continued to eat whatever was placed in front of him. Mrs. Paizak coaxed him to eat more.

"How about some more milk?" she asked, and without waiting for a reply, she would fill his glass again.

At long last he was full; he lifted his head, moved the chair away from the table a little, and burped twice. Throughout the entire meal we hadn't taken our eyes off him, and now he glanced at us, and for the first time smiled a faint smile. We in turn smiled, and then his mouth widened and his face beamed; then he giggled and finally laughed.

We laughed, he laughed louder, we joined him, and gradually the house was filled with peals of laughter. I laughed along with the others. But why I laughed I didn't know, any more than they did.

Again he sat there quietly, only answering the questions Mrs. Paizak was hurling at him, and even this he did in a whisper. As the clock on the mantelpiece ticked away he began to yawn. Mrs. Paizak turned to me.

"Kubush, show this man to the barn."

Was he going to sleep with me? What if he is indeed a German and plans to kill me during the night?

Mrs. Paizak lit the lantern and handed it to me. The man eased himself out of the chair, kissed Mrs. Paizak's hand, bowed to her and Genia, and said, "Good night."

I took him to the barn and showed him the sleeping place. He thanked me and lay down. I was afraid to lie beside him. The night wasn't warm enough to sleep outside and there wasn't room for me inside the house. I debated for a moment, then excused myself and ran back to the house. The door was already bolted. I knocked. Mrs. Paizak's voice came from inside:

"Who is it?"

"Kubush," I replied in a whisper, and I was sorry now that I hadn't gone to sleep. The door opened and Mrs. Paizak, half undressed by now and combing her long hair, stood in the doorway looking at me in surprise.

"What is it, Kubush?" she inquired.

I stood for a moment, the lantern in my hand, ashamed to tell her. Then, almost stuttering, my eyes pleading for understanding, I asked:

"Who is that man, Mrs. Paizak?"

She placed a hand on my shoulder, reassuring me. "Go to sleep, Kubush, he's a friend."

"Mrs. Paizak," I implored, "I think that man is not what he says he is. I think he's a German soldier in disguise, and he's here to kill me." I was sure she would laugh at this, but she didn't.

She drew me closer to her and said, "Don't worry, Kubush, this man is not a German soldier, he's a friend."

But when it became obvious to her that my mind was still not at ease, she asked, "Can you keep a secret?" I nodded my head. "He's a Russian. He escaped from the prisoner-of-war camp in Chelm, and no one must know he's here. No one, do you understand?"

I was relieved and indeed happy. "I understand, Mrs.

Paizak," I answered with a smile, and then ran back to the barn.

When I approached the Russian, his eyes were still open. How exciting, I thought, an escaped prisoner sleeping with me, and the fact that he was Russian made me feel safe. I had always known that the Russians were kind to the Jews, and treated them well. That's why my father had fled to Russia. Perhaps he knows my father. I'll have to ask him tomorrow.

The man stretched his hand out to me and said, "Ivan!"

I offered him my hand in return and said, "Kubush."

He shook my hand firmly, then turned on his side and fell asleep. I blew out the lantern and sank into the hay, but my mind was so active now that my eyes refused to close.

Mentally I made a list of questions I would ask him concerning my father, "Do you know by any chance a man by the name of Zelik Kuperblum?"

"What does he look like?"

"Well, he . . . "

What did my father look like? I couldn't describe him now. I tried to visualize him, but his image refused to come into focus.

I now saw myself as a very little boy sitting on wooden steps eating grapes. Out of a fog a stranger dressed in a soiled raincoat and creased fedora hat approaches me. With sad brown eyes he stares at me, and I look back at him with fear. The stranger picks me up, hugs me, kisses me, then asks:

"Do you know who I am?"

I tremble but I fear to cry. The precious grapes fall from my hand and I shake my head.

"I'm your father," and he squeezes my face towards his, scratching my skin with his unshaven face.

I see a silhouette against the workbench repairing shoes and I hear my father whistling Schubert's Serenade.

I see him at the table with earphones on, listening to the radio.

I'm running with him, bombs are falling.

I watch him walking through the rubble which once was our apartment, looking for his sewing machine.

I see his hands making a birdcage out of wood and then I feel his lips kissing me and faintly I hear his voice saying, "Good-bye, Jankele my child, we'll all be together soon. I'll send for you."

I see him framed against the doorway like a shadow and then I only see the doorway.

Then suddenly I remembered that my father had a scar on his left cheek from a tooth operation many years back. Yes, I consoled myself, that's how I'll describe him.

One thought led to another and it didn't take very long before I began to suspect that not only did this Russian soldier beside me know my father, but in fact maybe he *was* my father. Why not? It's possible, I assured myself. Well, he looks older, I reasoned, but that could be because of his beard. But if he is my father, surely he would have recognized me. How could he recognize me? He hasn't seen me in so many years, and wouldn't expect to find his son Jankele in this place. It's possible, I kept repeating to myself. But is it possible? After all, this man's name is Ivān. Maybe he changed his name. Sure, that's it, he changed his name. I'll have to wait until tomorrow. Perhaps then he'll shave and I'll look for the scar on his left cheek.

When I opened my eyes the next morning, Ivan was still sleeping, snoring heavily. I ate breakfast, unhitched my cows, and drove them to pasture, to a piece of grazing land far from the house.

That whole morning my thoughts centered around Ivan. Perhaps he'd already shaved by now, I mused. And wouldn't it be something if indeed he turned out to be my father? But what if he doesn't shavē, then what? How will I know? I must ask him if he's ever been to Pulawy, and if his answer is "yes," then I'll ask him casually if by chance he has a boy by the name of Jankele. Then if he is indeed my father, I reasoned, he'll look at me in surprise, recognize me, lift me into the air, cry, and cover me with kisses.

The sun seemed to play tricks with me that day. It appeared to me that it wasn't moving at all, and there I was impatiently waiting for noon and Genia's arrival. From Genia I might learn something about Ivan. But when the sun finally was above me, hard as I looked, I couldn't see Genia's figure in the distance carrying my lunch. I began to worry. Something had happened. Perhaps the Germans had discovered Ivan and arrested Mrs. Paizak and Genia along with her.

I became worried and restless, and when the sun had passed the noontime position—it was about one o'clock now —I decided to drive my two cows home and see what had happened. I was about to start home when there, in a cloud of dust on the road, I saw Genia's dancing feet running towards me. She seemed to run faster that day than at any other time.

She approached me, placed my lunch on the grass, and still panting, apologized for being late. I sat down to eat.

"Kubush," she said, "you won't forget the dishes when you come home tonight."

I looked up in surprise. "Aren't you staying for a while?"

She pinched my cheek. "I'm sorry, but I have to go back right away." She began to run.

"Wait!" I shouted after her. She stopped and turned around. "Genia, what about the stranger?"

"What about him?" she asked with a smile.

"Well . . . what I mean, Genia, is . . . that beard of his . . . has . . . has he shaved yet?"

Genia burst out laughing. "You're a funny kid, Kubush. Yes, he's shaved." She turned and ran.

I couldn't eat my lunch and waited impatiently for the sun to set so that I could go home and see Ivan. But on that day the sun refused to set and my desire to look at Ivan's clean-shaven face was so intensified that while the sun was still far away from the ground I drove the cows home, running all the way.

When I arrived in the courtyard Mrs. Paizak looked at me, turned to look at the sky, then back to me. "Why so early, Kubush?" she asked with annoyance.

"It feels like rain, Mrs. Paizak. I didn't want to be caught in it."

"Rain?" asked Mrs. Paizak in surprise. "Without a cloud in sight?" I just stood there helpless, my eyes cast to the ground. "All right, take them in for the night, but don't let it happen again."

I drove the cows into the stable and tied them up.

I wonder where Ivan is? Probably in the house. Shall I run in now? No, it must not be too obvious, first I'll wash up.

As I was about to leave the barn I heard a slight rustle coming from the hay. I stopped and listened, then tiptoed to where the noise was coming from. In my sleeping place in the hay lay Genia, and beside her, with his arms around her, lay a young man. He wore a clean white cotton shirt, open at the neck, and white cotton trousers. His hair was combed neatly to the back, and his face was clean-shaven. I looked closer at the face, and from the eyes I could tell it was Ivan.

They both looked up at me, not disturbed in the least by my presence.

"Home so early?" Genia asked.

I turned from them and ran out, shutting the barn door

behind me. I stopped, unable to move and trembling. Then I heard Genia's voice:

"Don't run away, Kubush, come and lie down with us."

I heard her laugh and say to Ivan, "He's jealous." And then they both laughed.

Suddenly Genia seemed to be grown up, and this made me feel more like a child. She was continually occupied with Ivan: talking to him, kissing him, going for walks with him.

The Sunday visits of other young men came to an abrupt end, but instead, as if they had fallen out of the sky, a new group of friends congregated in Mrs. Paizak's courtyard on Sundays, and in the evenings during the week as well. Most of them were about Ivan's age, though a few were older, and they too were escaped Russian prisoners of war. There was Nicolai; there was Dimitri, and Yoska, Boris, Yuri, Sergei, and countless others.

Some, like Ivan, were living with families in the village, while others less fortunate roamed the fields by day and slept in the forests by night.

While tending my cows in the field, I would now meet new companions almost daily. Sometimes by themselves, sometimes in twos or threes, they wandered aimlessly across the fields like lost sheep. I'd study their faces, always looking for a scar on the left cheek, and each and every one of them I'd ask the same question:

"Do you by chance happen to know Zelik Kuperblum?"

When I met with a blank stare, I would add that the man I was inquiring about had a scar on his left cheek. My questions led to questions from them, and they would sit on the grass and listen to my story, urging me to continue when I stopped for a moment. My companions would stay for hours hearing my story and telling me their own tales.

I appreciated having such interesting company, and I was only too happy to share my lunch with them as well as to provide them with slices of bread or a bunch of cherries, which I stuffed into my pockets in the mornings before leaving for the fields.

When the food was devoured and the stories came to an end and the evening was about to descend on us, my friends would leave, promising to inquire about my father, and often their parting words were:

"You'll see your father, boy; the war will be over soon."

The ones I got to know would go, never to be seen again, then new ones would appear, and then they too would soon vanish.

On some evenings a group of them would appear looking for Ivan. Ivan would don his raincoat, hide his rifle under it, and depart with them. In the early morning he would return, sometimes drunk and sometimes bruised.

Where do they go? Why do they carry rifles?

Eventually Ivan described to me in great detail a night's adventure: an ambush, a truck full of German soldiers, rat . . . tat . . . tat . . . tat . . . the truck turns over, the Germans try to flee, but there is Sasha with a grenade, he throws it . . . the Germans explode into the air, their bodies fall apart into small pieces. On other occasions an informer is shot in his own bed while asleep, a German garrison is set on fire, and so on.

These accounts fascinated me and I admired Ivan and the others for their courage and felt that at long last someone was taking revenge for all the terrible things the Germans had done to us.

Sometimes when Ivan described the bodies flying into the air, I would picture the blood gushing all over the roadside and imagine the horrible screams of pain shattering the still of the night. At times I even felt sorry for those who were killed in the ambush. Perhaps they were good ones, innocent soldiers who had mothers and fathers back home, I thought. Then something in me would say, Good Germans? What's the matter with you Jankele? After all that's happened, how can you have such thoughts?

But there *are* some who are good.

I'd like to meet one.

What about the one in Lublin?

Which one in Lublin?

The one by the truck, when they were deporting us, remember?

Yes, I remember. He was shoving us onto the truck as if we were cattle.

But don't you remember he offered you and Josel candy? Now if he was as bad as you say, why would he give you candy?

Candy? It was poison you fool. That's why Mommy wouldn't let you take it. She said it was poison. Did you forget so soon?

I remembered the scene vividly, and now before me I could see the German soldier with his outstretched hand offering us the bonbons.

"Take, please take," he pleaded. My mother drew us nearer to her, holding our hands in hers so that we couldn't reach. "Please take it. Let your children take it," he begged.

But my mother just stared at him and held us tighter. "Why?" he finally asked.

"Coming from you it must be poison," my mother replied.

The candy dropped from his hand. "I have two children at home. Your children remind me of them," and he began to cry. "I wonder if I'll ever see them again." He wiped the tears from his face and, with a slam, closed the rear of the truck, then shouted to the driver, "Filled up, take it away!" As the truck started to move he turned his back to us, but even from the distance I could sense he was still crying.

What if he was among those in the ambush? I felt sorry for him and for his children, for I knew how they would feel without a father.

Shame on you, shame! I heard the voice within me again. Go on, feel sorry for the German and for his children. You should feel sorry for your own family and yourself instead.

And so I argued with myself and only brought the argument to a satisfactory conclusion when I told myself that the German soldier with the bonbons was not among those killed that night. I was certain that he was still alive. Probably on leave visiting his children back home. Ivan and his companions only killed the bad ones, the ones that mistreated us. And now again I was glad, I was satisfied. They were getting what was coming to them.

But in front of my eyes I could now see the smiling face of another German soldier. Rudi was combing his blond hair, looking into a small mirror which hung on the side of an army truck. I was cleaning his motorcycle which was covered with mud from the previous day's maneuvers.

Every day he went on maneuvers and I was constantly cleaning it, polishing his boots, and brushing his uniform.

"Your name is Jakob," he once mused. "A good Biblical name," and he threw me a loaf of bread. "For your mother." Every day he stuffed my pockets with food to take home.

The bread my mother accepted without comment, but the pork sausage she threw out and forbade me ever to bring it home again.

I could now see the training camp on the outskirts of Siedliszcze being evacuated. Truckloads of German soldiers moving out. I stand by the gate and wait and then I catch a glimpse of Rudi. His motorcycle glistens and I'm proud of that. He sees me and pulls over to the curb and stops. He wears a long leather coat now, a rifle hangs on his back. His face shines and he forces a nervous smile.

"Where are you going?" I ask.

His face tenses and he answers, "To the Russian front."

He tries to smile but he can't. "Come along with me, Jakob, you'll clean my motorcycle there too."

"I can't leave my mother," I answer.

"Look at it, Jakob, thanks to you I'll have the cleanest motorcycle the Russians ever shot at."

"Move on!" shouts the soldier directing the convoy.

"Will I ever see you again, Rudi?" I ask.

He now reaches into a pouch and hands me three chocolate bars. "I don't think so, Jakob. I don't think I'll ever make it back. I'm afraid!"

"Move on there, soldier!" the man shouts again and Rudi and his sparkling motorcycle fall into line with the others.

He turned to look back once and waved his arm to me. His face was filled with fear, but he smiled.

There you go again, laughed the voice within me.

I closed my eyes and vowed not to think about it anymore.

On Sundays when the whole gang got together, Mrs. Paizak's house was filled with song and laughter. The vodka flowed freely and Mrs. Paizak served pierogy with sour cream to the guests with great pleasure.

Genia would not confine herself to Ivan alone; she sat on everybody's knees and gave all of them kisses without much prompting. Her mother was pleased beyond description, and urged each and every one of them to eat more.

This is more exciting than my Uncle Shepsel's cowboy tales, I told myself, and here I am among them, sitting and eating with them. Watching them polish their guns, and singing their songs with them. In time I even began to believe that I too was part of this band.

Apart from Ivan, the one I knew and liked best was Sasha. He was a tall man with curly black hair, a camel nose, and large dark eyes. He wore a heavy long brown coat, under which he always carried his rifle. He was lively, full of stories, songs, and jokes, but on occasion he sat silently and his eyes became sad, and his face looked as if his thoughts were far away. Sometimes Sasha would leave the others in the house, take me by my shoulders, and lead me out into the courtyard. Somewhere in a corner where it was quiet, he would sit and talk. I would hurl all sorts of questions at him about Russia:

"Is it true that Jews are well treated there? I heard that there are Jews in the army in Russia, and some of them are officers, and even generals. Will I ever find my father?"

Sasha would roll a cigarette, light it up, and answer all my questions, taking his time and elaborating at every turn.

I was mesmerized by his words as he told me about the town he came from, about the school he had gone to, and about the girl he loved and had left behind.

"What about your family?" I asked him one day.

He paused, looked into my eyes; then smiling he said, "Kubush, I, like you, have no family."

I now felt very close to him.

"You see, I'm an orphan; I've always been an orphan."

"What happened to your father and mother?" I inquired with a trembling voice.

He shrugged his shoulders. "I don't know, I never knew them. I grew up in an orphanage." Then he smiled a pleasant smile and pointed to his nose. "You see this?" I nodded my head. "It's a real hooker, isn't it? I think I'm one of your kind." I looked at him in surprise. "Yes, Kubush, I'm a Jew."

Is he telling me the truth or is he only saying this to comfort me?

"Can you speak Jewish?" I asked.

"I'm afraid not, but believe me, I've heard it said that my father was Jewish."

Sasha and I became very good friends, and every time we met he had a little present for me: a piece of chocolate, an empty bullet shell, a shiny button, anything he could pick up.

One day he taught me a song which he always sang or whistled, and from that time the song never left my lips, for it seemed to me it had been especially written for Sasha and me.

The song about Kubush the cowherd I put aside, and instead these words now echoed throughout the village of Kulik:

> Forgotten, I have forgotten
> My very young years.
> I remained an orphan
> And never had happiness in my life.
>
> In the forest by the valley,
> There a nightingale sings a song;
> I'm a fellow on foreign soil
> Forgotten by my people, forgotten.
>
> When I die, I will die,
> They'll put me underground
> And my countrymen will never know
> Where my grave is.

No one will come to see me,
No one will ever find me,
Only a nightingale in the early spring
Will sing a song over my grave.

"Tonight, Kubush, we're going to pay a visit to Siedliszcze," Ivan announced one evening. "There's someone there, who had a hand in deporting your mother, your brother, your uncle, and all the other mothers, brothers, and uncles. We shall try to repay him for his endeavors." He smiled, ruffled my hair, and departed with the others.

I couldn't sleep that night as I waited for their return, but there was no sign of Ivan or Sasha. The night passed and they were still not back.

The next day a story circulated in the village of what had happened the night before. Apparently, while the mayor of Siedliszcze was asleep in his elaborate bed with fine quilts and fluffy pillows, Russian partisans entered his mansion. They stripped his wife, tied her, and beat her with a strap. They destroyed all his furniture and took many of his belongings, including gold and money. Then they drove the mayor into the town square and hanged him naked from a tree.

All this was done under the noses of the German guards patrolling the town.

What happened to Ivan, Sasha, and the others? Mrs. Paizak kept sending me out to watch the road for some sign of them. Genia sat quietly by the table and finally broke down in hysterical wailing.

Every few minutes I'd run out, stand on the road, and look for approaching figures, hoping to hear a song, laughter, or just the sound of their footsteps, and then I'd go back to the house, wait a few minutes, and venture out to the road again.

I now saw a man approaching, but it wasn't anyone I knew. He wore a homburg hat and a heavy black coat with a fur collar, and he was swinging a silver walking stick in his hand.

I ran back into the house and informed Mrs. Paizak and Genia of the approaching stranger. They followed me outside and we watched this well-dressed gentleman come towards us. The face smiled when he entered the courtyard, and only then did we realize that this stylishly attired gentleman was none other than our own Ivan.

"What do you think of the new mayor of Siedliszcze?" he inquired, twirling the stick between his fingers. Mrs. Paizak gasped, Genia trembled. I was stunned, but happy to see him, and I wondered where Sasha was.

"Feel the fur," he indicated the collar. "Real fox."

That night Ivan tossed and talked in his sleep. I listened to his broken, senseless utterings and wondered how it was possible for one human being to kill another. How does it feel to watch a man die?

Then I tried to imagine, though I couldn't, how it must be to see a gun pointed at one's face, or to feel a rope around one's neck and know that the end has come. What goes through a man's mind at such a moment? What does he think? Or does he think? What did the mayor of Siedliszcze think? God, I prayed, I hope I never find out!

Days turned into nights and nights into days. The trees had blossomed, borne their fruits, and were now bare. The wheat had grown tall and was ready to be cut.

Thus the summer came to its end, and with it, Mrs. Paizak's excursions to the Warsaw Ghetto. There was too much work to be done on the farm, and entering and leaving the Ghetto had become too dangerous. On her last trip she had been caught, arrested, and interrogated for hours, and only a large bribe had saved her from being shipped to an unknown destination.

Furthermore, her transactions were not as profitable now as they had been at the start, for by now the town of Siedliszcze had come back to life. Poles from the villages and from other towns had moved into the deserted homes and stores, and once again, one day a week, there was marketday in Siedliszcze.

According to Mrs. Paizak and Genia, who rode in now and then, it was not the same as it had been. Again I tried to imagine what the town now looked like. Who occupies our room? Who looks through the window where I once looked, waiting for my grandfather to come home? And the people who walk the streets, what do they look like? And what do they talk about? And what do they think?

I pictured German soldiers strutting to and fro, their rifles hanging over their shoulders. I could see the officer, meticulously dressed, walking along the street like a wound-up robot. One . . . two . . . three . . his left arm would automatically straighten out, bend at the elbow, bring his wrist close to his eyes, and he would read the time from his watch. The arm lowered . . . one . . . two . . . three . . . and he would pace stiffly on. But here in the village, kilometers away from Siedliszcze, not one German was in sight.

It was harvest time and in the fields all around me the

sound of the sickle cutting the wheat could be heard. Ivan learned the workings of the farm, and in time became the man of the family. I marveled at his strength, but sensed that he was bored with cutting wheat and hoeing potatoes. He was much happier when his friends arrived, when they would eat, drink, sing, and then depart on a night's adventure.

One late afternoon upon returning from the pasture, I discovered sitting at the supper table a young man with blond hair. He was about nineteen or twenty years old, and was dressed in a neatly pressed blue suit, black shoes, white shirt, and a blue tie. His face was tanned, his fingernails free of dirt and closely clipped. He blew his nose into a white handkerchief and not into part of his garments.

When I entered, his cold blue eyes stared right through me. His face was serious, refusing to smile. I observed him, then nodded my head. He ignored my greeting and instead turned to Mrs. Paizak with a questioning expression.

"This is our Kubush," said Mrs. Paizak.

He focused his eyes on me. "So that's the Jew boy! What do you feed him? Or does he eat pork?"

Mrs. Paizak glared at him scornfully, "No, Stashu, leave that boy alone. He's part of this family."

He laughed under his breath, then said quietly, "There will be some changes made around here."

Mrs. Paizak went on with her duties at the stove and not even turning to him she said, "Any changes to be made around here will be made by me."

Again he laughed. "What would you change, Mother?" he asked and waited for a reply. When it didn't come he continued, "You should see the farms they have in Germany. If you only saw how farms are run! Not with horses and bare hands, but with machinery. You should see how they live there, what they eat, and where they sleep! Paved roads everywhere, and along those roads apple trees, free for anyone to pick and eat to their heart's content. Would you believe it, Mother . . . ? No, you wouldn't believe it." He stopped, waiting for a reaction from his mother.

"What wouldn't I believe?" she finally asked.

He stood up and approached her. "Everybody, but almost everybody, owns a bicycle." He paused and looked at Mrs. Paizak's face, hoping to see a change in her expression, but her expression did not change. If she was impressed, she concealed it from him. He sat down again, and as if speaking to himself, but staring at me, he said, "Yes, Mother, I tell you this Hitler is a good man. If he does for Poland what he has done for Germany, then I say he knows what he's doing."

At first I didn't believe his wild tales of paved roads and apple trees, abundance of food, and especially the fact that almost everyone owned a bicycle. That's impossible, I thought.

But in the days that followed, Stashek showed us photographs of the farm in Germany where he had served for one year on forced labor, and then I did believe him. It was indeed as he had described it. There was Stashek on top of a tractor . . . and Stashek, beautifully dressed, riding a bicycle along a paved road flanked by apple trees, and in the background some of his friends, all on shiny bicycles just like his . . . and there again was Stashek with a girl, both smiling. It was a different world, a happier world, a world without hunger, a world without poverty, a world without lice, a world without hard work, and most of all a world without fear.

Everything was done by machine, even the milking of cows. This I found hard to believe, but I accepted it as being true since by then I knew that Stashek was not a liar. The best proof of this different, superior world was Stashek himself. He insisted on changing his shirt every day, washed his body twice daily from head to toe, always wore shoes, cleaned and cut his fingernails frequently. Even his own mother was bewildered by his new ways.

Thoughts which I was ashamed of entered my mind, but hard as I tried to ignore them or drive them away, they refused to leave until I acknowledged them. Perhaps Stashek is right; Hitler is indeed a good man and is out to save the world, bring machinery, paved roads, and bicycles to every human being on earth. That's a good thing if only, if only he would let my people live. But he doesn't.

Why? I questioned. There must be a reason. Yes, he would not do it without a reason. Perhaps Genia was right, it's God's will. We killed Jesus Christ and now Jesus Christ has sent Hitler to avenge his death. Or perhaps, I thought, it has nothing to do with Christ.

Perhaps we are indeed inferior and stand in the way of progress: paved roads, free apples, and bicycles. Perhaps that's what it is. We're not like other people at all. We speak a different language, we have different holidays, in fact we do everything differently from others. Why do we celebrate our Sabbath on Saturday instead of Sunday? And worst of all, why do we circumcise little boys and make them suffer? It's cruel. And why do we . . . No. I mustn't think of that.

You'd better think of it . . .

I can't, it's a lie.

Is it?

Sure it is.

It's true! Jews kill little Christian children for Passover.

It's a lie! "I'll never believe it!" I said out loud, but deep in my heart I wondered, and felt ashamed, deeply ashamed, for my thoughts.

Stashek didn't approve of my presence, nor was he happy with Ivan or his friends. In the days that followed there were countless quarrels between him, Genia, and Mrs. Paizak on account of us.

Mrs. Paizak constantly reminded Stashek that she was still boss in her house, and he countered by pointing out to her the danger in which she placed not only herself, but her entire family, by harboring us.

When his shouting and arguments failed, he resorted to threats. He, personally, was going to inform the Gestapo of our presence.

This is the end, I thought. Surely Mrs. Paizak knew he meant every word.

Ivan began to pack, but Genia's crying and Mrs. Paizak's pleas stopped him. Perhaps I too should at least make some sign of wishing to leave, and avert a family tragedy, I thought. But what if I'm not stopped? What if they let me go? Then what? Where would I go?

"Go and inform your Gestapo friends. Don't wait, go right away," Mrs. Paizak shouted to her son.

"All right, if that's the way you want it, I'll go." He put on his jacket, jumped on the horse and galloped out of the courtyard in a flurry.

The rest of the day we spent in torment and suspense, waiting either for Stashek, or the Gestapo to arrive. Again Ivan made preparations to leave, and again Genia and Mrs. Paizak stopped him. Both assured him that Stashek was only threatening and would never inform the enemy.

I was not so sure. I felt Stashek was capable of such an act, but then I reasoned that by informing on Ivan and myself, he would at the same time endanger his mother and his sister, and this thought put my mind at ease. Nevertheless, the outcome was not yet clear. Who knows, I thought, what some men are capable of doing?

Late in the evening Stashek returned on the tired horse, and left the animal in the courtyard for me to attend to. He marched into the house, sat down at the table, and began to eat his cold supper. He didn't say a word to any of us, nor we to him. What was he up to? Had he informed on us? Were the Gestapo on their way, or had he spent his day visiting a girl in another village? His silence was frightening.

From that day on, the large Sunday gatherings of Ivan's friends stopped, to the great regret of everyone except Stashek.

Mrs. Paizak continued to stand up to him, but in reality, secretly, I sensed that she was now frightened of him as well. On many occasions she called him a fascist, a traitor, and not the son she once carried in her belly.

"Your father would return to his grave if he saw you now," she told him.

He continued to show displeasure towards Ivan and me, but somehow he tolerated us, especially Ivan. At me he yelled and screamed and shouted orders, calling me every name with the word "Jew" in it. With Ivan he was kinder. He didn't speak to him in friendly tones, but simply left him alone, ignoring him as if he didn't exist.

Ivan still came and went as he pleased, sometimes not returning for several days, or a week.

Sasha and some of the others, I saw only fleetingly now, in the fields, but none dared to come into the house, or even into the courtyard. Stashek had indeed succeeded in changing things as he had promised, and now I wondered what other changes he was contemplating.

It had rained that day; a heavy, merciless rain poured down from heaven, and in the late afternoon it stopped as suddenly as it had begun. It was too late to take the cows to pasture so Mrs. Paizak asked me to join her and the others in the potato field not far from the house.

For me this was a holiday, and a rainy day was like a day of rest. I used to pray for rain, heavy rain, torrential rain. If only it would rain forever, never stopping, then I would never have to sit in the field watching my two mischievous cows.

Digging potatoes was something different. We'd walk along the rows, pull out the plants, dig into the earth with our fingers, and produce large and small new potatoes from the ground.

Stashek was faster than any of us; when he'd completed a row we'd still be far behind. I was always at the end, and hard as I tried, I couldn't keep up with the others.

Ivan sang and we joined him, everyone except Stashek who hardly uttered a word. Occasionally he'd cast an angry glance at me and say, "This is hard work, eh? Not like selling herring, is it?"

The clouds moved swiftly, breaking up into smaller clouds, and eventually disappeared; all that was left was a gray, even-colored sky. Suddenly a shot rang out and a bullet whistled above our heads. We stopped singing, looked about. Another shot was heard but there was no one to be seen.

"Probably one of your boys got drunk," remarked Stashek, and we turned back to work, but not for long. Soon another shot, then another was heard, and then Stashek yelled, "Look! Over there!"

In the distance silhouettes of soldiers were visible against the sky.

"Some of our boys," said Ivan.

"Why are they shooting?" asked Mrs. Paizak with a worried expression on her face.

"I don't like it," said Stashek.

"Whatever it is, it doesn't concern us. Just go on working," answered Mrs. Paizak, and so we did though the bullets were now flying over our heads and the silhouettes in the distance were moving closer towards us.

When they were almost upon us we could see they were German soldiers and Ukrainian Brown Shirts, all carrying rifles and machine guns, fully equipped for battle.

"Quick, Ivan, you have to hide," shouted Mrs. Paizak, and dragging him by the arm she started off for the courtyard.

I ran after them, Genia following me. "Mrs. Paizak," I said, "shouldn't I hide somewhere?"

"No, just be calm. I'll tell them you're my son."

In the corner of the barn Ivan removed some rubbish, lifted two boards, kissed Genia, and jumped into a hole which I never knew existed. Mrs. Paizak replaced the two boards and with great urgency we piled a huge mound of freshly dug potatoes on top of the boards.

When we came out from the barn we saw a group of soldiers approaching the courtyard and Stashek with them. He was talking and laughing with them. He wouldn't hesitate to tell them who I am. If he does, I'll deny it.

But what if they pull my pants down, then what? The rabbi who circumcised me flashed through my mind. I imagined him an old man with a long black beard and a long kaftan, holding a large, sharp knife in his hand and looking down at my naked body and laughing . . . laughing with great satisfaction. I hated him now. I despised him. He was the cause of all my troubles.

Mrs. Paizak forced a smile, and Genia began to feed the chickens, trying to give the impression that the soldiers' presence did not disturb her.

The soldiers were entering the courtyard when Mrs. Paizak, panic-stricken, whispered in a trembling voice, "Run, Kubush! Hide."

My heart beat like a drum and in a split second my eyes surveyed the courtyard. It was too late to hide in the barn, in the house, or in the courtyard. There was only one route of escape. I opened the gate that led to the back fields and at that moment I thought I heard the voice of one of the soldiers calling after me but I didn't stop. I kept on walking and now I knew what it feels like when one is about to be shot.

I waited for the moment when I would be pierced with a bullet in my back. I could see myself falling, falling asleep forever. But where would I be buried?

I reached the back of the house, and to my dismay, found a German soldier armed with grenades and an automatic rifle ready in his hands. He was tiptoeing near the back window and peeking inside. I jumped with fright but quickly composed myself and smiled.

He didn't even glance at me. I began to whistle and walked along a path dividing a field of wheat from a field of alfalfa. I plucked a stem of wheat, placed it between my teeth, and then made my way further and further away from the house and closer to the river.

Bullets zoomed past my head creating shrilling sounds. I kept my eyes forward and walked in a slow, steady pace, never running or looking back.

I'm safe, I thought, the farm is far behind me. Then I hurled myself into a wheat field and lay panting. My heart was beating so loud that the vibration shook my whole body. The slightest sound of a bird or a field mouse made me jump and I imagined a German with a gun close by, aiming it at me. Any moment his bullet will leave his gun and penetrate my flesh.

It's only a mouse, perhaps a silly bird. Why are you shaking like that? You've got to take hold of yourself. That's right, nothing to be afraid of, just lie still. All this will stop in a few hours, the soldiers will leave, and you'll go back to the house.

I heard voices, German voices, marching feet. It's your imagination, you fool! Ignore it, don't stand up, my inner voice told me.

Yes, it must be my imagination. But the voices wouldn't go away and kept coming nearer and nearer and now I was able to make out certain words. I've got to look, I've got to see who's around.

There's no one around, lie still, you idiot.

You're right, I'll lie still, I'm only imagining. I stood up.

Below me in the valley, German soldiers by the hundreds were crossing the small, narrow river. Some of them were making a game of it by jumping across, and some succeeded, but not all. One soldier plunged into the water and his companions laughed. Others had already crossed over and were coming in my direction. I looked to my left and then to the right and there were soldiers along the banks of the river as far as my eyes could see.

They moved slowly, methodically searching every stack of hay, every bush with their pointed bayonets.

This is the end, I've been caught. They'll question my presence here, look into my eyes, and find a Jew staring at them. They'll pull down my trousers, laugh, and that will be the last sound I will ever hear.

A short distance away, a horse was grazing and a plow lay idle in the middle of a partially plowed field. A wagon was parked not far from it. I approached the horse, fear striking inside me not only from the oncoming soldiers, but from the horse as well.

"Please, horsey, don't kick me. Be kind," I pleaded. I touched him and he didn't seem to resist. "That's a good horse," I patted him on his forehead, then fetched his harness, and managed to put it on him. Then I led him to the plow and began plowing. I whipped the horse, gripped the handles of the plow, and yelled, "Vio!"

Plowing had looked easy enough when I watched others do it, but now I realized that it was indeed a skill to be learned.

The horse began to trot, obeying my order, but the plow refused to submerge, and slid along the top of the ground. I then pushed the handles with all my strength, forcing the blade into the ground. It went too deep, the plow fell, the horse stopped, and by now the Germans were almost upon me. I backed up the horse and started again.

As if by a miracle the plow moved along in a straight line. I began to whistle Sasha's song and tried to appear unconcerned about the armed soldiers who had surrounded me and were gazing at me. Pretending I didn't even notice them, I continued to bark orders and sometimes swear at the poor horse just like a boy or man of the village.

Then a voice called in German, "You!" I didn't look up. It called again. I brought the horse to a stop and looked up, acting surprised, as if this was the first time I was aware of their presence.

A round-faced sweating soldier approached me, pointing his rifle. Two or three others followed behind him.

"What are you?" he asked suspiciously in German. I understood German.

"I don't understand," I answered in Polish.

"Are you Ukrainian?" he asked looking at my dark hair. Again I said in Polish, "I don't understand, I only speak Polish."

He looked into my dark eyes. "Are you a Jew?" he asked with a grin. Again I repeated the same answer. "Do you know of any Russians hiding in the village?"

I smiled, looking straight into his eyes. "I'm sorry, I don't understand German, I can only speak Polish."

He stared at me for a moment, then burst out laughing. He turned to his companions. "These peasants are so stupid, they're all idiots!" He laughed again and this time I joined him in his jubilation. "Look at this imbecile!" he remarked to his friends. "Laughing at himself. If only he understood German!" Then he added, "What a waste of time!" and they moved on.

"Vio," I called out to the horse and began to plow and whistle again. I didn't dare lift my eyes from the plow until sometime later when I had finished plowing the entire field.

Slowly I raised my eyes and looked around me. The soldiers were not to be seen, but shots could be heard coming from the direction of the village. I set the tired and confused horse free and patted him affectionately.

"Thank you, horsey, I'll never forget you for this." The horse snorted and then taking a few paces he relieved himself. Having finished he walked slowly to an adjoining field and began to graze.

I lay down on the ground, but I felt unprotected. I walked over to a stack of wheat and crouched inside so that the wheat surrounded me, but after a few minutes I realized that a stray bullet could still find my body. I stood up not knowing where to hide, and then I saw my haven, the deserted wagon.

I didn't run, but walked over almost casually, climbed onto the wagon, and sat down on the edge, my feet dangling between the two back wheels. I surveyed the surrounding countryside and then matter-of-factly, slowly reclined, turned on my stomach, and boosted myself to the center of the wagon.

In case a bullet should come flying at me, I'll be protected. But soon it became evident that wood couldn't offer much protection, though I had no desire to run for another sanctuary. And there was nowhere else to hide, so at last I reconciled myself to fate, and closed my eyes. If I was hit, I didn't want to see the bullet, and each time I heard one whistle by I'd wonder if I was still alive, and sometimes I couldn't tell, but I didn't move or open my eyes.

At long last the shots stopped. I slowly opened my eyes, raised my head, and saw that night had fallen. Little stars were shimmering in the sky and all around me was darkness. I could hear the horse still grazing but couldn't see him now. In the distance, flickering naphtha lamps could be seen in the village.

I climbed out of the wagon. Perhaps what is before me is not the village of Kulik, but the land of the dead. I took a few steps and suddenly stopped.

"I'm alive!" I said aloud. Perhaps I'd better wait, I thought. The Germans are probably still there, waiting for me. Maybe they've found Ivan, and Sasha. I wonder where Sasha is? Did he have a hiding place? What should I do? Wait here? Why hasn't Genia come to look for me? I know why. They've found Ivan and shot everyone. No! They would never find Ivan. Poor Sasha, what if they caught him? Not only is he an escaped prisoner, but Jewish as well. How could they tell? I wondered if he's circumcised.

I waited quietly, listening to the sounds of the night: a dog barking here and there, a little wild animal running through the field. The night was cold and I shivered in my thin cotton pants and light shirt, I'll have to go back to the house and find out what happened there. I began to walk briskly, finding my way more by instinct than by vision.

When I approached the house, I could see coming from the back window the small flickering light of the naphtha lamp. Someone is home, I assured myself, and tiptoed to the window and peered in.

Mrs. Paizak was sleeping on the cot. There was no one else to be seen. I walked to the front of the house treading softly, still afraid. I opened the door, and the squeaking of the dry hinges brought Mrs. Paizak suddenly to a sitting position and she screamed.

She looked at me, rubbed her eyes, and said, "Your supper's on the stove." And she went back to sleep.

I had forgotten about food, but now that I was reminded, I realized how hungry I was. On the stove I found some cold potato patties left from the day before. I poured myself a glass of milk and sat down to eat.

Where are the others? I'd better not ask. I looked at Mrs.

Paizak; she was snoring heavily, turning nervously from side to side.

I had started on my fourth patty when I heard the sound of a motorcar. I jumped out from my seat and ran to the door. I opened it with the intention of running back to the fields, but it was too late. The car had come to a stop in the courtyard and a Ukrainian Brown Shirt was getting out of it.

I stopped dead, smiled, and casually walked back to the room and sat down to finish my meal.

The Brown Shirt entered, walking energetically, his black boots striking terror in me. He looked around the room; then, with the riding crop he held in his right hand, he hit Mrs. Paizak's behind. She jumped up screaming.

"Where's the boss of the house?" he asked in Ukrainian.

"I'm the boss here," replied Mrs. Paizak.

"I mean the man of the house," he said, his face showing no expression, as if it had been molded out of steel. "Your husband," he added.

"My husband is dead. I have a son," said Mrs. Paizak.

"Then where is he?" he snapped.

"He's still in the field. What is it you want with my son?"

"Call him!" he ordered.

Mrs. Paizak moved towards the door.

If she leaves, his attention will surely focus on me, and he'll ask questions.

I stood up and said, "I'll go and call Stashek." And I didn't wait for a reply.

I ran out of the house and into the barn. I unhitched the cows which were sleeping by now, and hitting them several times with my stick, I drove them to pasture in the dark of the night. As I passed the potato field I heard Stashek and Genia conversing and moving about.

"Stashek!" I called out.

"Is that you, Kubush?" came the reply from Genia.

"Yes," I answered, and then one of the cows mooed.

"Are those our cows?" came Stashek's angry voice.

"Yes," I answered meekly.

"Where in hell are you taking the cows at this time of night?" he shouted.

"To pasture," I yelled back. "They've been in all day; some fresh grass will do them good."

"You crazy herring merchant, take the cows back to the stable," he snarled at me.

"Your mother told me to take them out," I lied.

"She's as crazy as you are," he shouted back.

"By the way, Stashek, there's a Ukrainian soldier in the

house who wants to speak to you right away." Stashek was now silent.

I hit the cows again and again and ran. I couldn't see the road or the fields, and when I finally stopped I didn't know in whose land my cows were grazing, and I wasn't sure if they were grazing on grass or perhaps in someone's cabbage patch. I could hardly see them and only heard them chewing, but by the sound I could tell it was something good.

I sat down on the ground, my arms clutching my frail body, and trembled from the cold. I began to sing Sasha's song, and wondered, as I sang, whether the words in the song were actually meant for me.

Several hours later I heard Genia calling me, "Kubush! Kubush!" I hesitated to answer. Perhaps it's a trap? I knew Genia would never betray me. But maybe she was forced to? Maybe the Brown Shirt is with her, walking quietly behind her, and all he's waiting for is the sound of my voice. "Kubush! Where are you?" Her voice was nearer now. The chewing and mooing of the cows finally brought Genia close to me. "Kubush, why didn't you answer me?"

I couldn't reply. How could I tell her of my terrible thoughts? "Is he gone?" I finally asked.

"Yes, don't be afraid," she consoled me.

"What did he want with Stashek?" I inquired.

"A lot of questions, that's all."

We started back, the cows in front of us, their bellies now swollen.

"They didn't find Ivan?" I asked, afraid of an answer.

"No. I just hope he's still all right in there."

Am I being led into a trap? Are they waiting for me back in the house? No, I don't believe that of Genia. Then why am I not sure of her loyalty?

Run you fool, leave her with the cows and run for your life . . . away . . . away into the woods.

I didn't run; I had to prove to myself that Genia, above all, would never lead me to my death.

When we entered the courtyard, the car was gone. In the barn Mrs. Paizak and Stashek were feverishly removing potatoes from Ivan's hiding place. We took away the boards, and there, in a hole big enough for one man to squat, was Ivan, unconscious.

We pulled him out, poured vodka into his mouth, and a few moments later he revived. Half an hour later he was his old self again, lying in the hay, his arms around Genia, kissing her.

The following day was sunny and warm; the sky was clear and the sun covered the village and its surrounding fields with bright rays of light.

After breakfast I started to take the cows to pasture, but Mrs. Paizak stopped me. That morning a neighbor had brought news that the soldiers had spent the night in the village searching and questioning. They had found many Russians in hiding. And they had killed many others in the fields who were trying to escape.

Maybe they'll return and search our farm again. Where will I hide this time? and Sasha, where is Sasha now? Is he still alive? Or perhaps . . . And the others? Will I ever hear their songs again?

As I sat at the table I couldn't hear the conversation around me, for my mind was far away. Weeks and months have passed and Moishe has not shown up. What has become of him? And Sasha, my friend Sasha. Is it possible that he is . . . No! I'd better not think of it.

My father, God only knows of his destiny. And my mother, Josel, and my Uncle Shepsel: they are lost. But why am I so sure? I should not write them off the face of the earth so easily. There's still hope. I've got to have hope.

I looked up at Ivan and now I noticed how pale he was. He sat quietly on the couch listening to consoling words from Genia. Does Ivan feel the same way I do? Perhaps he does. I caught Stashek's gaze and felt uneasy. His eyes were telling me that I was in the way.

Suddenly there was a knock on the door. We froze to our seats and looked at each other. There was nowhere to run and hide now. Ivan pulled a revolver out of his pocket and stationed himself behind the door.

How daring! Could I do that? I wish I could.

He motioned with his hand for Mrs. Paizak to open the door.

Stashek sat on the bed trembling with fear, his eyes on the gun. Genia covered her mouth with her hands to prevent herself from screaming.

The scene reminded me of a cowboy tale told to me by my Uncle Shepsel, but somehow it wasn't the same. The sense of excitement and adventure was missing, and instead of being thrilled, I was frightened.

The knock was repeated, now a little louder. Mrs. Paizak made her way to the door and with quivering hands opened it.

I expected to see a German soldier or a Brown Shirt, a gun

pointed in our direction, and his eyes suspiciously looking at me, his finger pointing accusingly, his voice saying, "You're a Jew!"

"No!"

"We'll soon find out, pull your pants down," and at that moment Ivan would shoot him from behind. The soldier would fall, his blood gushing like water from a fountain. And then he would . . .

The door opened, and framed in the doorway stood a little man with a heavy moustache and a frightened face with large bulging eyes. He carried a straw hat pressed to his chest. With a handkerchief, he wiped the sweat from his almost bald head and perspiring face, and in a stuttering voice he greeted Mrs. Paizak who stood in front of him blocking his way.

"I've been sent by the sheriff." He stopped, cleared his throat, and asked for a glass of water. Genia handed him the water; he swallowed it in one gulp, and then he stuttered, "You'll all come to the center of the village today at noon, outside the sheriff's home."

"Why? What did we do?" asked Mrs. Paizak.

"The whole village has to come. There's going to be a big meeting or something. It's an order from *them*."

"All right, we'll be there," said Mrs. Paizak.

"Don't forget now, every one of you. After twelve they'll be searching all the farms and whoever is found will be shot on the spot." He departed, running like a wild rabbit across the fields to the next farm.

Mrs. Paizak shut the door, Ivan hid his revolver, Stashek sighed with relief, Genia hugged Ivan, and I began to worry anew as to where I would fit into the day's proceedings.

It was immediately decided that Ivan would hide in the same place, and the rest of us would go to the meeting at the appointed time.

Ivan slid into his dugout and again we piled the potatoes on top of the boards. Stashek washed and dressed for the occasion as if he was going to a wedding.

Solemnly, as if marching behind a coffin at a funeral, we left the courtyard. When we reached the main road of the village we could see other farmers leaving their homes, all walking in the same direction. Unexpectedly, Mrs. Paizak stopped and threw her arms around me.

"Kubush, I don't think it would be safe for you there. Go and hide somewhere, my child."

"But where?" I asked, my heart beginning to pound again.

"I don't know, just hide anywhere you can. Save yourself. Now run quickly." She turned and walked away, Genia and Stashek following her.

I stood for a moment looking at their backs, feeling abandoned. I turned in the direction of the nearby forest and began to run towards it. I stopped. The forest would be the first place they would comb for partisans. I thought of the fields and wanted to run there, but again I decided against it. Where then? I looked around and there was not a soul to be seen now.

"I have to get off the open road," I said out loud, and started towards the farm.

In the courtyard chickens were cackling and picking grain from the earth. How I envied them; they didn't have to hide or run. Perhaps I could hide in the chicken house. I ran in there. The place was small and covered with chicken droppings, and it offered no concealment. I left and ran into the house.

I studied the room, thinking of hiding under the bed, but that was too obvious a place. I looked at the ceiling and my eyes rested on the trap door leading to the attic. With the help of a ladder I made my way into it.

I had never been there before, and now I forgot my reason for venturing there, for so many things caught my eye and I examined them with some satisfaction. Then I remembered. Perhaps I should hide here, or perhaps there, under the pile of grain. Inside this trunk . . . Yes, that a good idea, I'll climb inside it. I closed the lid on top of me. It was dark; a terrible moldy odor filled my lungs, but I was safe.

Then I remembered the ladder. How am I to get rid of it? It's no good, I'll have to abandon the trunk and the attic, and look somewhere else.

Quickly I climbed down, left the house, and entered the barn. Upon seeing me, the cows mooed as if reminding me that I had neglected to take them to pasture. Perhaps I could hide in the hay. That's an idea, I'll bury myself in the hay. But what if they search the barn or set it on fire?

I looked at the piled potatoes and now I envied Ivan. He was safe under there, protected in that hole. No, the barn will not do, I'll have to find a place they'll never think of searching. But I can't waste much more time; they may be on their way this very minute. Perhaps they've entered the courtyard now.

I left the barn, and as I shut the door behind me, I saw my hiding place staring at me. On the other side of the courtyard stood the cooler. It was a hole dug in the ground, covered by a straw roof, and it had a small opening in the front. From the outside, the cooler resembled a small house with only the roof showing, and its walls were deep in the ground. In the summer the cooler was used to keep milk, cheese, and butter fresh, but its main purpose was as a storage place for potatoes during the winter. Now it was empty.

I walked over to it, scanned the area around me to make sure I was alone, and then I slid through the opening and jumped in. I squatted down in a corner.

The ground was cold and damp and the air had a stagnant odor. I looked on the earth beneath my feet, gazed at the earthen walls around me, and saw hundreds of minute bugs and insects busily engaged in their own little world. I envied them, for they were free to do as they pleased and didn't have to hide.

If only I could be a little bug! A small ugly insect, in fact anything at all but a Jew. If only I could be a cow, a horse, a bird in the trees, or a frog in the pond. Anything at all. I'd have a better chance of surviving.

Why did God create Jews anyway? There seems to be no reason for our existence. My mind wandered from one thought to another as I squatted in the corner, not daring to move at all, not even to brush off a fly when it landed on my nose. I was glued to the earth.

From the outside I could hear the birds chirp and sing sweetly; the crows cawed in the fields; the cows mooed now and then; and the rooster gave out with a loud cock-a-doo-dle-doo. Periodically I heard the bark of a dog somewhere in the distance, but otherwise it was quiet.

Several hours later I heard footsteps approaching from the distance. Perhaps I'm only imagining them, or perhaps the Paizaks have returned.

I waited and listened, but didn't move. The footsteps came closer, and closer, and then I heard voices, German voices. Two soldiers were conversing. Their every step now was like a shot, and I could visualize them, although I couldn't see them.

The barn door opened. Silence. Then I heard their voices again. The door to the house opened . . . a few moments of silence . . . footsteps running up the ladder . . . some other sound . . . then their voices, again coming from the courtyard. The door to the chicken house opened, more conversation . . . laughter . . . more footsteps . . . now far away . . . now   closer . . . closer . . . closer . . . and now the shadow of a soldier fell into my hiding place and onto one of the walls as he bent down looking in.

I could hear him breathing. Does he see me? He must see me, and even if he doesn't, he must hear my heart pounding. It sounded like a loud drum. The shadow stayed there, moving only slightly. What is he waiting for? Why doesn't he order me to come out? Perhaps he's afraid. Perhaps he doesn't hear my heart beating after all. Wait a minute, I know what he's up to: he won't order me out, he'll simply throw a grenade in and blow up the whole structure and me with it. If that's what he intends to do then I'll show him. Once the grenade lands, I'll grab it and throw it right back at him and blow him up with his own weapon. I've got to keep my eyes open for the grenade. I'll have to work fast.

Oh, God, what will I do? I have to sneeze. Will I be able to repress it? I could feel it coming. Why doesn't he throw the grenade and be over with it?

I now heard the other voice, "Something there?"

"Just bugs. It's amazing how well organized they are!" came the reply.

"All right then, let's get to the next farm."

The shadow straightened itself and disappeared. I heard footsteps moving away, and then silence. I now swallowed my sneeze.

Why did he leave? He must have sensed someone was here. Perhaps he thought I was a Russian partisan and was as much frightened of me as I was of him. No, they haven't left, they're still there. They know there's someone in here. It's a trap. They want me to come out into the open. Someone is at the side of the entrance, waiting, waiting for me to stick my head out. I have to deceive them to the end. I was not going to move at all, though by now my knees were giving way and felt as if they would break.

In time I couldn't feel them at all, as if they had been disconnected from the rest of my body. I was numb. My eyes were wide open, staring blankly at the earthen wall. Perhaps the German has thrown the grenade into the cooler and I am now dead, that's why I can't feel my legs. If so, then there isn't much reason to fear death, it's quite sudden and painless. Alive or dead, I continued to stay in the same position and lost all sense of time and sound. I heard nothing, saw nothing, and eventually thought of nothing.

Hours later I realized I was being called. "Kubush! Kubush! Where are you?" came Genia's pleading voice. "Come out, everything is all right now." Then I heard Mrs. Paizak's voice calling me, but still I didn't answer, and then I heard Genia sobbing. "They found him, Mamma, they've found him! He's probably dead by now," and she cried hysterically.

"So they found him," Stashek said.

I tried to stand up, but couldn't. My legs wouldn't straighten. I crawled over to the opening, looked out, and saw that night had fallen.

"Here he is," cried Genia upon seeing me, and ran towards me and embraced me. "Holy Mother, Kubush is alive!"

Mrs. Paizak's eyes were wet, Ivan was drinking water by the well, and Stashek looked at me with angry eyes and said, "Afraid, eh? I bet you shit your pants." And he laughed, but no one laughed with him.

At the supper table, Mrs. Paizak recounted what had taken place outside the sheriff's house. As she was telling the story, her eyes would fill with tears; she'd wipe them with her sleeve, continue the sad tale, and then she'd cry again. Genia begged her to stop, but she insisted on telling what her eyes had witnessed that day.

When the villagers were gathered in the center of the village, a Ukrainian officer delivered a speech about the danger of hiding Russian escapees. The German authorities were lenient, he said, but if the inhabitants of the village continued to give refuge to these bandits, the whole village and its occupants would be bombed and obliterated from the face of the earth. He also added that in the two days of operation, they had found and killed dozens of Russians.

Sasha, there was no word from Sasha. Was he safe? Or . . . I began to tremble now and his song, his sad song ran through my mind. Sasha has to be alive, he's probably hiding somewhere. They'll never get Sasha.

She told how they had made an example of one elderly man from the village whom they accused of hiding Russians. They cut off his tongue, pulled out his fingernails, and then his toenails. The onlookers cried and wailed and hid their faces, but the soldiers standing by threatened to shoot them all if they didn't watch. They extracted the old man's teeth, ripped the skin off his body, then gouged his eyes out one at a time with a hot iron bar. The poor man finally died a slow, agonized death.

Mrs. Paizak now wept beyond control. Genia tried to soothe her, and Ivan, who had sat silently throughout, now said quietly, as if to himself:

"I'll leave."

Mrs. Paizak threw herself on him, held him tightly, and cried, "How can I let you leave? You're like a son to me. Better than a son, much better than my own son." And she continued to sob until the naphtha in the lamp burned out.

The next day we received reports of the deaths of Nicolai, Dimitri, Boris, Yuri, Sergei, and countless others, but there was no word of Sasha. We listened with heavy hearts to the details of how our friends had met death: some in the fields running away, others in the forest defending themselves until they were out of bullets, and still others, found hiding in a well or a barn or a haystack.

Mrs. Paizak and Genia cried. But Ivan was silent and so was I. I wanted to cry, but hard as I tried I couldn't, and only succeeded in recalling the many Sundays those now dead had sat at the table, eaten, drunk, and sung.

In the evening, an old woman who lived at the end of the village by the forest arrived in our courtyard. "One of them was shot in the bushes near my house," she informed us in a shrill voice. "He's still lying there." And now a silly grin crossed her face, as if she took delight in bringing us this news. She was all excited and proceeded to recall with great relish how the bullet had struck the runaway Russian in the back, how he had limped for a while, shot back several times, and finally fallen screaming like a wild animal.

Stashek wanted no part of it, and since it wasn't safe for Ivan to be seen, Genia and I followed the woman to bury the dead man. As we walked along the road leading towards the forest, I prayed silently, and begged God to spare Sasha, and that it shouldn't be he who was lying dead in the bushes. But my prayers must have been too late, or else God ignored me, or perhaps He didn't understand me, or else I didn't pray hard enough, or recite the right prayer, for when we reached the dead body, I recognized the face with the hooked nose immediately.

We began to dig a hole, but the earth was hard and full of rocks and tree roots. As if the earth was refusing to receive him.

But somehow we managed, and laid Sasha to rest. When we had covered the grave, Genia kneeled in front of it, crossed herself, and prayed silently. I, too, wanted to pray for Sasha, but I didn't know a proper prayer for the occasion, and at the same time, I began to wonder if there was after all anyone in heaven who listened to prayers.

We stood at the grave for a long time not saying a word, but just staring at it, and during that silence I realized how accurately Sasha's song had predicted his fate.

> In the forest by the valley,
> There a nightingale sings a song.

But where is the nightingale? I looked about me hoping there would be one, for I wanted the song's prophecy to come true. On a branch of a young poplar tree, I now spotted a bird. I wasn't sure if it was a nightingale, and it probably wasn't, but I took it to be one. The tiny bird hopped from branch to branch and finally stopped and chirped; but I imagined that it sang. Sasha's prophecy had come true. How could he have known?

The next day Ivan left. He was dressed in the mayor's coat and hat, and under the lavish garment bulged his rifle.

"Going somewhere?" I asked as he passed me.

He stopped and smiled. "I'm going away for good, Kubush."

"Where are you going?"

"I don't know. Good-bye!"

"Good-bye," I answered, and watched him disappear across the fields towards the river.

The countryside was deserted and quiet, and a cool breeze blew to and fro. Gone were my companions forever, gone were their songs, their stories, and gone was their promise to find my father.

I began to sing:

> In the forest by the valley,
> There a nightingale sings a song;
> I'm a fellow on foreign soil,
> Forgotten by my people, forgotten.

TWO

☐ In the late afternoon of a cold fall day, my eyes caught sight of an approaching figure in the distance. The walk was familiar, the feet shuffling rather than walking. It couldn't be! I thought. And yet I wanted it to be . . . How I hoped that it would indeed be my Uncle Moishe! How wonderful it would be to have someone, anyone!

Perhaps it is Moishe. But once the figure comes closer it will be some stranger. How many times before had I imagined someone in the distance to be Moishe, only to be disappointed?

I was so accustomed to this that on this cold day as I sat on the grass, my legs crossed under me, my eyes on the approaching stranger, I refused even to stand up. And yet the walk was so much like his. Unmistakably Moishe, my Uncle Moishe! But why risk being hurt again?

I sat there. The figure came closer, and now stood beside me. I looked at my Uncle Moishe, barefoot, with torn pants and a cotton shirt. I wanted to jump up and kiss him, hug him, I wanted to laugh and be happy, but I did nothing. I simply sat there choking with oncoming tears.

He sat down beside me not uttering a word, and then both of us started to cry. I wanted to stop the tears. I tried desperately to stop them, but I had no control. Finally we stopped crying and sat silently looking at each other.

"I knew you'd come looking for me, Moishe," I said to break the long silence.

"I would have come sooner," he answered, "but they wouldn't give me a day off."

"I'm so happy to see you Uncle Moishe. Now I'm not alone. Now you'll have to come to see me more often and I'll come to see you."

Moishe nodded his head and smiled. "Don't worry, Jankele, everything will be all right. I won't abandon you."

"When do you have to go back?" I asked.

"Oh not until later tonight, maybe not till tomorrow."

"Good!" I exclaimed. "Then you'll sleep over."

"Won't Mrs. Paizak mind?" he questioned.

"I'll ask her," I assured him. "I'm sure she won't mind."

It felt so good to have my Uncle Moishe beside me. We lay awake for a long time talking about Warsaw, about Siedliszcze; then Moishe told me a joke, and that's how I fell asleep.

The next morning we had breakfast together. Moishe thanked Mrs. Paizak for her hospitality and said good-bye to her, to Genia, and to Stashek. Mrs. Paizak invited him to come back whenever he had a day off. I drove the cows to pasture, and Moishe came along to the field. From there he was to take his leave, but when we got there, he sat down on the wet morning grass and began to talk again about all sorts of things, and before long he was making up songs about Hitler. He tried to make the lines rhyme, though they did not always make sense.

When the sun was directly above us, Genia brought me lunch.

"Are you still here?" she asked, looking at Moishe.

"I'll be going soon," he answered unhappily.

We shared the lunch, after which I implored him to go.

"What's the matter, Jankele, you're tired of seeing me?"

"I wish you would never have to go, Moishe," I said, "but I'm afraid they'll be angry with you for being late."

"So I'll be late," he joked.

"Please, Uncle Moishe, go. Tell me where you work and I'll come visit you next week." He fell into silence.

Late that afternoon he still hadn't left and finally, to my complete surprise, he said, "The truth is, Jankele, I have nowhere to go."

"What about your job?"

"There is no job. They told me to leave."

"But why? What did you do?"

"I did nothing wrong, Jankele. They're afraid of keeping me on. But don't worry, I'll find another job around here. We'll be able to see each other more often."

"Uncle Moishe," I said, "wouldn't it be wonderful if we could be together?"

He smiled. "Do you think Mrs. Paizak could use me?"

"I'll ask her," I said, and ran off.

Mrs. Paizak listened to my plea as I pointed out what a good worker my Uncle Moishe was and what big muscles he had, and after all he was thirteen and capable of greater tasks than I. Mrs. Paizak was amused.

"Sure, Kubush, we'll find something for him to do. He may stay."

"Oh, Mrs. Paizak, thank you, thank you." I ran back to the field. "Moishe! Moishe!" I yelled with joy. "You can stay."

He lifted me into the air and placed me on his shoulders in

the same manner I remembered him doing in the Warsaw Ghetto.

"Gee up, horsey," I yelled, and he galloped around the field until he fell from exhaustion and I on top of him. We rolled on the grass and laughed. The cows stopped grazing and stared at us.

How good it felt not to be alone!

Every day another plot of land was cleared of its crop, and now the fields lay empty waiting for spring. The trees shed their leaves, and the winds grew fierce. On some days it was even too cold to take the cows to pasture.

Mrs. Paizak was happy with most of her crop, but she complained bitterly about the cabbage. She said, "There's no justice in this world. Across the river some son-of-a-bitch has a healthy batch of cabbage, every head as big as a pumpkin." Stashek looked at his mother and she turned on him. "Don't look at me like that. I'm only saying what nice cabbage is there, and if you want cabbage soup this winter it wouldn't hurt to help ourselves to some of it."

It was an extremely dark night when we set out across the river with long, sharp knives in our hands and burlap bags over our shoulders. We could hardly see where we were going, and had to feel our way along quietly without whispering a word.

In the dark of that night, Stashek, Moishe, and I let our knives go at the cabbage, and after six or seven trips the cabbage patch lay bare.

In the house Mrs. Paizak and Genia were shredding and packing the cabbage into barrels so as to destroy the evidence immediately. Mrs. Paizak was drunk with victory, and slapped us on our backs.

"This is not the end, only the beginning." We looked at her in surprise. "Tomorrow night," she continued, "I have another mission for you."

From the beginning I was aware that what we were doing was wrong, but there was a certain excitement about this work, so I almost looked forward to it and even hoped it would continue forever.

The following night we raided a cabbage patch directly across from our house. We didn't go to sleep; it was too late for that. Instead we sat at the window and looked across the fields, our eyes on the ravaged cabbage patch.

The sun came up; a figure appeared there, then another. We heard conversation, then more people came, and later we heard a woman crying.

What if they find us out? What will happen to us?

That evening when I saw a stranger arriving with a horse and wagon I was certain he'd come to claim his cabbage.

"How is life treating you, Abraham?" he asked me as he descended from the wagon and went into the house. Later I saw Mrs. Paizak lead him into the pigsty. There was some haggling; he gave Mrs. Paizak some bills, loaded a pig onto his cart, covered it with some boards, whipped the horse lightly, turned to me and said, "Good-bye, Abraham," and rode away.

I shook with fear.

"What's the matter?" Mrs. Paizak asked.

"I was afraid he came looking for his cabbage."

"What cabbage?" asked Mrs. Paizak with a completely straight face.

"The cabbage we stole," I said innocently.

"Kubush!" exclaimed Mrs. Paizak. "What are you saying? Who steals cabbage?"

"But, Mrs. Paizak," I protested strongly, "what about the cabbage in the barrels? Where did it come from if not . . . ?"

"From our garden, Kubush. We had a very good crop."

My fear was still there, but the excitement of stealing was gone. I felt cheated, as if it had never happened, and that woman's crying haunted me for many days.

Dressed in a short leather coat with a scarf around his neck, Mr. Kowal's only son was making his way towards our house. Looking at him I realized how cold it was and I began to shiver from the wind.

He had never been warm towards me, but always quite friendly. Now as he entered the courtyard he avoided even looking at me or saying good day.

"Where's your boss?" he asked coldly, as if he didn't know me.

"In the house," I answered.

From inside the house I heard voices, low, unintelligible voices. Minutes later he departed without even throwing me a glance. When I entered the house I found Mrs. Paizak seated at the table, her eyes wet with tears. She pulled me towards her and held me tightly against her body.

"Dear Jesus Christ," she murmured. "Please guide me. What shall I do?"

"What is it?" I asked.

Mrs. Paizak released her hold, bit her tongue, and instead of answering me, broke down, crying hysterically. Frightened, I ran out of the house into the fields, running like a wild rabbit.

"Moishe! Moishe!" I screamed, and fell into my uncle's arms. "Something terrible has happened."

"What happened?" asked Stashek, who was also in the field.

"I don't know, she's just crying."

Stashek dropped his pitchfork and ran towards the house. We followed him. In front of the portrait of the Holy Mary, Mrs. Paizak was praying. She stood up and dried her eyes with the end of her cotton apron.

Then the reason for her sorrow unfolded in sentences that were broken and sometimes interrupted with more crying.

The Germans had issued a decree that day which commanded every farmer who employed a Jew to bring him to the Gestapo within forty-eight hours. Any farmer caught disobeying the order would be shot, together with his family and ten surrounding neighbors.

Now I realized the Kowals' concern: they lived only a few houses away and they feared reprisal.

When she had finished telling us this terrible news, Mrs. Paizak joined our stony silence, and that's how the rest of that particular day was spent, in silence.

Genia had heard the news in the village and when she came home she too was silent. We ate our supper in silence, and went to sleep in silence.

Moishe and I hardly looked at each other, and in a deadly silence we covered ourselves with fresh hay and fell asleep.

In the morning Mrs. Paizak served us breakfast, and then she proceeded to mend my coat.

I recalled the day when my mother and father had taken me to the tailor to have it made for Passover. I must have been about six years old then. It had been a great occasion. Now the coat was too tight.

Her eyes still on the needle, and in a trembling voice, but trying to sound firm, Mrs. Paizak said, "You'll have to leave, boys. They would have to kill me first before I'd lead you to your death, but at the same time I can't keep you here any longer."

"When do we have to go?" asked Moishe.

"Right away," came the reply. "I'll pack you some food to take." And into a cotton bag she packed two loaves of bread, a bottle of milk, and several pieces of ham.

"Where will we go?" I asked.

She didn't face me. "I don't know. That you'll have to decide, but you have to go."

I wanted to cry but then I looked at Moishe. He was calm and collected. He must have a plan, I thought, and so I too became calm. I said good-bye to Genia. She pulled me towards her and kissed me on my cheek, then fell onto the bed, stifling the sound of her crying. Mrs. Paizak walked us outside the door.

"Where do you plan to go?" she inquired. I looked at Moishe for an answer.

"That we'll have to decide," he said, smiling. I marveled at his confidence.

"Listen to me," she said. "I've done everything for you that was possible. If I could, I'd keep the two of you for as long as you'd want to stay, but what can I do? I have to think of my family and my neighbors. Your presence here endangers the whole village. Your tragedy is not of our doing. The Germans have brought this on you. Nothing and no one can help you now. Your fate is sealed. Why don't you go to Chelm, there's a ghetto there. You'll be among your own. If you wander around this district, sooner or later the Germans will catch you and then you'll implicate us. Give yourselves up, for our sake."

I should have been surprised by her advice, and yet I wasn't. For I understood the instincts of fear and survival. I wasn't surprised, but somehow I was sickened. The same Mrs. Paizak who fed me, who bathed me once in a basin of warm water, who once even told me that she thought of me as her own son. This same woman wished to sacrifice me now.

Moishe listened attentively and then, to my complete surprise, said, "I think that's a good idea. We'll go to Chelm."

"No!" I shouted. "We will not give ourselves up."

"Don't you understand, Kubush . . . ?" Mrs. Paizak began to plead with me.

"No!" I exclaimed again. "We are going to live. We won't die!"

She turned to Moishe. "Take care of him, you're older."

We started down the back road.

"May God look after you," I heard Mrs. Paizak whisper, but I didn't turn back to look at her. We passed Stashek in the fields, but he turned his head as though he hadn't noticed us.

The day was extremely cold and we shivered in our rags. Moishe had acquired an old, torn suit jacket which didn't protect him much from the bitter wind. The fields were almost deserted and the naked trees seemed to play a melancholy symphony as they waved in the wind.

"She's right, you know!" said Moishe. "There's nowhere for us to go except to Chelm."

"No!" I shouted. "If we give ourselves up they'll kill us."

"Don't be crazy. We'll steal our way into the ghetto, and no one will even know how we got there."

"No!"

We had reached the river. Several boys bundled in heavy winter coats were sitting around a glowing fire baking potatoes. Their cows were close by, enjoying the last days of fresh grass before the snow. One of the boys recognized us and called to us. We sat down and warmed ourselves, and later filled our stomachs with baked potatoes which we washed down with the milk Mrs. Paizak had given us.

We cherished every moment by the fire, but it had to end. At dusk the boys drove their cows home, saying, "We'll see you tomorrow."

How I envied them for having a home to go to! Moishe tried to keep the fire alive, but soon night fell and we began to look for a place to sleep. How cozy and warm Mrs. Paizak's barn seemed now! What we wouldn't have given to sleep there that night!

"Look, Jankele!" exclaimed Moishe, and pointed to a haystack. We made a hole in the hay, climbed in, and fell asleep.

The next day we waited anxiously for the cowherds to arrive, but they didn't show up. It was too cold. We sat in the haystack and devoured the remains of our food. We looked across the fields and in all directions there was hardly a soul to be seen. In the distance we saw Mrs. Paizak's farm, and now and then we caught a glimpse of Mrs. Paizak, Genia, or Stashek.

We sang songs, old ones that we knew, and new ones which we composed. All of them concerned Hitler in one way or another.

At the end of the third day we were too hungry to sing. When the sky was covered with darkness, Moishe suddenly announced, "Wait here, I'll be back."

"Don't leave me," I pleaded. "Let me go with you, Uncle Moishe."

"You stay here, Jankele. I'll be back in no time at all with food." He left. I sat waiting and when, what seemed hours later, my Uncle Moishe still wasn't back, I began to worry that he had deserted me, or worse, that perhaps he had been caught.

Along the horizon, lamps flickered in windows. To have a home, a mother, a bed, I mused. To belong to someone, to be loved, to be cared for, to have a piece of dry black bread. How lucky some people are!

"Jankele!" I suddenly heard Moishe calling. "Look what I've got." From under his coat he produced half a loaf of bread, from his pockets, a few raw potatoes and sugar beets. We ate half the bread, leaving the rest for the next day. We felt good again. It was good to be alive. Another day had passed and we'd survived. For another day we had cheated death.

One day, after weeks of existence in this manner, Stashek searched us out. He threatened personally to drive us to the Gestapo unless we left the area immediately. We listened without protest and we were frightened, but as much as we wished to go, we had no place to go to.

One very bright moon-lit night soon after we were awakened by sharp stabs from pitchforks. I heard voices, whispers, coughing, then stabs, heavy stabs all around me. Hands reached from all directions, and held us firmly. Suddenly I found myself standing on the ground and about a half-dozen pitchforks facing me, like machine guns ready to shoot.

"Kubush!" I heard a voice call. "Who is your friend?"

"My uncle," I replied, studying a man's face. Then I recalled having worked for this man one day, helping him build a fence. He had offered to pay me for my labor but I had refused, and I remembered how thankful he had been then.

"Shall I blow the bugle?" asked one of the farmers.

"No!" said my acquaintance. "What's the point? Look at them. They don't have a penny."

"Do you have any gold?" asked another. "If you give us some gold we'll let you go. If not, we blow this horn and other men will arrive with a horse and wagon, and drive you to the Gestapo in Chelm."

"We have nothing," said Moishe.

"That's what they all say," said the man with the bugle.

"Search us then," said Moishe.

A man approached us and was about to search when the farmer I knew shoved him aside, then turned to us and said, "We are volunteer policemen. Our job is to catch Jews and Russians before the Germans do, understand? If the Germans catch you here, the whole village will go up in flames, and this we want to avoid. We'll let you go if you promise to leave this area. But if we catch you here again we'll be forced to run you in."

We didn't sleep the rest of that night, but talked and pondered. Moishe was all for going to the Chelm ghetto. I was against it, but had no alternative plan to offer.

"Let's go into the forest then," said Moishe, "and join the partisans."

I had heard how the Germans combed the woods daily, searching for escaped Jews and Russians. "Not the forest," I said, "that's the first place they search." We argued and argued, and in the end we decided to explore a new district.

In the morning we wandered across the river into another village, but when night fell and we were hungry, tired, and had no place to sleep, we returned to the haystack.

Our nights were now sleepless, for we feared that the men with the pitchforks would return, but several nights passed and no one showed up.

Then one day Stashek came with bread in his hands. To our complete amazement, Stashek not only offered us the bread, but was extremely sympathetic. While we devoured the loaf, picking up every crumb that fell from our hands, he explained how he needed our help.

"I need some lumber," he said. "There are a lot of trees in the forests, but it's illegal to cut them down. If you boys would give me a hand tonight, I'd let you sleep over in the barn and give you a good supper."

We were overjoyed. At dusk we entered Mrs. Paizak's house again. How good it felt to be in a house with a fire burning in the stove!

"Get to sleep," said Stashek when we had finished eating. "We have a busy night ahead of us."

We entered the barn and lay down in our old, familiar sleeping place. That it was only for one night didn't seem to matter; our stomachs were full, and our bodies were warm. It felt good to be alive.

At midnight, Stashek was to wake us. Again I felt the excitement I had experienced with stealing the cabbage. For the moment we weren't simply hiding. There was a purpose in our being.

In my sleep I heard the barn doors open and then a voice, "Moishe!" It's Stashek, I thought in my sleep. "Moishe!" Then I heard other voices. I opened my eyes; a torch flashed, then another. "Moishe!"

Moishe turned in his sleep, jerked his head, and yelled out, "All right, Stashek, we're . . ."

My hand covered his mouth and he began to struggle. It was too late, the flashlights were now upon us, and hands were reaching for us. We scurried like a pair of mice, trying to find shelter.

"I've got the big one," I heard a voice say. "Get the other one."

Flashlights, feet, hands all around me, and then I was blinded by a light shining directly into my eyes.

"This time we'll have to take you in. Blow the bugle."

"Please, please, I don't want to die," I began to scream. "I don't want to die. Please let us go."

"Blow the bugle," said the voice again, and again I screamed and then began to cry hysterically. Moishe tried to calm me, and when he couldn't, he became annoyed with me.

"Wait here," said another voice. They left the barn, locking us in. Outside, Mrs. Paizak was pleading on our behalf, and swearing at Stashek and wishing him every imaginable plague.

"We have to be rid of those two lice, Mother, once and for all," he was yelling.

"You scum!" she shouted at him. "How could you have ever been born from my belly?"

I heard the door to the house open and close, and then more quarreling, but it was too difficult to hear what was being said. I waited for the bugle to shatter the quiet of the night. Two white horses will come galloping, pulling a wagon driven by a husky farmer. Like a couple of pigs being taken to market, that's how we will be driven to Chelm. On the way people will stop and stare. What a horrible end! We'll be herded to the Gestapo, ordered to dig our own graves, shot, and . . . there'll be no and . . . that will be it. That's all forever . . . no one will ever know, remember, or care.

The doors to the barn opened and again I felt the flashlights upon me. I fell to my knees and cried, "Please let us go, we haven't done anything. We have nothing to give you. Take mercy, please let us go!"

A hand pulled me up, making me stand up straight. I looked into the face of my acquaintance. "Stop crying, Kubush!" he said. I tried to stop, and choked on my tears. "We've warned you once before, but you didn't listen."

"We had nowhere to go," I explained.

"Go anywhere you like, but away from this village. This is your last warning."

I pulled Moishe by his coat and we walked out into the courtyard. Mrs. Paizak approached us pleading, "Please go away, take mercy on me and go away. Go to Chelm, give yourselves up."

We walked past her to the back of the house and then began to run. We ran and ran until we were almost upon the river, and there stood the haystack. Instinctively we went to it, and sat down exhausted and shaking with fear.

Above us the moon shone brightly, like a searchlight pointing us out. This time we resolved to abandon the haystack and venture into new territory.

"We'll be picked up in no time at all," said Moishe. "Look at us, a couple of runaway Jews. We would stand a better chance if we separated." I protested. "Let's try it out for a week," he begged. "We'll meet here at the end of the week."

"Promise me you'll come back," I begged him.

"Don't worry, Jankele, I'll never desert you."

We parted. He turned left and I right. We drifted away from each other. Two lost figures on a vast, deserted early morning landscape.

The first part of the day I wandered in the fields, but by late afternoon hunger drove me to the village across the river. Farmers passed and, to my amazement, ignored me. Dogs barked and sometimes chased after me, but otherwise I attracted little attention.

When I reached the last house of the village, I resolved to enter and ask for food. Then fear overtook me and I imagined myself being chased from the house with a stick or else being apprehended and driven to the Gestapo.

I moved towards the courtyard of what looked like a well-to-do farmhouse; there was a huge barn and a separate stable. A dog's barking brought a man out of the stable. He stood and looked at me, his face cold and suspicious. I wanted to turn and run, but something inside of me said, Go on, don't be afraid.

I approached him. His eyes were on me, studying me.

"Could I have something to eat?" I asked looking straight at him.

He pulled out a pipe, lit it, then said, "Follow me," and led me inside the house.

An old man with a head of white hair sat at the window. A fire burned in the stove and an aroma of food permeated the air.

"Take off your coat," said the farmer. I removed my hat and coat and looked around the room. My feet were aching and felt swollen. My shoes were too small and made my toes curl under.

"Over there," he pointed to a large table in the center of the room. I sat down, and when I looked up, he was bringing me a plate of soup and a piece of black bread. I looked at him, then at the old man; they in turn were watching me.

Obviously he knows I'm a Jew, I thought. That's why he doesn't ask about me. I bit into the bread and was about to pick up the spoon when his voice rang out:

"Don't you cross yourself before eating?"

The spoon fell from my fingers and my heart began to beat so loud that I'm sure the two men must have heard its sound.

"I'm sorry," I said. "I'm so hungry that I forgot." And quickly made the sign of the cross and then attacked the food in front of me. I guess they don't know I'm a Jew after all.

"What do they call you?" inquired the old man. I raised my eyes and paused for a moment.

"Kubush," I answered meekly.

"What?" shouted the old man, turning one ear in my direction.

"Kubush," I repeated.

"Louder," said the younger one. "My father doesn't hear too well." And turning to his father he yelled out in a voice that almost shook the whole house, "They call him Kubush!" The old man either still didn't hear or simply didn't care. He turned towards the window and looked out again as if waiting for a messenger who would never arrive. The son picked up some logs and threw them into the fire.

"Where are you off to, boy?" he questioned.

I wasn't prepared for such questions and almost choked on the last spoonful of soup.

"Looking for work perhaps?"

"Yes, yes, I'm looking for work."

"How would you like to work here?"

"I would, very much."

"There isn't much work now, but you could help around the house and barn, and in the spring I could really use you to look after the cows."

"That I know how to do well," I said, my face beaming.

"Really?" his eyes opened wide, waiting for an explanation.

"I looked after cows this past summer."

"Where?"

"In the next village. In Kulik . . . the Paizak family."

"Oh? Why aren't you there now?" he asked inquisitively.

I had blundered. I should never have mentioned the Paizaks at all, but now it was too late. I looked up at him and he was waiting for an answer.

"I would rather not talk about it," I finally said.

He sat down beside me and refilled his pipe. "That's all right, you don't have to tell me. If you would like to stay with us, we'll treat you well!" I nodded my head and smiled. "Very well, Kubush, you're hired." He extended his hand and I shook it. "My name is Mr. Cybulski."

I filled a burlap bag with straw, placed it on the floor near the warm stove, and this became my lodging for the night. I began to undress for sleep feeling very uneasy, for Mr. Cybulski and his father were doing the same. I prolonged my undressing as long as I could, watching them and imitating their every move so as to appear like one of them. When they were down to their winter underwear they kneeled in front of their beds. Quickly I too kneeled. From the corner of my eye I watched them: their lips moved silently, their hands in praying position and eyes closed. I moved my lips without saying a thing. A few moments later they crossed themselves, stood up, and jumped into their beds. I too made the sign of the cross, miming every gesture to its minutest detail.

"Blow out the lamp, boy," grunted the old man. I walked over to the table and extinguished the naphtha lamp and then jumped into my new, warm bed on the floor.

How fortunate I am! There must indeed be a God in heaven.

The crackling of the fire beside me and the heat it produced induced me to sleep, but as I wallowed in my new-found comforts, my thoughts turned to Moishe and I suddenly felt guilty. Where is he right now? Is he sleeping beside a warm fire? Is his stomach full like mine? Is he still alive? If only he had come along with me, then the two of us could have found shelter here.

From Moishe, my thoughts wandered to other things, and suddenly it occurred to me that I was in danger of betraying myself. What if I dream and in my sleep I should speak in Jewish? I'll have to start thinking in Polish, I'll have to dream in Polish. What if I succeed so well that I even forget my real name, my father's name, my mother's name? No, I won't forget. But for now I have to become someone else. I began to feel groggy.

Dear God, then immediately I clarified, Dear *Jewish* God, don't make me dream tonight. I know I've been breaking the laws. As you have seen tonight I've even kneeled and crossed myself, but you know, dear God, that I'm only pretending. My heart isn't in it. Please, dear God, forgive me and help me.

Outside, the branches from the trees were beating against the window panes and the wind lashed without mercy; when day broke there was snow on the ground and frost on the windows. I looked sadly across the white, deserted fields and wondered where my Uncle Moishe was.

Nothing eventful occurred during the first days. I arose in the mornings, mouthed my prayers, made the sign of the cross before each meal, and tried to look devout. I peeled potatoes, swept the house, fed the pigs and the other animals, and tried generally to make myself as useful as possible. Mr. Cybulski was pleased with me and complimented me on several occasions.

On the fifth day of my stay, Mr. Cybulski put on his Sunday boots, and as he was buttoning up his winter coat he announced, "I'll be gone for a while, Kubush." He instructed me to feed the animals and take care of his father.

In the early evening he returned covered with fresh snow, his nose red from frost. He warmed himself by the fire, had some soup which he had prepared that morning, then inquired if everything was in order. He filled and lit his pipe and spent the rest of the evening puffing on it, refilling it, and puffing again. Then it was time for bed. Again the three of us got undressed and knelt to say our nightly prayers. By this time I had mastered their mannerisms though I still didn't know one word of the prayer. I crossed myself when unexpectedly a voice rang out:

"Why don't you say your prayer aloud, Kubush?"

I froze, then turned my head. Mr. Cybulski was standing beside me.

"I never say prayers aloud," I answered. Then I added, "Neither do you, I notice."

"I'd like to hear how you pray. Just this once, perhaps you'd be good enough to recite the Lord's Prayer."

"I'd rather not, Mr. Cybulski," I pleaded, my face turning red.

"I don't think you know the prayer."

"Of course I know the prayer."

"Then why don't you recite it?"

"I'm shy," I answered.

He smiled. "Stand up boy, I know all about you."

"I know the prayer, I tell you I know it!" I shouted.

He sat on his bed. "I was in Kulik today." My heart jumped. "I spoke to Mrs. Paizak." I lowered my head. "You'll leave tomorrow morning." He blew out the lamp and went to bed.

I couldn't sleep and when day broke I dressed, and while the others were still snoring, opened the door and left.

It's all for the best, I reasoned. God knows what He's doing. Tomorrow I have to meet Moishe anyway.

I left the farm and headed towards the haystack.

The river was frozen and I began to walk across it, but the ice gave way and I fell and slid deep into it. With all my strength I fought and eventually succeeded in rescuing myself. I was dripping wet but not for long. The frost turned me into a winter scarecrow, icicles hanging from my body.

I reached the field where the haystack had been, but now it was gone. Everything was gone. Only snow, snow all around as far as my eyes could see. Even the little houses in the distance looked like piles of snow and only the smoke coming from the chimneys was visible.

I have to find shelter. But where? Where do I turn? Who will have me? What about Moishe? I was expecting Moishe the next day and if I left he wouldn't know where to find me. I will freeze to death if I don't find a warm place.

In the distance stood the Paizaks' farm. I'll hide in the barn, I reasoned. They don't have to know that I'm there.

I reached the back of the barn and peeked in through a crack between two boards. No one was there. I pried a loose board open and squeezed in. The cows were sleeping in their dung. I looked for a place to hide and finally decided to lie down with the cows under their trough. I lay waiting for the day to pass. Tomorrow Moishe will come!

The ice melted and now I was drenched with water, but it was warm. Suddenly I heard the door open and heard Mrs. Paizak's voice.

"Gee up, princesses." But the cows just lay there. She hit them with a stick and they jumped up. She sat down on a stool and began to milk.

I couldn't see Mrs. Paizak's face, only her hands pulling the cow's udders. I saw her legs and I could also see right up her skirt. To my complete surprise, in this terrible cold, Mrs. Paizak was not wearing underpants. I felt ashamed for looking and yet there was a certain fascination I experienced.

I wanted to call out to her. I knew she'd be pleased to see me, but I hesitated, for I feared she'd be frightened suddenly to hear a voice.

If only I was a cow instead of a Jew, then I could stay here all winter long without fear, I mused.

By noon I began to feel cramped. My eyes wandered, surveying the barn, and finally rested on the ladder which led to the landing. There I dug a hole in the straw, climbed in like a rat into its nest, and fell asleep.

When I opened my eyes I didn't know where I was, and because of the total darkness, I imagined that I was dead and that this was the other world. So I've died, I guess I've been shot. I accepted my thoughts calmly. Death seemed painless and I felt no different than before. Then I remembered. I rubbed my eyes, and through a crack in the boards I looked out.

It was dark. The barn door suddenly opened. I jumped back. Below me, making her way towards the pigsty, was Genia. I almost called out to her, but controlled myself.

Out of a wooden bucket she dumped freshly cooked potatoes into the trough. How appetizing those potatoes looked! Their odor reaching my nostrils made me realize that at that moment I would have been happy to change places with one of the pigs.

She hummed a Russian melody, patted one of the cows on the rear, and left.

I should have spoken to her, I now blamed myself. She would have brought me some food. The pigs were shoving each other, fighting for every potato. I climbed down, stuffed my pockets with their food, and back on the landing had my meal for the day.

How good those potatoes tasted. I had made my kill and now went back to the nest. I began to feel like a wild animal, a rat perhaps.

I recalled my feelings towards rats and now I knew what my enemies thought of me. What careful preparations they were making in setting the trap to catch me!

"What's this for, Daddy?"

"A trap, Jankele, to catch a big ugly rat," said my father, and the next morning the spring had sprung, the door was locked, and inside the cage was a big black ugly rat. What a revolting looking creature! We drowned him that day, but that was a long time ago.

How cruel, I now thought. Who knows what went through that rat's mind when we threw him into the water?

The door to the barn opened and closed many more times that day, but I didn't move.

The next day I kept watch through the crack so as not to miss my uncle. I had a good view of the fields, the river, and the place where the haystack once stood. I reasoned that once I saw Moishe in the distance I would break out of the barn and run towards him.

Below me, Stashek was whistling and cleaning the horse. I became motionless, afraid to move.

Outside it was calm, clear, and the land lay frozen. I had turned my head to give my eyes a rest, but when I looked out again I saw Moishe walking directly towards me.

"Moishe!" I screamed.

Stashek's whistling suddenly stopped and before I realized what I had done he was pulling me down the ladder.

"You filthy little herring dealer," he was yelling, twisting my arms behind my back. "Get out of here!" He pushed me out of the barn and into the courtyard. "If I catch you again I swear by Jesus Christ I'll tie you to the horse's tail and personally deliver you to the Gestapo!"

Moishe entered the courtyard and I fell into his arms. Now Mrs. Paizak and Genia were there too.

"Come inside quickly," Mrs. Paizak ordered. "Someone may see you," and she led us into the house.

Stashek, raging mad, clenched his teeth and yelled, "Mother, if they stay here I'm leaving." She closed the door in his face.

"Stashek is right, boys," she said. "It's too dangerous for you to stay here. The Germans are all around here every day. Without notice they search and question." She began to plead, "Why don't you go away. Please go to Chelm." Then she became silent and pointed to the table for us to sit down. We did, and with her trembling hands she served us food. "You can stay overnight," she finally said, "but don't show your faces outside."

"Don't you think it's dangerous, Mrs. Paizak?" asked Moishe, his face turning to a grin.

What's he saying? I wondered.

"Coming here, I saw a truckload of Germans headed in this direction."

Mrs. Paizak could hardly speak now, as if she was paralyzed.

Moishe broke into laughter. "Look how afraid you are."

"Leave right away," she blurted out. "Please go. If you're caught, you don't know me, remember. I've been kind to you; don't give them my name." Moishe laughed louder.

"Come, Moishe," I pulled at his sleeve.

"I was only joking," said Moishe. "I saw no Germans."

"Go! Go! Leave me in peace!" shouted Mrs. Paizak.

We turned the corner of the house and headed towards the river. Not a word was said until we reached the place where the haystack had once stood. A farmer muffled in his winter clothes passed by. It was as if we were ghosts and he couldn't see us. All around was snow and ice, as far as the eye could see.

"Where do we go now?" I asked.

"To the Chelm ghetto," came the reply.

"No ghetto for me," I said.

"There is no escape, Jankele, we'll go to the ghetto."

"I won't go to the ghetto."

"You'll go where I tell you to go, understand?"

"I don't have to listen to you," I answered in anger.

"Look, you squirt, I'm your uncle and don't you ever forget that."

"That doesn't mean you have the right to lead me to my death."

"A little respect, please; after all I am older than you. Therefore, I'll make the decisions."

"You're only thirteen," I said.

"But I *am* older."

"That doesn't make you smarter. Why did you have to frighten Mrs. Paizak? We could have stayed the night there, but no, you had to joke. I was doing all right without you and then the minute you came back I'm out in the cold again." I was sorry for saying that, but I didn't apologize, for I feared this would weaken my position.

Moishe fell into a long silence, then finally said, "Perhaps I'm in your way, Jankele." I was quiet. "Perhaps without me you'd be better off. You don't look as Jewish as I do. They see me coming and they let the dogs loose. What I've been through this last week is worse than death."

"Nothing is worse than death," I answered.

"I envy you, Jankele, you still have such a will to live."

"We'll live, Uncle Moishe," I said, "or at least, let's try."

"I'm going to Chelm; come with me. I don't want to die alone."

"I won't go," I said, holding my own.

"Then you leave me no choice but to go alone."

"Then go if you like." I felt certain he wouldn't leave me and that all I would have to do was to stand firm and refuse to join him.

"Jankele, perhaps you'd be good enough to give me the two pieces of fur."

In my coat pocket I carried the fur pieces from my mother's coat, and without hesitation I handed them to him.

It's all part of the act, I thought. He just wants me to go with him, but all I have to do is pretend to be unconcerned about his leaving and he won't go.

"You sure you don't want to come?" he asked.

"Never!" I answered. "I won't give myself up."

He turned, facing the river. "Good-bye."

"Good-bye," I answered coldly, and turned to face Mrs. Paizak's farm.

We walked away from each other in opposite directions. I wanted to turn back, but restrained myself. He'll come running after me any moment. Perhaps he's following me. I turned to look.

A small, hunched figure, shuffling rather than walking, reached the river, jumped across, stopped, and looked back. Immediately I turned and walked on. When I turned back again, my Uncle Moishe was not to be seen.

He'll come back; all I have to do is wait. By midday my body was frozen, I could hardly feel my toes and fingers, and Moishe was still not in sight. He's probably waiting for me on the other side of the river, but I'll hold out, I can't give in to him. If I do, we'll both end up in Chelm.

By staying in the field much longer I risked freezing to death, but I vowed never to return to the Paizaks. I began to walk. I should have cried; I wanted to cry; in fact I felt there was something wrong with me for not crying. Instead, I began to sing a Russian song.

I had visions of myself as an escaped Russian prisoner of war. I am Ivan or Sasha; under my coat there is a gun, and the next German I see, I'll shoot. How romantic! How daring! Nothing and no one can harm me. Suddenly I was marching instead of walking. I wasn't cold any more, my arms outstretched, swinging, my voice alive, singing loud and clear. I had completely forgotten who I was, where I was, and what I was looking for. I didn't feel the cold, the hunger, or the sorrow.

"Jew boy!" a voice called out. I ignored it. They didn't mean me. "Jew boy!" I stopped singing. Staring me in the face was the old woman who lived at the edge of the woods. Her face reminded me of death. "Jew boy, run for your life, they're in the village." I stood gaping at her. "Hundreds of them. German and Ukrainian pigs; they're searching every house, every barn. Run, hide or you'll die." She wanted to touch me but I drew away. "Poor Jewish boy," she uttered, and went on her way.

Again I was afraid. Looking about, I found myself standing on the main road of the village, familiar houses all around me. Everyone knew me here; anyone could have recognized me. I looked and spotted a dilapidated, deserted house with broken windows and no door. I ran in and found it filled with stalks of wheat. I climbed to the top of the heap and again like a rat I dug myself in, making a nest. Perhaps they won't find me here. But what if they have dogs? They could sniff me out.

Several shots rang out in the distance. I dug deeper into the wheat. Later I heard more shots, voices, shouting, footsteps.

I imagined someone was looking into my hiding place, that someone with eyes like a cat's was standing in the doorway ready to leap on me once I stirred or murmured.

How many times had I witnessed this scene? A cat waiting patiently, endlessly, for the mouse to come out of its hole. I closed my eyes and hoped that if I were shot I would be spared seeing my killer.

Outside it was quiet. Is he still waiting? How long will he wait? Perhaps it's only my imagination.

When at long last I opened my eyes and looked out the glassless window, night had fallen. The village was as quiet as a graveyard, yet I was afraid to move. I filled my empty stomach with kernels of wheat and retreated to my hole.

Three days went by. Outside, streaks of smoke were rising from the chimneys. Oh, to sit near a burning stove, I mused. I rubbed my hands trying to make my blood flow again. I could hardly move my legs or the rest of my body. I had lost all touch and taste.

The wheat, even though in abundant supply, did not satisfy my hunger. At times I regretted not having gone to Chelm with Moishe.

I heard footsteps in the snow. Quickly I retreated behind the window. When the approaching figure came nearer, I recognized him: a neighbor of Mrs. Paizak's.

"Jan!" I called out.

He turned sharply. "Kubush!" he exclaimed. "What are you doing here?"

"I'm hungry," I answered.

"Wait here," he said, and disappeared.

Now I was sorry I'd called out to him. I didn't know him too well and the enemy had many guises. I decided to run, but when I had reached the door Jan appeared again.

"Get inside," he ordered me, looking all about. "Someone may spot you. From under his coat he pulled out half a small loaf of black bread and threw it at me like a football. "You're frozen," he said.

"Are they gone?" I asked.

"I don't know. I'm off to the village now. You sit tight, I'll be back tonight." And he left.

I retreated back into my hole and for the longest time only stared at the bread, admiring it. It must have been weeks old, for it was as hard as stone. With all my strength I finally managed to break off a piece, only to lose some crumbs deep in the straw. I plunged after them, searched until I found them, and ate each one. Then I ate the broken piece of bread, taking small bites and chewing them slowly, turning the bread in my mouth dozens of times before swallowing it. The first piece had been devoured, but my stomach refused to be satisfied. Just one more small piece, perhaps? I broke another piece, then another, and another. There was only a small portion left, which I was determined to put away, but the voice in my stomach kept urging.

Treat yourself, it said. Go ahead and enjoy it.

What about tomorrow? I asked.

Tomorrow? The voice laughed. How sure you are of yourself. What makes you think you'll be alive by tomorrow?

I reached for the remaining piece and bit into it.

When the sky turned dark, Jan's voice called, "Kubush, come out!"

"Are they gone?" I asked.

"Yes," he whispered. "Follow me quietly."

He led me to his house. In the corner of the room sat his wife, her left breast exposed, feeding a newborn infant.

I removed my hat and sat down at the table. Jan, his hands shaking as if he was made of springs, served me a bowl of cabbage soup.

"Up there, you'll find some hay." He pointed to a ladder leading to the attic. I thanked him, nodded to his wife who stared at me, and climbed up.

There was little hay in the attic. To keep my hands warm I slid them into my pants and kept them near my genitals. Rats and mice were all around me, and I had the feeling of being their king and ruler.

The door to the attic opened two or three times a day and Jan would appear with a bowl of soup or a piece of stale bread.

One evening he invited me to come down and have supper with his family. When the meal was over and his wife was clearing the table, he turned to me.

"If you had some money or valuables," he said, "then I'd be able to keep you on." I believed him, for I knew he was extremely poor. His farm consisted of a small piece of land, one old cow that hardly gave any milk, and a few chickens.

"I have nothing to give you," I answered.

"Didn't your parents leave you their gold?" he asked.

"No, we had no gold."

"If only you knew where they buried it," he said, almost to himself.

"I tell you we were very poor, we had no gold."

He glanced at his wife and smiled, then turned back to me. "You're too young to know, Kubush. All Jews have gold."

Did my parents or grandparents have gold? If so, why were

we so poor? How many times, even before the war, did I go to bed hungry? How many times did I have to cry for one grosz to buy a candy? Did my parents lie to me? Were they in fact wealthy like all Jews are supposed to be?

"When you get hold of some money or valuables, Kubush," I heard Jan say, "then come and see us. You're a good boy, we'd like to see you save yourself."

The next morning I was given another piece of stale bread and I departed. As I walked across the fields I saw coins, diamonds, and gold glittering all about me. When I touched them and held them in my hand they simply melted away, turned into water.

I resolved to find my uncle and within me a voice whispered: keep looking, he's wandering somewhere on the road.

The day was coming to a close when I found myself in foreign territory; houses, little houses covered with snow; a dog barked here, a cow mooed there, a voice shouted, someone laughed, and in front of me was an endless, winding road covered deep in snow and only visible because of the tracks left by a sleigh that had passed that day.

No sign of my Uncle Moishe. Perhaps he did go to Chelm after all. A terrible guilt took hold of me. I drove him to Chelm. I should never have let him leave me. Instead of turning away from him, I should have sat down and cried.

My eyes continued to search, my feet to trudge along the road, filling my undersized shoes with snow and drenching my feet.

"He should never have left me," I said out loud. "After all, he is older, he should be looking after me, but perhaps I was in his way. Maybe he's found a refuge somewhere."

At a crossroad, a sign spelled out a familiar name of a village and then it struck me that this was the village where Moishe had once worked. If I could only find his former bosses, perhaps they would know of his whereabouts. Then I had another thought: Moishe is there, of course! Where else? But how can I find them without knowing their name?

On the side of the road a young boy about my own age was aiming at a bird with a slingshot. He pulled the rubber band, a stone shot up into a tree, and a small bird fell down beside me. He ran up to the bird, picked it out of the snow, and held it in his hands.

"That's the third one in one day," he said, waiting for a compliment.

I recalled how I used to kill frogs in the pond at the Paizaks. I'd sneak up on a huge frog and with one heavy blow I'd end his life. The frog would float on the water for a while, then as the water would enter his body and make him heavier, he would sink, never to rise again.

"Why do you kill the birds?" I asked.

"Are you some kind of a nut?" he asked. "For fun, stupid."

That's why I had killed frogs, for fun. I killed frogs for fun, he killed birds for fun, and others killed Jews for fun.

I then recalled the German officer in my hometown of Pulawy who couldn't eat his lunch unless he'd killed two Jews for fun.

I looked at the dead bird in the boy's hands, its head limp, its eyes closed, a drop of blood showing below its wing.

Someday I may look like that. Who knows who may want some fun one day, see me wandering along the road, and . . . ?

The boy eyed me suspiciously. Any minute he'll call me a dirty Jew, I thought.

"Three birds is nothing," I finally said. "With my slingshot I never miss. I kill as many as twenty birds a day." He looked skeptically at me. "If you don't believe me, come over to our farm some day and I'll prove it to you."

"Where do you live?" he asked half-heartedly.

"In Kulik."

"If you're such a good shot, here." He extended the weapon towards me.

"No thanks, perhaps next time I'm around here." It was getting dark. "Jesus!" I yelled out, "I'll be late. Say, perhaps you can help me. I'm looking for a cousin of mine who lives in this village."

"What's his name?" the boy inquired.

"That's just it, I forgot his name. I do know he's got four cows and a horse."

"That's not much help," said the boy.

"Last summer he had a dirty Jew working for him; perhaps that will help."

The boy's eyes lit up. "Come, I'll show you." He led me to a house and I thanked him, promising to bring along my slingshot on my next visit. The boy turned and ran home. I walked to the door and entered.

Sitting by the open fire was an elderly woman mending socks. The back door opened and her husband entered, carrying a load of chopped wood in his arms.

"I am Kubush," I announced. The man dropped the wood and took off his coat and hat, all the time staring at me. Obviously my name didn't mean a thing to them. "Moishe is my uncle." They looked at each other, then back at me. The man rushed to the window and looked out, then turned to me and inquired in a frightened manner:

"What do you want? Moishe is not here."

"I thought he might be," I answered.

The man paced the room, back and forth, then turned to his wife and whispered something in her ear. She nodded. While he threw some fresh logs on the fire, she poured a glass of milk and cut a slice of bread.

"Eat," she said, and placed it on the table. I sat down and ate.

"About a week ago," began the man, "Moishe stopped here on his way to Chelm. We gave him a loaf of bread and he left us this." Out of the linen chest he produced the two pieces of fur.

He threw them on the table for me to examine. I just stared.

"Did he say he was going to Chelm for sure?" I asked.

"He was going to give himself up."

I finished eating and now sat feeling uneasy, for their eyes were upon me and seemed to be saying, "Please leave, we're frightened." But the room was so warm, so inviting. The rest of the bread lay before me, but I didn't know how to ask for another slice. I intended to prolong my stay by asking more questions, but the man cut me short.

"We're glad you looked us up, but for your sake and for our sake don't come here again. It's too dangerous." I found myself rising and putting my hat on. "Go to Chelm, boy," I heard him say as I bade them good-night and left. Behind me I heard the door being bolted and facing me was darkness, darkness all around me, waiting to embrace me.

I passed the house where the boy with the slingshot lived and imagined how he was now getting ready for bed, or per-haps was already asleep, his head on a soft pillow, his body covered with goose-feather bedding. I walked not because I had a destination, but rather because it was better to walk than simply to stand still.

Soon the lights in the windows were extinguished and even the dogs were asleep for the night. My feet still tramped in the snow, nothing around me except the stars up above. I walked and counted the stars, keeping my eyes upwards. One . . . two . . . three . . . a few more steps, another house, eleven . . . twelve . . . more snow, a turn of the road, snow . . . snow. Thirty-six . . . thirty-seven . . . and suddenly I fell into a pit of snow. Quickly I wiped the snow off my face and looked around. The road was not to be seen, for the stars had led me into a field.

A terrible lonely, melancholy feeling took hold of me and I felt I would never survive. Moishe was right, there is no escape. At that moment death would have come as a welcome relief. I looked up at the stars and began silently to cry. The snow felt warm, I lay back and covered myself with it as if it was bedding.

Please let me fall into an everlasting sleep, I prayed. From above, the stars looked down upon me and then they seemed to twinkle, to go out of focus, and finally they disappeared completely.

The brilliant rays of a winter sun woke me from a deep sleep, and when I opened my eyes I was glad I was still alive and that God hadn't taken my plea of the previous night seriously.

Quickly I freed myself from the snow and headed towards the road. My feet moved briskly through the snow as a new village appeared in the distance. To an onlooker I must have looked like a boy with an urgent message to deliver, and yet I still had no idea where I was going.

The thought of going to Chelm occurred to me, but I feared not finding Moishe. Most of all, I feared losing my own life, and in the end I somehow accepted the loss of Moishe the way I had accepted my previous losses, and began to worry about my own immediate needs: food and shelter. I was a wild animal looking for easy prey.

As I walked I looked down at my shoes and after a while I saw a large pair of winter boots instead of my own cramped shoes. The boots belonged to my grandfather Shie Chuen, the shoemaker from Warsaw.

Perhaps he walked along this very road I'm walking at this moment. He most likely knew every house, every farmer by name, and every curve in this road and all the other roads in this district.

Now more than ever, I realized the shame and humiliation my grandfather must have gone through to keep us alive, and yet he never complained; he only told us of his good fortune and never of his bad luck. How many times must he have stumbled and fallen on the ice or in the snow! How many times must he have been called abusive names and shamed! And yet he always greeted us with a smile and an amusing story. My poor grandfather . . .

How our eyes were glued to the little frosted window that night, waiting for his return! Only to see his shadow or hear the sound of his footsteps! But night fell and darkened the streets, and though we sat up waiting till the small hours, his knock on the door never came. It seemed impossible to me then. It was as if the man with the burlap bag had been swallowed up deep inside a village somewhere, or else had grown wings and disappeared into heaven.

It disturbed my mother greatly that her father, always a man full of pride, should suddenly have become a beggar, and she would cry upon seeing him arrive home tired and worn after a day's journey. But he would calm her by recounting an amusing incident of the day.

"There is no shame in begging," he would say, "there is only shame in stealing." And when saying it he would invariably look in my direction, as if addressing this message to my young mind so it would lodge itself there forever.

Now I saw myself in his image. I was walking in his footsteps, contemplating becoming a beggar as well. But how to walk into a stranger's place and ask for a piece of bread I didn't know, though my hunger would have driven me to steal if it had been possible.

I passed houses on my left and on my right. I wanted to enter. I wanted to ask. I started, then turned back. I was ashamed.

Then my grandfather's words came back to me, and I resolved to enter the next house, but fear overtook me and I passed it by. My poor grandfather, if only he had grown wings and flown to heaven!

"I won't be afraid, I'll go in and keep my head up high," I said out loud. Yet, the next house I came to I quickly passed by as well.

You're afraid, eh? said my own voice.

I'm not afraid. That house looked too poor. I doubt whether the people living there have enough bread for themselves.

Then what's wrong with this house? my other self asked as I came upon a prosperous-looking farm.

Here I'll enter, you just watch me, and I trembled as I opened the gate and made my way towards the house. Suddenly three chained dogs barked. I opened the door and entered. The house was dark and it seemed there was not a soul in it. Then I saw the back of an old man sitting in the corner.

He turned, opened his mouth, and said something like, "What is it you want?" But at that moment it sounded like, "Get out, dirty Jew."

I leaped out the door and fled. In my mind's eye I could

see the man's rotten teeth, and kilometers away I could still hear the dogs barking at me.

You fool, the voice said again. How frightened you are! And it began to laugh. Then I heard myself laughing.

I'll try again, I said, and this time nothing will frighten me. I shouldn't be afraid of people, I reasoned. After all, the worst they can do is refuse me.

To my right stood a small old house in terrible need of repair. Poor farmers, I observed. Poor people are usually kinder. I decided to enter. When I opened the door, a gust of steam enveloped me.

"Come in and close the door," a woman's voice said.

Through the mist, a woman washing clothes in a large wooden basin became visible. On the stove, water was boiling in several large metal pots, and at a small table by the window sat three children, two of them crying.

"I'm hungry," I said. "Could you give me something to eat?"

"We're all hungry," answered the woman. I started for the door. "Don't go away," she shouted. "If you wait I'll make supper as soon as I'm through with this."

"I'll wait," I answered.

"Good. Take off your coat and perhaps you can shut up my brats for a while."

I recalled how my Uncle Shepsel used to quiet me whenever I cried for bread. He would draw me a picture of Tarzan or else a cowboy, or an ice-cream vendor on a Warsaw street. Those drawings had fascinated me to the point where I'd forget my hunger completely.

I now performed the same magic. On a piece of old, faded paper I sketched a tank with a German soldier in it. The children marveled and asked for more. I drew a cow with a cowherd, and a dog beside them.

"Draw some soldiers," one child said. I drew a line of German soldiers with rifles ready to shoot.

"What are they shooting?" asked another.

"I'll show you," I said and drew another line of people. When I had finished, to my great astonishment, I realized that I had drawn armbands with the Star of David on the arms of all the people about to be executed.

The kids laughed; then one said, "I know, those are Jews."

"That's right," I answered, and though my heart jumped, I laughed too.

"You'll have to leave now," said the woman when we had finished supper and she was putting the children to sleep. I thanked her and went for my coat. That moment, the children began to cry.

"We want him to stay," they shouted. "He'll make us more drawings."

"He has to go," replied their mother. "I have no place to put him."

"I can sleep in the barn," I said.

"It's too cold in the barn."

"I don't mind," I answered, throwing her a smile.

"Let him sleep with us," begged one of the children.

"All right," she said, "but only for one night."

The children screamed with joy and began to throw pillows at each other. That night and the following night as well, I slept in a crowded but warm bed, and when I finally did leave, I left the children the same way I had found them, crying. But this time they weren't crying for food. They were crying for me.

The shame still lingered deep inside me, but I tried to hide it. In time I learned not simply to ask for food; instead I offered to perform some work. In some cases I'd be given a small job to do, but most of the time people stared at me blankly and said, "Work, in the wintertime?" But seeing my sad face, they'd ask, "Are you hungry?"

"Yes," I'd answer, though at times my stomach was full and what I really needed was shelter from the bitter cold. Once my hat and coat were off and the offering devoured, I'd chop some logs for the fire, or feed the pigs, or peel the potatoes. Where there were children, I'd immediately ask for a piece of paper and commence drawing.

In this way the day would pass and I was assured of lodging for the night. The next day I would move on to the next house.

In time I enlarged my repertoire and told stories to children, stories my mother had told to me and others which I made up as I went along. I learned to diaper babies and put them to sleep with a lullaby or a Russian song.

My young soprano voice attracted so much attention that eventually I was in demand for gatherings when neighbors would congregate in the evening.

They'd laugh and applaud and ask me to sing more. I also performed card tricks which I had learned from my Uncle Moishe. Those even of a very simple nature held my audience spellbound, and soon they began to believe I was blessed with godly spirits.

Whenever I was asked about my past I told of a terrible stepmother who beat me constantly, and claimed that my father, a farmer in a village near Pulawy, had been taken away to Germany on forced labor.

After listening to this story, one farmer asked, "Why did you leave home?"

"I couldn't stand the beatings," I answered him.

He smiled and said, "It's all right, you don't have to lie to me." I looked at him as if insulted. "I can tell you're a Jewish boy."

I protested; then he went on to tell me he was a Sabotnik * and that he too had been persecuted for his religion and knew what it felt like. With a Bible in his hands he went to great pains to explain how the Jews had erred by not accepting Christ.

"That is the reason for your sorrows."

He read passages from the Bible, stopping to enlarge on them now and then. I shook my head as if I understood, but in reality I was only pretending.

What would my mother think of me listening to a Christian teaching me religion? And so I hardly listened. But he went on reading until my eyes closed.

In the morning when I was leaving, he shook my hand and advised me, "Believe in Christ and He'll save you. It's never too late."

I gradually became aware of a constant itch all over my body. I felt as if I was being devoured.

When my family had first arrived in Siedliszcze and had been billeted in a house, six families to one room, the lice then had not only been in my hair and under my armpits; one day I had seen an army of them crawling on a wall. But the plague that kept me awake every night now was even worse; it was beyond description.

My experience with hunger did not shatter my being as much as the infection with these little vermin. Sitting at someone's table, I would suddenly feel them crawling all over my body, but I didn't dare scratch, for the discovery that I was infested would have made me most unwelcome, even though my hosts themselves had an adequate supply of their own lice.

I'd suffer silently through the day, waiting for night to fall, and then work feverishly to rid myself of the pests. It was of no use, however; the more I killed, the more I could feel them eating slowly away at me.

One day behind a barn, I took off my coat and shook it. What I saw sickened me: hundreds of lice had fallen from

* Seventh-Day Adventist

my garment and were now crawling in the snow. I'll have to
have a bath and change my clothes, I reasoned. But where?
In the summer I could have stopped at some river, but this
was freezing winter.

My suffering reached such proportions that one night I
cried because of it. My thoughts went back to the last time I
had had a bath:

It rained that evening. Mrs. Paizak boiled four pots of
water which she poured into a small wooden tub, and she
ordered me to undress. In the room were Genia, Mrs. Paizak, and a neighbor. How shy I was! I began to unbutton my
pants, my eyes downcast.

When I looked up, the three were watching me.

"Come on, Kubush," said Genia, "don't be shy."

I finally undressed, turning my back to them and getting
into the basin backwards. They all laughed. With a bar of
soap, Mrs. Paizak scrubbed me from head to toe except my
privates which I kept covered with both my hands.

"Don't worry, Kubush," Mrs. Paizak laughed. "You can
let go; I won't bite it off," and the room shook with laughter.

When I had finished and was ready to go to sleep, Mrs.
Paizak said, "It's raining outside. Why don't you sleep in the
house tonight?"

"With me, in my bed," added Genia, smiling. "Don't be
afraid, Kubush!" I opened the door and ran. When I reached
the barn, drenched with rain, I could still hear them
laughing.

Now as I recalled that incident I longed to relive it. To
bathe in warm water, to have on a clean, lice-free shirt, to
have my hair washed and combed! And the more I thought
about it, the more I was drawn to visit the Paizaks again.

On a moonlit night I found myself again crossing the river.
Gently I knocked on the door and waited. There was silence
all around me, and from the darkened interior I heard snoring. My second knock brought a tired voice to my ears.

"Who's there?"

"Kubush!" I answered. The door opened and Mrs. Paizak
stood in the doorway, her coat wrapped around her body,
her hair disheveled from sleep, and her eyes only half
opened.

"Holy Mother!" she uttered. "You're still alive, thank God
for that." She inquired about Moishe. "Go to the barn," she
said. "I'll bring you something to eat, then you must go
immediately."

"I didn't come for food."

"No?" She looked surprised.

"I came to have a bath."

"Holy Mother! You poor child, how can I give you a bath now? Stashek is out, but he'll be back any minute, and if he should find you, it would be terrible." She began to cry. "He has joined the village police, you know, the ones with the pitchforks." She wiped the tears and blew her nose on the end of her sleeve. "Some policemen they are! They're bandits, Kubush, worse than the Germans. Everyone they've caught they've turned in. If he finds you here Kubush . . . he'll . . ." She suddenly looked past my shoulder. "Listen!" she said. "It's Stashek coming down the road."

The familiar terror gripped me and I turned to run, and once again I was inside the cooler. It was now filled with potatoes so I had to lie on my belly, unable to move.

Stashek's footsteps and then his whistling came closer and closer; then the door to the house opened and closed. I didn't move.

Some time later Mrs. Paizak came out, "He's asleep." I crawled out, hardly able to hold my balance now. She shoved something into my hands. "Take this and go."

"Good-bye," I whispered.

On the other side of the river I stopped to examine what she had given me. A pair of Stashek's long winter underwear unfolded in my hands.

In the next village I eyed a man's shirt dangling on a clothesline, and quick as a fox, I had it off the line and was headed for a place to change.

I felt clean that day, but that very night my body itched again. My companions had returned. To add to my discomfort, I awoke with a rash on my hands. In the crevices between my fingers were little itchy pimples which, when I scratched, opened and spread and itched worse than before.

Wherever I went now, I had to keep my hands out of sight. I tried eating with one hand, I kept my hands in my pockets, and many times I succeeded in not being found out, but quite often I'd be discovered and I'd be thrown out like a sick dog.

"Out, you're diseased!" they would shout.

Word spread quickly that the boy with the golden voice had a terrible contagious rash, and many doors were now shut in my face. Again I went hungry and now lodged in barns, spending my nights scratching.

On one such night I heard the doors to the barn open, then saw the shadow of a figure coming towards me. There was a rustle in the hay and later, breathing. I feared to scratch and lay there silently in terrible agony.

When I awoke in the early morning, a man's face popped out of the hay beside me. He was unshaven, his eyes were like those of a wild animal, and upon seeing me, he looked as if he was going to run, or else attack me. We stared at each other and then the stranger asked in a broken voice:

"Boy . . . could you bring me a piece of bread?"

From his accent I knew immediately he was a Jew.

"Where will I get bread?" I asked.

"Ask your mother for a small piece, just some crust will do."

I wavered for a moment. "I too am hungry," I finally answered. He stared at me, questioning me with his wild eyes. "I don't belong here," I explained. "I got in here the same way you did." He looked at me suspiciously. "I too am a Jew," I blurted out. His eyes opened wide as if in disbelief.

"You are?"

"Yes," I answered.

"But you don't look Jewish, and your Polish is so good." He scratched under his arms. "It's so much easier when you're young," he sighed.

I felt good to have found someone of my own kind, but then I feared that he might attach himself to me and with his pronounced Jewish accent betray both of us. I felt ashamed for my thoughts.

I showed him my hands and he picked himself up and headed for the door.

"Please help me," I begged him. "Tell me how to cure it." He laughed. "You need medicine, boy, and where will you get medicine here?"

"Wait!" I called after him. "Let's talk for a while."

"There's nothing to talk about," and he vanished from my sight forever.

A pair of lady's black gloves were hanging on a fence. I picked off the first glove, but when I reached for the second one, I heard the sound of a door opening, and fled. Several days later I stole another glove, this time a red one, and unfortunately, like the first, it too was for the left hand.

With covered hands, I now moved into new territory and again began to entertain children with drawings and adults with songs and magic. I changed my name to Stefan and told a different story about myself.

Because I never removed the gloves from my hands, even when eating, people asked many questions.

"A dog bit me," was my standard reply.

Everything within my reach would attach itself to my

gloved fingers. My pockets were filled with trivial items: a few nails, a pair of old broken scissors, a pair of pliers, a pair of false teeth which I stole from inside a glass full of water.

One night I knocked on a door and was greeted by a woman attired in a long dress and smelling of perfume.

"Who is it?" I heard another woman's voice call from the back.

"A little Jew," she answered.

Two other women, almost identically dressed and of about the same age, were suddenly in front of me, and now the three of them were looking me over.

"What do you want?" asked one of them.

"I'm hungry," I answered.

"Come sit down, we're just baking bread, but then you'll have to leave."

I scanned the room. Now and then one of the ladies would exit into another room from which the aroma of baking reached my nostrils. In the corner stood a piano with sheet music on it. One of them sat down and began to play "Gloomy Sunday." The melody filled the room and brought back fragments of memories to my mind.

I was deeply lost in recollection when suddenly a voice called, "Look! He's coming." The playing abruptly stopped and all three looked out the window. I jumped up to look.

Through the frosted little window pane, the shape of a man dressed in a long fur coat, fur hat, and leather boots could be seen approaching. "What do we do with the Jew?" asked one.

"He has to leave," cried another.

"He can't now, it's too late," said the third.

"He can't stay here."

"Quick, he's by the barn, do something."

I was pushed into the other room. It was dark and the heat from the oven made it extremely warm so that I looked for a window or door: there was none. My body began to itch beyond description. I scratched and held myself back from screaming.

Voices now reached me, and from the conversation I gathered that the three ladies were sisters. The gentleman in the fur coat and hat was the sheriff of the village, a widower, and he was courting the three old maids. He told dirty stories. They all laughed. The piano could be heard again and they drank. The visitor now sang, and then they remembered the bread. One of the sisters offered to inspect the oven, and the visitor, now drunk, insisted on going with her. The others tried to hold him back, but couldn't stop him. The door burst open and I jumped behind it.

"How hot it is in here!" exclaimed the lady as she opened the door to the oven.

"It's hot wherever you are, my lamb," said the visitor, his smelly breath almost upon me. There was a bit of shuffling now, something fell to the floor creating a terrifying noise, and then I heard the sound of a kiss. The lady giggled.

"Come, you devil, the bread isn't done yet," she said, and they left.

"It's getting late," I heard one of the spinsters say.

"Let it be late," said the sheriff. "Let's live while we're young," and he began to sing again.

I hadn't eaten that day and now felt faint. I opened the door to the oven, yanked out a chunk of a half-baked bread, and ate it. There were more songs, and more laughter. Again I opened the oven and devoured another piece of hot dough. When at long last the sheriff was finally escorted to the door, the sisters came rushing in.

Instead of finding three loaves of bread, they only pulled out two. They looked at me sympathetically and said nothing, except to invite me to stay the night.

Desperately I tried to sleep, but I couldn't. The knowledge that two large loaves of bread were lying in a cupboard within an arm's reach prevented me from even closing my eyes. My stomach was full now, but I feared tomorrow. Tomorrow I might go hungry all day. I opened the cupboard and pulled out a loaf. I broke off a piece and munched on it. In this fashion I managed to finish the second loaf, but I still couldn't sleep. I lay waiting for dawn to come, and when it did, I donned my coat, and under it hid the third loaf of bread. I unbolted the door and headed towards the forest to have breakfast.

To add to my problems in midwinter, I began to wet at nights. Not only did I have to hide my lice and my diseased hands, but a wet floor every morning as well. When I'd lie down to sleep I'd dread the thought of waking, for I knew that my clothes would be wet, and that emanating from my sleeping place would be a small puddle of water. Which would bring anger from my hosts and embarrassment to me, and as a result I could never stay and wait for their reactions; instead I'd rise early and flee.

Some nights, sleep would overtake me and in my deep slumber I'd dream I had to urinate. I'd search for a basin, and then out of nowhere a large, beautiful golden basin would appear in front of me. I'd sigh with relief and urinate with great satisfaction, only to discover the terrible truth in the morning.

In desperation I tried several remedies, but without success, the last of which was a bottle attached to my penis. In the morning the bottle was empty, but my bedding was wet as usual.

An angry voice awakened me one night. I looked up and saw my host, Mr. Bogusz.

"You're wetting the floor," he shouted.

"I'm sorry," I pleaded. "I don't know how it happened." I dressed, removed the mattress, and wiped the floor.

"I can cure you of this, boy," he told me, and lit the naphtha lamp as it was still quite dark. He asked me to sit and then in a low voice so as not to awaken his wife he said, "I think you're a Jewish boy." I laughed. "Shush! I don't want my wife to know."

"You're mistaken," I said. "I'm not a Jew."

"You don't have to pretend with me," he continued. "I won't betray you. If you're not a Jew you can stay with us. We have no children, you'll be like our own."

Again I said firmly, "I'm not a Jew. What gave you that idea?"

"I would have to be sure," he said. "Pull down your pants and let's see if you're circumcised."

His wife stirred in her sleep and got out of bed.

"I don't mind," I said, "but your wife is here."

"Come then," and he led me into the barn.

I unbuttoned my fly. Perhaps he can't tell the difference, I thought, or perhaps in the morning light my penis will look like any other normal one; or perhaps God will perform a miracle.

"You're a Jew, just as I thought."

I buttoned up my pants and laughed confidently. "Mr. Bogusz, this is a very serious accusation."

"You don't have to be afraid," he said again.

"I'm not afraid." I now pretended to be angry. "You're mistaken."

"I know what a circumcised penis looks like, and only Jews are circumcised."

"Perhaps I'm circumcised, but I'm not a Jew," I still protested.

"What's the matter with your hands?" he now asked.

"A dog bit me."

"Let's see," he said, pulling off my gloves and studying my hands carefully. "There's a very simple cure for dog bites."

Obviously I fooled him this time, I thought.

"Urinate daily on them," he advised me, "and in several weeks your sores will be gone."

For lack of a better cure, I took Mr. Bogusz's advice and for many weeks urinated on my hands, but without success.

If I ever survive this war, I thought, I'll come back here, call all the villagers together and present them with a statue as a lasting monument to their kindness. I longed for that day and imagined myself surrounded by all the surprised faces when they heard me saying, "I'm a Jew!"

The snow began to melt and here and there a patch of green grass could be seen. The roads became muddy and the sky turned brighter. Winter's end was almost in sight, but there seemed no end to my hiding, lying, and searching for a place to stay.

My feet walked along a muddy road in an unfamiliar village. I looked at the houses scattered along both sides of the road and debated which one to enter. On the right stood a prosperous-looking structure with a barn and a large stable, on my left, smoke was coming out of a small, though well-kept hut set far back from the road. I turned to the left and walked over to the door. A young woman answered the door, and without asking me what I wanted, she invited me to come in.

In one of the rooms a young man was repairing shoes by the light of a naphtha lamp, and coming from the other room was the disturbing sound of a baby's cry.

"Take off your coat and sit down," said the woman as she closed the door behind me.

"Is it cold outside?" asked her husband.

"Not too cold," I answered.

"It will be cold tonight," he said, driving another nail into a shoe.

I took off my coat and stood watching him. He reminded me so much of my own father repairing shoes.

My father, I wonder where he is. Our little flat in Pulawy, Josel, my mother, my father's mandolin playing. If only I could wake now and find it was all a terrible dream!

"Whose boy are you?" I suddenly heard a voice say.

Startled, I looked at my host and smiling I said, "I come from far away."

"You must be hungry then," he said, then called to his wife who was now attending to the baby. "Wanda, bring some of that tasty soup of yours."

Between spoonfuls of hot cabbage soup with beans, I repeated my story of being an orphan, of how my father was working in Germany on forced labor, and what terrible beatings my stepmother gave me, and how finally, unable to take it any longer, I had run away from home. I told of my wanderings throughout the winter and of how impossible it was to find employment.

The man dropped his hammer and listened, his mouth half open and his eyes upon me. His wife sat in the corner wiping the tears from her eyes. At the end of my story the man rolled a cigarette, lit it, then asked me my name.

"Franek Zielinski," I answered.

"Well, Franek, you won't have to wander any longer."

I looked up. "You need someone?" I asked with joy.

He looked at his wife, then back to me. "I wish we had more room, we'd keep you on like our own son. I know what it's like to be all alone. I too was an orphan, kicked from house to house. This is the first place I can call my home." He took a deep puff on his cigarette, then continued, "But I have a wealthy cousin, and he's a very fine man and I'm sure now that summer is coming he'll need a boy like you to look after things."

"Where does he live?" I asked.

"Near Siedliszcze. I'll drive you there tomorrow."

When I lay down to sleep, my eyes wouldn't close. In the darkness of the room I could still make out the tools and several pairs of old worn-out shoes on a shelf; some required mending, others were already repaired.

My thoughts again wandered back to Pulawy, to the front room of our apartment where my father had worked. I could almost hear him whistling Schubert's Serenade as he sat near the door working feverishly on a pair of shoes, occasionally lifting his head and stealing a look at the church across the street, or waving to a person passing by.

"When will you make Jankele a pair of sandals?" my mother used to ask.

"I'll get around to it," he'd answer, and continue to whistle.

That same day, catching sight of a redhead orphan of the town, he opened the door and called him in. The boy stood in the doorway puzzled.

"Come in and sit down," my father ordered. "Let me see your feet." He took his measurements and told him to come back in a week's time for new shoes for Passover.

"What about shoes for Jankele?" my mother pleaded.

"Is Jankele an orphan?" he replied, and resumed whistling.

My mother instilled in me a fear of God, and though she was not fanatically religious, she nevertheless carried on a sense of tradition. On Friday nights she lit the candles and on the Sabbath she did not work; all the food she prepared was strictly kosher, and of course she had two sets of dishes, one for milk and the other for meat.

My father did not prevent her from carrying out these rites, but he himself was not religious. He never wore a hat when eating, and never went to the synagogue on the Sabbath or even on the High Holy Days. This created some friction between them, especially concerning my upbringing.

I was on my mother's side, and when on a Friday night I would run to the synagogue which was in a courtyard behind our house, I would sip the wine from the cup which was passed around as part of the ceremony, and I would usually be questioned by the townfolk, "Where is your father tonight? How come he isn't here?"

"He's sick," I'd answer with shame.

"Sick again? What is it this time?" they'd tease.

"He has a toothache," I would reply, and run, only to be confronted by another one.

"And what's the matter with your father now?"

"He's sick."

"Don't tell me, I know, a toothache. Will he be here next week?"

"He'll be here for sure if he doesn't get sick," I'd answer.

"Please, Daddy, why won't you go to the synagogue?" I would plead with him, and then cry.

The shame of having an irreligious father was more than I could bear.

Sometimes he'd hold me on his knees and say, "To be good to others, to be kind, to be strong and healthy and live a clean life, that's what's important, not sitting in a smelly old synagogue and praying to someone who doesn't exist. The world needs help, my child, but it's not an invisible thing called God that will help it. Someday when you grow up you'll realize how the masses are poisoned with fairy tales about a God in order to make them forget how hungry they are."

I listened, but refused to accept his teachings, for I could clearly picture an enormous old man with a long white beard sitting in heaven and watching my every move and listening to my every thought. And everything was written down in a huge book. When it thundered I knew God was angry at someone, when it rained he was probably urinating, and when it snowed I reasoned that perhaps his wife was changing the feathers in the bedding. I felt deeply sorry for my father for not believing in God, and feared that He would punish him with death.

On cold winter nights our place was always very lively. In the workroom my father carried on political debates with several of his friends. And always, perhaps as a sign of protest, at all such meetings there was a package of sliced smoked ham. And it always lay on a newspaper; my mother would not give one of her plates for it.

On such occasions, in the kitchen, my mother, and two musical companions and myself would carry on with a sing song. Shie, the town barber, my mother, and I would sing, and Kisel, the street musician, would accompany us on his mandolin. Between songs my mother served potato pancakes and hot tea with lemon in a glass.

My father was very gentle with me, but if I disobeyed him, he did not hesitate to pull my pants down, put me over his knees, and lick me until I screamed. As a result I began to fear him. So much so that when one day, walking home from school, I saw him coming towards me, I turned and ran.

He called, "Jankele!" and began pursuing me. I ran, turning one corner, another corner, hearing his footsteps and his voice behind me, "Jankele!" In the marketplace I finally lost him. I now feared to return home, all the time wondering what bad deed I had performed.

When night finally brought me to the door, trembling from the cold, he was sitting at the workbench, his eyes red from tears.

"Why did you run from me?" he asked. "I only wanted to give you money for chocolate. Jankele! Jankele!" The voice seemed to fade now from my memory.

Then I heard whistling, my father's whistling, Schubert's Serenade. I turned my head towards the window; in the dark of the night the wind outside was whistling its own melody.

Early the next morning we set out on the journey. The ice covering the roads was now melting, and caused the poor horse to slip several times. Along the way the young shoemaker gave me words of hope and told me that someday I too would grow into manhood and have my own family and farm. He told me of his sad life, of how his parents met death in a fire while he was still an infant, and of how he had found his way in life.

At about noon we turned off the road into a small, neatly kept courtyard and brought the horse to a stop. "This is my cousin's place," he said proudly. "What do you think of it?"

"It looks fine to me," I answered as we descended from the wagon.

"He's a good man, you'll like him. Come."

A petite woman met us at the door. She was meticulously

dressed and the interior of the house had an almost clinical look about it. Everything in its own place and not a speck of dust anywhere.

"I brought you a boy," said my friend, addressing her.

She examined me casually and said, "How wonderful! Where did you ever find him?"

"His name is Franek Zielinski; he's an orphan."

"Bogdan will be very happy," she said, leading us into a large kitchen where a fire burned in the stove.

"Where is Bogdan?" asked the shoemaker.

She looked at him, then at me, and as if divulging some mysterious secret she said, "On business."

"And Ina, where is Ina?"

The woman looked out the window and pointed. "Here she comes now."

A girl of about fifteen greeted the shoemaker and asked him endless questions as she took off her coat and beret. He introduced her to me, and then we all sat down to lunch.

"Well I have to get back," said my friend when he had filled his stomach. He shook my hand warmly and wished me good luck. I thanked him for everything and watched him through the window getting into the wagon. He looked back and waved when he reached the road. I smiled and waved back.

Ina, her eyes downcast, acted as if I didn't exist, and when she had to address me, she still refused to look at my face.

"My husband will be home in the evening," said the lady of the house. "I'm sure you'll like it here."

Late in the evening the husband returned. Mother and daughter ran out to greet him and help him unharness the horse. Their voices, full of excitement, reached my ears as they told him of my presence.

The door opened, and framed between his wife and daughter stood the master of the house. He wore a dark suit that looked sometimes green and at other times blue, a shirt with a tie, and neat black shoes; his hair was cut and combed neatly. He hardly looked like a farmer, but more like a city doctor. His face had a kind look about it, for it never ceased to smile. I liked him immediately, for there was something very gentle and kind in his manner. His hand outstretched towards me, he said, "I'm Bogdan Golombek."

I approached and offered him my gloved right hand. He shook it warmly and glanced at it. "Why the gloves?"

"I'm a little cold," I answered, and smiled broadly at him. He returned the smile and then stared at me without saying a word. I stared back and now at close range I recognized him and understood the reason for his stare. He was the same man who had bought a pig from Mrs. Paizak. At that time he had called me "Abraham."

"What is your name?" he asked. My voice somewhat shaking now, I answered:

"Franek Zielinski."

"Franek Zielinski," he repeated, as if to himself. "That's a nice name, a very nice name."

He knows who you are, a voice whispered within me.

Perhaps not, another voice answered.

The first voice laughed, Oh, how optimistic you are! The man is no fool, he's recognized you.

So what? The worst he can do is ask me to leave.

The first voice laughed loudly. Or else turn you in. How do you know you can trust him?

He looks kind.

So that's how you judge people now? How do you know that the ones who took your mother away didn't look kind as well?

I trust him.

Very well, wait till tomorrow, said the other voice, when he'll leave in the morning on some pretense and return later in a car with the Gestapo.

The two voices within me continued to argue, and when I was shown a cot to sleep in and lay down to close my eyes, they had still not finished.

You can't trust anyone, the first voice kept telling me. Especially those who look kind and smile. Don't you remember Bromberg in the Warsaw Ghetto? Remember how he smiled? And he was one of us. A Jew, a friend, and look what he did.

My mind traveled quickly back through time and space and recalled the day when Mr. Bromberg, an old acquaintance of my grandfather's, walked into our basement apartment on Pawia Street and said, "Shie Chuen, my old friend, I'm clearing out of the ghetto." My grandfather was extremely pleased.

"But how?"

"It's costing me plenty, don't ask. But before I leave I want a good pair of leather boots."

My grandfather served him tea with lemon in a glass and proceeded to show him a selection of remodeled boots. "That's all you have, Shie? Only old junk?"

"What is it you're looking for, Bromberg?" my grandfather questioned. "New boots you won't find in the ghetto; surely you know that we had to give up all the new leather to the Germans."

"I know all that," said Bromberg, "but I thought a clever man like you might still have a piece of good leather hidden here or there, and after all I am a friend, and I'm willing to pay well for it."

My grandfather reached for his hammer, turned the dining table upside down, and began removing nails from boards which formed a false bottom to the table. "Is this what you want, Bromberg?"

Bromberg walked to the overturned table. His eyes popped as he knelt and touched several skins. "That's more like it," he said.

"It will be expensive," said my grandfather.

"I don't care how much it costs me," answered Bromberg.

"In that case, make your choice, brown or black leather, and let me close the vault."

Bromberg fingered the leather again, and a smile formed on his face. "Shie, do me a favor; let me call my wife, she has such better taste than I have."

"I can't keep this in the open too long," said my grandfather with a frown.

Bromberg slapped him on the back. "It won't take long at all, I'll be right back," and he left.

Within minutes he *was* back, but not with his wife. A large black limousine drove into the courtyard and out of it sprang several Gestapo men led by Bromberg. Like a sudden tornado they broke into the apartment, and without saying a word, began to slap and kick my grandfather. He fell and got up, but each time he got up he was hit again.

"How could you do this to me?" he asked, his face bleeding. "I'm your friend."

Bromberg stood in the corner of the room, smiling and munching on a chocolate bar. My grandfather's question turned his smile into laughter.

"Don't be so surprised, Chuen; several days ago I turned my own father in."

I became convinced that Bogdan Golombek knew who I was and that in the morning he would turn me in.

Leave now, go! the voice within me kept urging, but my eyes closed and I fell into a deep sleep.

When I awoke, Mrs. Golombek and Ina were cleaning the house and preparing food for the pigs. I asked if Mr. Golombek was still sleeping, and they informed me he had left hours ago.

"Where did he go?" I asked.

They looked at each other, then Mrs. Golombek answered, "To Siedliszcze."

My heart jumped. He went to inform on me. "When will he be back?"

"Tonight," came the reply. "Did you want something?" asked Mrs. Golombek, throwing me a pleasant smile.

"No," I answered, "I only wondered."

"You relax, Franek, take a look around the barn, see the animals. There won't be much for you to do until all the snow melts."

I felt I was in real danger, but I hesitated to leave. The house was so warm and inviting, my new hosts were friendly, and it seemed to me that if Mr. Golombek hadn't recognized me, then I might have found a good home to stay in. I took a walk around the courtyard, chopped some wood, and pulled up a bucket full of water from the well; then I walked into the barn and stared at the animals. I was still debating whether I shouldn't pick up my coat and on some pretense leave and never return.

As my mind wandered and the two voices within me renewed their quarrel, I suddenly heard the sound of an approaching car. I rushed to the barn door and looked out. A German car was making its way along the muddy road.

I've been betrayed. He has turned me in.

Within me the voice said, You should have listened to me. I told you this would happen. You can't trust a kind face or any other face.

The car came to a stop now, facing the Golombek farm. I moved back into the barn feeling trapped. If I run out surely they'll pick me off with a rifle.

I waited behind the door, my eyes peering out through a crack. The car stood for the longest time; then two German soldiers got out of it, and to my horror headed in my direction. As they passed the barn I could see their revolvers swinging on their hips, and then I heard a knock on the door, the door opening, conversation, and then Mrs. Golombek's voice calling, "Franek!"

I began to pray, "Dear God, if you can hear me, please help me. I don't want to die. Dear God, please save me." It suddenly occurred to me that perhaps the Jewish God didn't exist, that he had got very old and died, or else perhaps that He did exist and could hear our cries, but didn't care. I could think of so many people who had prayed to Him and He never saved them. Didn't my mother believe in Him? He certainly didn't listen to her prayers. What about all those rabbis and scholars who did nothing else but pray day and night? Why weren't they spared? What happened to all those people I used to see in the synagogue?

"Franek!" the voice called again.

"Dear Jesus," I began, my eyes closed, "perhaps *you* can save me; please save me and I'll believe in you."

"Franek!"

I walked out of the barn knowing I had been revealed. The two Germans looked at me.

Where is Mr. Golombek? I wondered. Where is my betrayer? Probably sitting in the car, ashamed to face me, munching on a chocolate bar.

"Franek," said Mrs. Golombek, pointing to a white-washed structure surrounded by some tall trees, "run over to that house and ask if they can lend us some eggs."

"Eggs?" I inquired, my voice cracking.

"Yes, these gentlemen want to buy some eggs."

A broad smile suddenly covered my face. "Right away," I said, and jumped into the air almost flying.

In no time at all I was back. The soldiers paid Mrs. Golombek and after patting me on my head they walked towards their car and drove off. I re-entered the barn, closing the door behind me, and leaning against the wall I began to laugh.

Jesus saved you, said one of the voices.

Jesus shmesus, said the other, nobody saved you. There was nothing to be saved from. They came here to buy eggs, not to look for Jews.

They came here for you, but Jesus intervened and made them ask for eggs instead.

I felt deeply ashamed. I had indeed saved my life, but by doing so I had betrayed my religion. I had given up my mother's God, my God. The God for which my grandfathers had died. I now saw myself as an outcast: small, despicable, loathsome, and unworthy to continue to live. I was a betrayer.

At that moment, I remembered the cool summer evenings when the neighbors would congregate on our doorsteps in Pulawy. Kisel would be there with his mandolin, strumming a melody; Itche, a fat, bald-headed man, selling newspapers; the baker from down the street, complaining about his wife; and other assorted characters, waiting for night to fall and cool the air. I recalled a woman in peasant-like clothes, wearing no shoes. As she passed by, the playing and conversation would stop, and all eyes would stare at her. Several in the group would spit on the sidewalk as if spitting on her footprints and then others would call her terrible names.

I did not understand the reason for this behavior until

one day my mother explained that this woman had once been a nice Jewish girl of the town; her father was a learned and pious man. Then she fell in love with a farmer in the village across the bridge. They married and she converted to Christianity. From that day on, I too spat when I saw her walk by.

God will never forgive her for this sin, I used to say to myself.

Now I had a vision of myself being spat at by my mother, my grandfathers, my brother Josel, and almost everyone I had ever known. "Convert! Christ lover!" I could almost hear them shouting at me. I became terribly frightened of the conjured vision, and so I said to myself, I was only pretending, I am still a Jew. I don't believe in Jesus Christ!

At that moment, a shot rang out, then another, and another. Am I still alive? I ran out of the barn and looked towards the road. The German car appeared in view, headed towards Siedliszcze.

That evening when Mr. Golombek returned, his wife told him about the visitors we had had and the shots we had heard.

"Oh yes," he said, biting into a potato, "I heard about it."

"Did someone get shot?" asked his daughter.

"Yes," he answered, "a Russian escapee."

"How terrible!" exclaimed Mrs. Golombek.

"Yes, it is terrible," he said, "but guess how he was dressed." He smiled. "Remember the mayor of Siedliszcze?" His wife shook her head. "Well, he wore his fur coat, hat, shoes, and even carried his silver cane."

My heart jumped, for I knew that Ivan was dead.

On my third day with the Golombeks I decided to remove my gloves. Ina noticed the sores on my hands, and when I caught her stare, she turned her eyes. Soon after, I heard her whispering to her mother. Immediately I put the gloves back on.

When Mr. Golombek returned that night, I again heard whispers from the other room. I looked out the window and wondered where my feet would carry me next.

He came out of the room. Smiling and in good humor, he asked me how I felt and if I liked the farm. Later on, almost as if out of casual curiosity, he looked at my gloved hands and said, "Ina tells me you have a rash, Franek." Immediately I wanted to protest and to tell him that a dog had bitten me, but because of the calm way he confronted me I couldn't lie to him. I didn't answer. "Nothing to worry about," he

assured me. "If you have a rash, we'll find a way of curing it."
Still I didn't answer him. He reached for my hands and carefully pulled off the gloves. "You poor soul! How you must
suffer!" I turned my eyes downward, ashamed because of his
kindness. He patted me on my shoulder and said, "Tomorrow
I'll go to Siedliszcze and bring you medicine." With that he
threw my gloves into the fire. I lifted my head and saw him
smiling at me. I smiled back.

The following evening he came home with a bottle of ointment. After supper the women of the house were ushered
out of the main room and Mr. Golombek rolled up his shirt
sleeves and began pouring water into a barrel.

"Start undressing!" he said to me.

"Everything?" I questioned.

"Everything," came the reply. I hesitated. "What's the
matter, Franek, don't you like a bath?" he asked.

"It's not that," I answered.

"What is it then?" he asked.

I began to undress slowly, all along trying to find a way to
get into the barrel without Mr. Golombek catching sight of
my penis. When I had taken everything off except my long
underwear, I stopped and began to fidget.

"Come, come," he called, "the water will get cold."

I had begun to undo the button on my fly when Mr. Golombek left the room to get more firewood. I dropped the underwear onto the floor and jumped into the barrel.

Upon entering, he gathered my clothing and threw it into
the still warm oven for sterilization; then with a rough brush
and a bar of soap, he scrubbed me. That done, he ordered me
out. Again I hesitated, but finally had no choice but to leave
the barrel. I maneuvered myself in such a way that he could
only see my back, but no sooner did I feel a sense of success
than his hands were upon me with a large towel, drying my
body energetically. I kept turning my back to him and this he
eventually found annoying.

"Will you please stand still, boy," he shouted at me.

I froze and closed my eyes, for now he was in front of me,
drying my legs, my penis facing him.

He's noticed it now, I thought. Any moment now he'll stop
and say, "Why, you're a Jew!" But to my surprise he said
nothing; instead, he poured the ointment into his right palm
and began to apply it all over my body.

That night when I lay in bed, I wondered why Mr. Golombek hadn't noticed my circumcised penis. And, when for the
next six days the same treatment was repeated and Mr. Go-

lombek still hadn't made any mention of it, I came to the conclusion that his knowledge of penises was quite limited.

My body was now free of those terrible sores and lice. I could now sleep peacefully at night and eat my meals without having to hide my hands.

In no time at all I felt part of the Golombek family, and sometimes I had to remind myself who I really was. At those times too, I realized somewhat sadly that I had forgotten my Jewish, and now thought and even dreamed in Polish.

I teased Ina as one teases an older sister and even argued with her and pretended to be put out with her for days. She in turn treated me like a brother, but when on occasion I would not obey her, she would remind me that I was a servant.

Ina's girlfriends would visit on Sundays and spend endless hours listening to me sing.

"You'll be a heartbreaker when you grow up," they'd say, and then ask for another song. It seemed I never ceased singing, not only on Sundays, but throughout the week as well, from dawn to nightfall.

"Why do you sing so much?" Mr. Golombek asked me one day.

"Because I'm happy," I replied.

"I wish Ina had an ear like yours," he said. Ina was slightly deaf and this affliction had disturbed him. He had given her mandolin lessons but nothing had come of it. "Perhaps next year, Franek," he said, "you'll take mandolin lessons." I beamed with joy.

Mrs. Golombek, too, treated me well. She sewed shirts and pants especially for me, and always made sure I had second helpings at the table.

"You're a growing boy," she'd say, and without asking would empty the pots onto my plate.

I still wet my bed at night, but nothing was said of it; instead, Mr. Golombek began waking me in the middle of the night.

In late spring we planted a cherry tree near the fence in my honor and named it Franek.

I tilled the land, sowed it, looked after the cows, and took care of countless other duties. At times there were functions which I couldn't perform; then Mr. Golombek would stay home for a day and we'd work together, but most days he was away buying pigs.

We would all wait for his return, and on those occasions when he had a pig with him, the killing would take place that very night.

All animals were numbered by the Germans and no farmer was allowed to kill an animal for his own use. But there were some illegal pigs without numbers, and Mr. Golombek dealt in these, selling the meat wherever he could. If caught, he would have been shot, which is why the work was always performed in secrecy.

In time I learned how to kill a pig, how to cut it open, drain the blood, and slice the meat up into smaller pieces. After each killing, Mrs. Golombek would make blood pudding and on that, accompanied by some vodka, we would feast until very late into the night.

I took great pleasure in these nights, not because I enjoyed the killing of an animal, or the taste of blood pudding, but because I knew we were doing something illegal and undermining the regime.

Mr. Golombek praised me daily for the way I was carrying out my work and I was pleased, for it made me feel secure and wanted.

I made several friends in the village. On some Sundays I would visit them and sometimes they would visit me. We would play cards, tell stories, or climb trees, and they, like everyone else, came to know me as the Golombeks' boy, and very few asked any questions.

"How would you like to go to town, Franek?" Mr. Golombek asked me one day.

The thought frightened me, but I decided to go, not so much out of curiosity to see Siedliszcze again, but because I didn't want to arouse suspicion in Mr. Golombek's mind.

We drove through the town, my head turning from one side of the street to the other, and I could hardly recognize it. German soldiers were walking to and fro. Polish police and farmers were all about, and when we approached the house where I had once lived, I feared to look in case someone should notice my gaze.

The crop grew taller and eventually it had to be harvested. The weather changed and it was fall, and then winter. The snow fell, covering the fields and roads.

It seemed to me that I had never known any other life, that I had always lived with the Golombeks and that, no matter what, I would always remain there. I could see myself grown up, getting married to one of the village girls and raising a family on a local farm.

The Germans, the war, fear, and the fact that I was a Jew completely vanished from my mind. I continued to cross my-

self at mealtimes and pretended to say prayers, but this too
I accepted as being quite normal.

It was a Sunday; Mrs. Golombek and Ina had gone to visit
a distant cousin and Mr. Golombek had fallen asleep. When
he awoke he felt quite hungry, having missed lunch.

"How would you like to have some eggs and onions,
Franek?"

"Not for me," I said.

"I thought you people liked onions," he said.

Suddenly I stiffened, as if waking from a dream. Jews ate
no more onions than anyone else, but for some reason it was
said, "You can always tell a Jew, he smells of onions."

From that day on, I stopped singing. Does he know? I
wondered. Why did he say that? Perhaps he meant something
else. If he knows, why does he keep me? My head turned at
night and nightmares invaded my sleep.

Two weeks before Christmas he called me to his side. His
voice and manner were serious. "It hurts me to say this; I've
been wanting to say it for several months, but didn't know
how to." He looked at his feet. "Franek . . . I'm afraid we'll
have to let you go." He looked up again and took hold of
my shoulders. "You understand, boy . . . it's getting too
dangerous . . . I've heard rumors that the Germans are
planning a house-to-house search." My body stiffened as I
listened. "I've kept you on as long as I could . . . but now
I'm afraid. . . . You don't know what a loss this will be to
us. You don't know how much it has meant to me, having a
boy like you. I've always wanted a boy and I hoped that
somehow I could save you and that you would stay with us
like our own." He pulled me towards him. "God only knows
how I've tried. I've tried, but I'm afraid now." He released
me and sat down. I looked out the window and watched the
heavy snow blowing across the deserted fields.

"How long have you known?" I asked.

"I knew, Franek, I knew from the first day. I remembered
you from the Paizak farm."

The next afternoon, the three Golombeks stood at the
gate of their farm courtyard waving handkerchiefs and crying hysterically at my departure. As I closed the gate behind
me, I glanced at the cherry tree which now looked so fragile, surrounded by snow and tormented by the wind. I wondered whether I would ever pick cherries from its branches.

Deep and wet was the snow, and far and wide the horizon.
Where do I go now?

I crossed the fields and soon stood in the doorway of a
friend's home. I had visited there quite often to play cards.

"How nice that you've come to visit us," said his father.

I sat down and we played twenty-one. But when night fell and they were ready to eat, my friend's father said, "Franek, you'd better head home, it's getting late." I cast my eyes down and didn't move. I could feel his gaze upon me throughout the long silence that followed. "Would you like to have supper with us perhaps?" he finally asked. I indicated that I would by nodding my head. "What seems to be the trouble Franek?" he asked much later. Again I was silent. "Had a disagreement with your boss perhaps?" he prodded.

"No," I answered.

"Something must have happened."

"May I stay here for the night?"

The man looked at his wife and she at him; then, again after a long silence, he said, "You may, if you tell me what happened." He motioned to his wife and son to leave the room, then sat down across from me, rolled a cigarette, and said, "You can tell me, Franek."

My eyes still cast downwards, I finally muttered, "I'm a Jew and Franek is not my real name, and if you want you can turn me in. I don't care anymore, I've nowhere to go and I'm tired of lying and hiding, and it seems that I'll have to do this forever."

"Where are your parents?" he asked.

I told him my whole story.

"You should move away from here and start anew in a new village," he advised. "It's too close to Siedliszcze here. Lots of Germans around. You certainly fooled me, you don't look like a Jew."

"Where should I go then?" I asked.

He thought for a moment, then drew me a map of how to get to a certain village in the district of Chelm.

At noon the next day, I entered a house in a distant village and asked for something to eat. When the woman of the house left for the barn to milk the cows, I quickly explored the interior. On a dresser in the bedroom lay a bright silver medallion with the image of the Holy Mother engraved on its surface. Beside it lay a small prayer book. I slipped them into my pocket.

Once on the road, I hung the medallion around my neck and left my shirt unbuttoned so it was visible.

In one village when I stopped a man to ask for directions, he looked at me suspiciously, then broke out laughing, revealing his rotten teeth.

"What's so funny?" I asked.

"You're a Jew, aren't you?" and he pointed to the medallion and the prayer book in my hands. I didn't answer. "You're too obvious," he went on. "Do up your shirt and put the book in your pocket." I turned and ran, but several kilometers later I took his advice.

The roads were covered in deep snow and only occasionally did a sleigh with horses pass, driven by a shivering farmer dressed in heavy clothing.

In late evening I arrived at my intended destination. I looked about me at the deserted village road, then heard a voice calling, "What is it you're looking for?" I turned and saw a young man inside a blacksmith shop.

"Is this the village of Malinowka?" I asked.

"It is," he answered. "Who are you looking for?"

"I'm looking for work."

He extracted a piece of hot metal from the fire and said, "Wait a minute." Then he began banging on the metal, shaping it in many different forms. When he finished, he wiped his hands and said, "My name is Mr. Sidlo, what's yours?"

"Zigmund," I said, deciding to change my name.

He led me into the adjoining house. "This boy is looking for work," he announced to his sister and mother when we entered.

"Sit down," someone said, and then they hurled questions at me.

I answered them one by one. The sister, a tall, lean girl with a most pleasant smile and a rather prominent nose, became terribly upset by my story of how I was beaten by my stepmother and finally took to the road in order to escape her heavy, brutal hand.

"I know someone who may need a boy like you," she said, and tears ran down her cheeks.

Suddenly a German soldier appeared at the window, tapping on its pane. The girl motioned for him to come in.

He entered, and greeted everyone cheerfully in German. They all smiled and the girl returned his greeting in broken German. He sat down at the table beside me, hardly looking at me. The girl put on her coat and boots; then turning to me she said, "I'm going out for a walk with this gentleman, you wait here until I get back." I nodded my head. He stood up, clicked his heels, bowed, and they left.

Hours later when the black night had covered the village, the girl returned and immediately led me to a house nearby.

"I brought you a boy," she said when we entered.

The house was large and extremely filthy. The family was congregated in the kitchen by the fire. In a corner stood a

Christmas tree with candles, cookies, and other decorations adorning it. Unwashed dishes littered one table. On the floor two half-undressed children were playing with a black cat. The man of the house, a rather sturdy figure in his underwear, sat on a stool removing his boots. His wife, a nervous woman with sharp, piercing eyes, was combing her long, dark hair and searching for lice.

"Who is the boy, Maria?" asked the woman.

"A poor orphan," answered the girl, and she left.

The Wajdas, I found out, were from the Ukraine and had once lived under Soviet rule. As a result, Mrs. Wajda hated the Russians bitterly, but even more, she hated the Jews, whom she blamed for every wrong in the world. The Jews were responsible for the war and all the communists, fascists, bandits, swindlers, and devils were Jews.

The dilapidated house which they now occupied had, before the war, belonged to the only Jewish farmer in the village. No one knew what had happened to its owner, a Mr. Goldman, except that he had vanished one night, leaving everything behind. All that was wrong with the house or the land, Mrs. Wajda blamed on no one but its former occupant.

I sat listening, agreeing, and sometimes even adding a few anti-Jewish remarks of my own.

In comparison to his wife, Mr. Wajda was a tolerant man, but extremely boorish and bear-like in his manner. He talked so fast that one word overlapped the next. He constantly shouted, especially at me, and I never once saw him smile or say a kind word. He didn't blame the Jews for his misfortune, but everybody around him.

The Wajdas had countless violent arguments, she threatening to break his head wide open with an axe, and he shouting back in half-intelligible sentences made up mostly of filthy, vile words.

"I should never have married you!" Mrs. Wajda would cry.

"Whore," he'd call her, and spit in her direction. "You slept with all the Bolsheviks."

When they didn't quarrel, their two children, Wanda, seven, and Kasha, three, romped about the house, tearing pillows apart and sometimes scratching at each other's eyes.

Christmas came several days later, but they celebrated little, except for a few Christmas carols and Mrs. Wajda's telling the story of how many, many years ago Jesus was born and then later was crucified by the terrible, terrible Jews. The candles flickered on the Christmas tree, the cookies and other goodies were soon devoured by the children, and before

long the Christmas tree was chopped for firewood and the
holiday was over.

A merciless cold winter had set in and refused to depart.
Without gloves and with only wooden slippers on my feet, I
had to fetch water from a neighbor's well a block away.
Since there was no clear path to the well, my slippers, which
were too large for my feet, would lodge themselves in the
high snow. I'd find one and take another step, but only to lose
the next slipper. An hour later I'd arrive back at the house
with only half the water, my face and hands numb from the
frost, and my feet and legs frozen stiff.

"What took you so long?" Mr. Wajda would shout. And
when I would sit at the stove to warm and dry my feet, again
his boorish voice would shatter my ears with, "Let's go, let's
go, boy. There's work to be done in the granary."

There, for hours without rest, we would chop straw for the
animals' feed. When I'd complain about the bitter cold, or if
I asked to rest, he would immediately remind me that I was
a servant and must work if I wished to continue to eat.

He was an extremely fast eater; in fact it seemed as if he
didn't eat, but rather made his food disappear. The fact that
it took me longer angered him. "Let's go, let's go, Zigmund!"
he would shout.

In time I learned to keep pace with him, and whenever
he left the table, I left with him, sometimes leaving food on
my plate.

Once during that winter the Wajdas went to the city of
Chelm. Mrs. Wajda prepared a large potato pudding in the
morning for our meals and instructed me to take good care of
the children. I tried to entertain Wanda an Kasha with stories and drawings, but they soon tired of that and wanted to
play games. The day seemed long and endless, and it was
more out of boredom than from hunger that the three of us
devoured the pudding before lunch. I searched the cupboards
for more food, but there was nothing to be found except a
bottle of home-brewed vodka. The two children egged me on
to drink it, and as part of the entertainment, I took a sip.

"More," they shouted, "like Daddy." I took another sip,
then another. The children were laughing and jumping up
and down on their bed.

The room felt warm and I felt free and unafraid. Everything around me seemed so pleasant. I took another drink,
and though it burned my insides, I continued to drink.

"You're drunk like Daddy," said Wanda. But I protested
that I wasn't, which I proceeded to prove to her by walking in

a straight line and bumping into the cupboard and causing several plates to fall to the floor and break.

Wanda was alarmed, "What will Mommy do to you?"

"Nothing!" I replied. "They're only dishes and I'm not drunk. Let me show you again."

The room now swayed in front of my eyes and sometimes turned upside down so that I thought I was standing on my head. The children were so far away that I only heard their laughter faintly.

"I'm not drunk," I shouted. "I can walk a straight line." And again I bumped into something. They laughed louder and now began to throw pillows at me. I threw them back, and soon they tore and goose feathers engulfed the room. "It's snowing," I yelled. "Warm beautiful snow is falling and I'm not drunk I'll show you I can walk in a straight line."

Then the door opened and the Wajdas stood in the doorway, their faces cold and horrified.

"They think I'm drunk," I said beaming. "But I'll show you I can walk in a straight line." And I began to walk towards them. Mr. Wajda's face seemed to get larger and larger; eventually I could see the texture of his pimply face and the hair protruding from his nostrils.

I heard someone being slapped. I heard Mrs. Wajda swearing, I heard the children laughing and yelling, "He's drunk!" More slaps, the room turned like a spinning wheel, and I heard myself laughing and wondered who was being beaten.

The next day when I gazed into the mirror, I knew, for my face was swollen and covered with black bruises.

In time, the bruises disappeared and in time the snow melted and vanished beneath the ground. Suddenly all sorts of new faces were to be seen. People who had only stared out of their windows during the winter months now left their houses and were moving about the farmyards and roads. Soon they took to the fields and so did I, with the Wajdas' two cows and three sheep.

Occasionally Wanda would come along to help, but most of the time I'd go alone, and there I made new friends with boys and girls my own age.

On a late spring afternoon a group of us were sitting telling stories when we heard shouts. We looked up and saw a man running towards us like a wild rabbit, and chasing him were about a dozen cowherds.

"It's a Jew, catch him!" the pursuing voices were yelling.

Someone in our group jumped to his feet and yelled, "Let's get him." Everyone jumped up. I found myself hesitating; then a voice said, "Let's go, Zigmund."

I too jumped up, and before I knew what I was doing, I was running with the others and shouting, "Jew! Jew! Catch that Jew!"

The man seemed trapped; we had encircled him, but somehow he broke out of the ring and headed towards the forest. We pursued him. I caught sight of him jumping over a ravine, stumbling, falling several times, and disappearing among the trees. At times I wondered if it wasn't I who was being chased, but I didn't linger on those thoughts for long.

"Jew! Catch that dirty Jew!" I shouted along with the others.

"He's gone now, we'll never get him," I said when we were deep in the woods.

"We'll get him, let's go," said a young bully.

"Forward, march," shouted another, and they marched on.

"I have to go back," I said. "I can't leave my cows."

"The devil with the cows, we've got a live Jew to take care of," said the bully. "Come, Zigmund."

"If my cows stray I'll be in trouble, I have to go back." And I did. Who is this man? Where is he from? I wonder how much longer he will live. How will he die?

And then the group returned, bitter and disappointed, with a wornout left shoe as the only reward for their chase.

"It got stuck in the mud," said someone. "If only we could have gotten the right one as well."

"Next time we'll get the right one," someone else said, and then we all laughed.

"We can use it as a football," one of the crowd suggested and immediately kicked it into the air.

For weeks we played football with the shoe. A pang of guilt stabbed me every time I had to kick it. I felt better, however, the day the shoe fell into a pond and was lost forever. But this did not help to clear my dreams; endlessly I saw the man in my sleep, limping on one foot, running, and looking back. Sometimes his face was that of Moishe, sometimes that of my father, and sometimes the face was my own.

THREE

☐ It was now late summer and the days were long and hot. At times I would completely forget who I really was, and sometimes I couldn't even remember my real name. When it would finally come to me, I would repeat it several times so as not to forget it again.

Why, I didn't know, but something within me urged me not to forget who I was, where I was born, who my mother and father were. It was difficult remembering my real identity, for almost daily throughout that summer I had told tales of my imaginary life.

The other boys and girls would sit on the grass listening intently as my stories of beatings would unfold. Sometimes I'd be asked to repeat a particular tale; other times I'd be requested to tell a new adventure. In all of my stories, however, my non-existent stepmother was a despot, my father, a simple kind man whom she maneuvered cleverly, and I, a poor orphan being beaten constantly for things I wasn't responsible for.

On occasion these stories would evoke tears from my listeners. My tales seemed so believable that at times I too thought my name was Zigmund and that all these woes had actually happened to me.

I was, therefore, quite shattered when a chubby young girl with stringy blond hair said to me one early morning, "My daddy says you're a Jew."

I fell into a stony silence, but then quickly I smiled and asked, "When did he say that?"

"Last night. He says one of these days the Gestapo will arrive and shoot you, then burn the whole village. He says that someone should turn you in."

They know, obviously they all know. I'll have to move again, but where to?

I looked towards the forest, and the tall trees looked back at me. Deep inside the forest I imagined partisans with rifles and grenades, fearless, strong. I could see the man with the one shoe, my Uncle Moishe; perhaps my father sent from Russia was their leader, and Kisel, perhaps Kisel with his mandolin. Stories circulated about partisans. Now and then a farmer would be killed in the middle of the night for collaborating with the enemy.

"Tell your father he should watch what he says."

"He's not afraid of you, Jew," she replied, mocking me.

"He should be afraid of the partisans, though," I warned. "Perhaps he hasn't heard what they do to informers." The girl was silent. "First they kill the informer, then his whole family, and then they burn the house and barn. Tell that to your father." I was amazed at my own words. The girl remained silent, her eyes filled with fear. When I saw her next, she was still silent.

Occasionally I saw her father, and he too was silent; in fact his eyes gazed past me, through me, but never at me.

The long summer days dissolved into cold fall days. All over the fields, farmers were collecting the harvest. The trees were changing color and the wind and rain became frequent visitors.

All summer long I had gone barefoot without much trouble, but now several extremely large white blisters appeared on the soles of my feet. It became almost impossible for me to walk; I had to alternate between walking on my toes and my heels. I cried with pain and asked for help, but the Wajdas turned their heads as if they couldn't hear my pleas.

Running through freshly cut wheat fields became almost unbearable, but I had to run there, for that was where my cows and sheep were grazing now. I sometimes begged my flock not to stray into other fields, and at other times I simply sat down and cried bitterly and called out, "Momma! Mommy, help me . . . help me."

Every day without fail I had to take the flock to pasture. One day to this field, another day to that piece of pasture. Sometimes near the cabbage patch, which Mrs. Wajda was extremely proud of.

"Watch those cows, Zigmund," she would warn me. "If they so much as eat one of my cabbage leaves, you'll be sorry you ever left your stepmother."

With this kind of fear instilled in me, I guarded the cabbage patch with special care.

In the nearby field grazed two young cows supervised by the same chubby girl with stringy blond hair. She kept constantly disappearing into her house, leaving the cows to their own devices. Without fail, they'd end up in Mrs. Wajda's cherished cabbage. I kept driving them out.

"Mind your own business," the girl would shout at me when I would reprimand her.

"I'll tell Mrs. Wajda," I'd warn her.

"Go on, tell her. See if I care!"

I was afraid to tell, and I watched the cabbage patch

slowly diminishing. Some heads were completely gone, others half chewed away, and still others destroyed by the cows' hoofs.

The day came when Mrs. Wadja went to harvest her prized cabbage heads, only to find a bare field. That evening she was waiting for me with a long, heavy dried-out stick. Like an animal gone mad, she chased me around the room, into the barn, out of the barn, into the kitchen, and around the house, beating me with all her might and screaming and shouting the worst names imaginable.

I pleaded with her, trying to explain, but she couldn't hear me.

"My cabbage, my cabbage! How I worked on that cabbage!" she shrieked, and kept covering my body, head, and face with blows until the stick broke in half. But this didn't stop her, for now she attacked me with her bare hands, pulling my hair. "My cabbage! My cabbage!" Her fingernails ripped into my skin and she screamed, "I'm going to kill you . . . I'm going to kill you!"

Finally, her husband pulled her away and led her into the house. I stood outside behind the house, and resolved to go away.

I waited and saw night descend and the moon appear in the sky. Still crying and now shivering from the cold, I appealed to my mother, but the only reply was the distant howling of dogs.

I waited for the Wajdas to come looking for me, at least to ask me in for supper. I decided to refuse as a protest. I waited and waited. The sky got darker, the clouds moved on, the dogs ceased barking, and then the naphtha lamp inside the house was extinguished.

They don't care if I don't eat, I realized. I have no one in the world who cares what happens to me. And this pained me more than the beating itself.

When I saw the chubby girl next, she studied my bruised face and said, "This should teach you to keep better watch on your cows next time," and she laughed.

The Wajdas' cat gave birth to several kittens. Most of them died at birth or soon thereafter, but two little black kittens survived.

At first everyone was happy with the two new pets, but several weeks after their arrival, Mrs. Wajda discovered they were both sick. Some bloody substance protruded from their rectums, and on a neighbor's advice, the kittens were to be disposed of.

Kasha and Wanda protested and cried and delayed the execution, but a few weeks later, when the little creatures had not improved, but in fact were getting worse, Mrs. Wajda ordered me to get rid of them.

It's not nice for a Jewish boy, I suddenly seemed to hear. In what way am I different? Why is it that I'm repulsed even at the thought of killing the two kittens? Perhaps it is true that Jews are cowards! It must be true, for deep inside me I'm afraid. I'm scared not only of this, but of many things. I'll have to change. I'll have to become brave. I'll have to behave like the rest of them! How many times had I witnessed a farmer chopping the head off a chicken? He never gave it any thought at all. What do they possess that I don't? Is it because I'm circumcised? Perhaps that makes me a coward!

"Get rid of them, Zigmund," I heard Mrs. Wajda say.

"Yes, Mrs. Wajda, right away, but how?"

She looked at me in annoyance. "What do you mean, how? Haven't you ever seen anyone get rid of cats? Sometimes, Zigmund, you give me the feeling you weren't brought up on a farm."

My heart quickened. Does she suspect?

"Drown them," I heard her say. "You know how to drown kittens, don't you?"

Without hesitation, I replied, "I've done it many times."

"Then do it," she snapped, and left the room.

I picked up the two kittens and walked out into the courtyard, past the barn, and through the back fields until the Wajdas' house was out of sight. The kittens meowed and looked up to me as one looks up to a friend. I held them in my arms and felt like a third bleeding kitten rather than their executioner. I wanted to flee with them, to keep going further and further, perhaps to the forest, perhaps to some distant land, perhaps . . .

The small pond was now in front of me, and when I looked into the water I saw my own sad reflection. I sat down and soaked my feet, and felt the cold water. I looked up at the sky and hoped for some kind of miracle, but a miracle did not come. I thought of letting the kittens loose, but I feared they would find their way back home, and how would I explain this to Mrs. Wajda?

The act has to be performed, but how can I perform it? I'll have to be brave. Brave like the others. Brave . . .

I stood up, closed my eyes, and threw the two kittens into the water, then turned my head. I heard painful meows that sounded like pleas directed at me. I was deeply ashamed.

I could imagine my grandfathers and grandmothers, my whole family for generations back, standing around me, their heads bowed in shame.

Suddenly I felt something brush against my ankles. I opened my eyes and looked down. The kittens were huddling against my bare feet, shivering from the cold water. I wanted to pick them up and embrace them, but instead I broke out crying and once more threw them into the water. They submerged for a moment, came up, and paddled back to shore.

I became hysterical and began to scream, "Please, you rotten kittens, drown! Drown!" And again they came out and ran towards me for protection. I held them close to my chest and cried, burying my face in their cold, wet fur.

When I looked up, two familiar boys stood on the other side of the pond observing me.

"Why are you crying, Zigmund?" asked one.

I wiped my tears, "It's these rotten kittens." I tried to sound brave, "They've scratched me . . . Look, they're sick and I have to drown them."

The two boys approached me now. "You need a bag."

"What for?" I asked.

"How else will you drown them? You put them in a bag and fill it with stones, then you drop the whole mess into the water, and it goes down like a bomb."

"I'll run home and get a bag then," I said.

"What for?" said the other boy. "Here, let me show you. There's another way, too." He took two stones, and with some strong reeds which he plucked from the pond, he tied the stones to the cats' necks. "Watch this," he said, and dropped the two kittens into the pond.

For a moment they submerged, but they soon came up, swimming towards shore.

"I told you, you need a sack. These stones aren't heavy enough," said the first boy.

"Don't let them out," shouted the other, and he began hitting the kittens with a stick as they attempted to climb out. The other boy joined him, and it only remained for me to pick up a stick and do the same.

I did not want them to know how I felt, what I really felt, so I too beat the kittens.

We laughed, we shouted, and screamed, and watched the two helpless little black kittens struggle in the water, pleading for mercy, trying to survive, but in the end, drowning.

I am brave! As brave as they are! I thought on the way home. But I was still troubled, for I knew I *felt* differently. Something prevented me from being like them.

Why, why can't I be like them? God, dear God, make me the same. Make me brave.

The cows were tied in the stable for the winter. Outside, the winds blew without mercy, and inside the Wajdas' house, as in all the other homes in the village, a fire burned in the stove and everyone sat around it. Some delousing their hair, others reminiscing or telling riddles, and still others worrying about the Russian partisan army which was called the Bulbowcy because it was commanded by a General Bulba. It was said that they hid in the forests by day and attacked the enemy by night, disrupting trains and telephone lines, and attacking and blowing up army posts.

Word quickly spread that they invaded villages, stealing and ravaging everything in sight.

Mrs. Wajda became panic-stricken when listening to these tales. And she would retell her stories of the rape and horror brought on by the Bolsheviks.

I listened silently, shaking my head now and then to denote that I was in agreement with her. Secretly, however, I hoped that the Bulbowcy would invade the village and take me with them.

My thoughts wandered and soon I saw myself in uniform, riding a horse and carrying a gun at my side. German soldiers were fleeing from me, begging for mercy as I came upon them.

My thoughts led me now to my father, and I began to think that perhaps my father was among this army of soldiers.

It's possible, why not? I imagined a soldier in Russian uniform breaking into the Wajdas' house and looking around the room; then pointing to me, he would say, "Your name is Jankele."

"How do you know this?" I would ask.

"Because I'm your father."

At this point I would fall into his arms crying, "Papa, Papa, I knew you'd find me."

One night, as if swept by the tormenting wind outside, the village of Malinowka was invaded by the Bulbowcy. The sound of horses galloping and general turmoil woke us up.

Mrs. Wajda shook with fear, and pacing the room she began to pray and to cross herself without stop. "The bandits, the rapists, we're finished," she muttered.

There was a loud knock on our door. We waited in silence.

"Open up!" shouted a voice in Russian.

Mr. Wajda trembled and hid in the corner like a child.

"Open the door!" his wife ordered him in a whisper.

"I'm afraid," he said in a broken voice.

She composed herself and unbolted the heavy door. Two tired figures dressed in winter uniforms, with unshaven faces and automatic rifles over their shoulders, stumbled into the room.

"Welcome, welcome," said Mrs. Wajda in a pleasant voice. Her husband laughed nervously and repeated the greeting. The soldiers scanned the room and approached the hot stove. One took off his gloves, extended his hands to the fire and rubbed his palms together. "Please sit, sit," said Mrs. Wajda in Russian. They sat down and gazed at us through tired, wind-beaten eyes.

"We would like something to eat if you can spare it," said one of the soldiers.

Mrs. Wajda obliged by cutting several slices of black bread and a few pieces of pork fat, and handing it to the visitors.

Without removing their heavy coats, they sat like statues and ate without much pleasure.

I studied the stranger sitting next to me, and in the glow that emanated from the stove, he looked like my father. I wanted to ask his name, his place of birth, his age, and whether he had children, but while these thoughts were running through my mind I heard him say, "I have two children at home. I haven't seen them or my wife for a long time and I don't know whether I'll ever see them again."

Everything fits, I thought. If only I could find out his name. Then his friend addressed him by a strange, long name, one I'd never heard before. He could still be my father, I thought. He may have assumed a Russian name. I have to let him know I am here.

Suddenly I blurted out, "I am from Pulawy, have you ever been there?"

The soldier didn't answer, but pinched my cheek and said, "Perhaps by the time you grow up there will be no wars."

"When will the war end?" Mrs. Wajda now asked.

"Another year," came the reply. Then he added, "But I won't be here to see it. Five thousand of us started out of Russia two months ago; there are only two thousand of us left. I don't think one of us will return alive." He stood up and woke his friend who had fallen asleep in a sitting position. "Do you have a horse?" he asked Mr. Wajda.

"Yes," answered Mr. Wajda, then added quickly, "but he's no good, he's too old."

"That's all right," said the soldier. "We'll take him."

"Please," begged Mr. Wajda. "If you take my horse you might as well cut my arms off."

"We'll give you a young horse in exchange. He just needs food and rest, and we have no time for that."

They opened the door and headed towards the stable. We heard the stable door open. We looked out the window and saw our horse resisting as he was led out.

Mr. Wajda sat down on the floor and cried like a baby.

The same scene was repeated in every house in the village that night, but in some cases, besides trading their horses, the partisans also ransacked the beds for pillows, which they used as saddles.

The next morning the village was quiet, and what had happened the previous night seemed almost like a dream. I cast my eyes along the road, but there was no sign of them now. The road, the fields, the village itself, were deathly still. The Bulbowcy had vanished as abruptly as they had appeared.

"You never told us you were from Pulawy, Zigmund," Mr. Wajda said to me weeks later. I was silent and didn't look at him. "The head of the village has heard about you and wants to know why you've not registered. You must have some documents on you, don't you Zigmund?"

"No," I answered, smiling, "I forgot to take them when I left home."

The next day a man with a bushy, overgrown moustache appeared in the courtyard. He was so tall that he had to stoop in order to enter the house. The Wajdas greeted the visitor with unusual cordiality. He drank tea with lemon in a glass and ate butter cookies. Later, Mr. Wajda placed a bottle of vodka on the table and the two of them had several glasses. They talked about the crop, the snow, the pigs, the village, gossiped about the neighbors, and eventually the guest turned to me.

"So this is the boy, eh?" he said, and took a pad of paper and a pencil from his pocket. "It's dangerous for you to live here without being registered, boy. You could be picked up by the authorities, and seeing you have no documents, they could mistake you for a Jew."

They know, they must know, I thought. They're only playing with me.

"I understand that you have no documents on you," he went on. "Nothing to worry about, though; I'll send away for your birth certificate, and in no time we'll have you in the books."

A terrible fear stabbed me. Where will he write to get my birth certificate?

"Now then," I heard him say, "what is your name?"

"Zigmund," I answered.

The man scribbled on his pad, then lifted his eyes. "Yes, yes, Zigmund what?"

I hesitated. If I give him a made-up name and place of birth, and should he write and find that no such person was ever born there, that may be my end. I suddenly recalled a Christian boy with whom I had played back in Pulawy. He was about my age. If I give them his name then surely they will find it on record, I reasoned.

"Well, boy, what is your name?" the man asked again with some impatience.

"My name is . . ." Everyone's eyes were now upon me. "My name is Piotr Kuncewicz," I finally blurted out. Mr. Wajda tried to say something, but began choking. Mrs. Wajda stared at me, ready to devour me.

"I thought your name was Zigmund something-or-other," shouted Mr. Wajda, his face now angry as a bull's.

I looked down. "I'm sorry," I said. "I gave you a false name. I feared my stepmother might find me." The village head looked at me, then at the Wajdas, then turning to his pad, he wrote my new name.

"Where were you born?"

"Pulawy," I replied, assuming that my friend Piotr Kuncewicz had been born there.

"How old are you?"

"Eleven," I answered.

"That's fine," he said. "It shouldn't take too long to have a reply from Pulawy," and he departed.

Mr. Wajda now turned to me. "You have been here almost a year and yet never, but never, in all this time have you written one letter to your father or your stepmother."

"I would write my father if I had his address in Germany," I answered quickly.

"Then why not write your stepmother and ask for it?"

"I don't want her to know where I am," I replied.

"What's there to fear, boy? You're far away from her, she can't beat you from that distance. Why not write to her and at least tell her you're alive?"

"I refuse to have anything to do with her."

"Perhaps you want me to write for you? Maybe you can't write? Tell me."

"I can write," I insisted.

"Then write her a letter. I insist. She's probably worried about you."

I laughed. "You don't know my stepmother, she's happy to be rid of me."

"Zigmund," and he paused, "or should I call you Piotr?"

"Piotr is my real name," I answered.

"Are you sure about that? Perhaps you don't even have a stepmother."

I looked up; he stared back at me. "Do you think I'm a liar, Mr. Wajda?" He didn't answer.

I had sleepless nights again, for now I worried that Mr. Wajda might attempt to look at my penis while I slept. I felt that I was constantly being observed: at the table, at work during the day, and at night while sitting by the stove. Where before there was lots of talk, quarreling, and even fights, it was now unusually quiet. No one looked directly at me, but I could feel their stares wherever I turned. They know; they know. But what do they plan to do?

To dispel their suspicions, I found paper and pencil one afternoon, and sat down and wrote:

Dear Stepmother,
It's been a long time since I left home, and you're prob-
ably worried by now not knowing what has happened to me.
At present I am with a very good family. They are called
Wajda, and they feed me very well and don't beat me . . .

I had written about two pages before attracting Mr. Wajda's attention.

"What's that?" he asked.

"A letter to my stepmother, Mr. Wajda."

"I thought you didn't want her to know where you were?" he looked quizzically at me.

"You made me realize that I was wrong. Perhaps my father is back from Germany." I turned back to writing. He stood over my shoulder; then like an eagle, his heavy hand descended on the letter and he snatched it from the table. This will convince him, I thought. How lucky for me that he's reading it!

He paced the room reading the letter, then dropped it on the table. Looking into my eyes, he said, "You know something?" I waited. "You don't write like a Polish boy." I forced a smile. "You write like a Jew." I turned my head sharply, for I knew my expression would surely betray me.

Leave at once, something within me urged. They know. Leave before it's too late.

Someone knocked on the door, and when Mrs. Wajda opened it, an elderly priest entered accompanied by an assistant. The latter remained in the doorway while the priest shook hands, smiled at us, and asked questions concerning our health and crops. Then, dipping a whisk into a container of holy water, he recited a prayer in Latin and sprinkled the room. He had kind words to say to Kasha and Wanda, and it was then that he noticed me.

"Is this your boy too, Mrs. Wajda?" he asked.

"An orphan from Pulawy, Father."

The priest's face shone like the summer sun. He touched my face with his palm, and then asked me my name.

"Piotr Kuncewicz," I answered.

Again he dipped the whisk into the holy water, and saying a prayer he sprinkled the water over my head.

"Poor boy, poor boy!" he mumbled. "May Jesus Christ watch over you." He reached into one of his pockets, and from a small wallet extracted a silver coin and handed it to me.

Mrs. Wajda now produced several paper bills and extended them to the priest saying, "For the church, Father."

The priest pointed to his assistant, and the man near the door took the money, bowed, and stuffed the bills into his coat pocket. The priest wished us all a merry holiday, bowed, and waving to me, he and his assistant departed.

"How much did you give him?" growled Mr. Wajda.

"Why?" his wife shot back.

"They're all thieves, those priests. All year long when you're struggling, working, sweating, you don't see them. Once a year at Christmas time he shows up with all that black magic."

"Shut your mouth, a little respect for something at least."

"Since when have you become so religious, Holy Mary?" he came back at her. "You haven't set foot in a church since you were baptized."

I knew that the water the priest had blessed me with was the same water I had seen used to baptize babies. By all rights then, I now thought, I am baptized. Unknowingly the priest had made me a Christian. I am not a Jew. I don't have to hide or lie any more. But then again I felt the familiar guilt and quickly washed myself in the hope of removing the holy water from my skin. I still feel the same. I am still a Jew, I told myself.

For weeks in every household, the ovens were kept busy with cabbage cakes, kasha cakes, cookies for the Christmas trees, raisin breads, and all sorts of other goodies.

Outside, the boys and girls went from door to door singing carols, and inside every house songs were heard till late in the night.

While the villagers were celebrating, I tried to find a way to escape. Where to run next?

I walked towards the village road; deep snow had covered the fields as far as the eye could see so that the road was hardly visible.

If only I could fly! I mused. But then, even if I could, where would I fly to?

A sleigh pulled by two healthy looking horses appeared in the distance and now came closer. It drove into the smith's. From it stepped Maria, the girl who had originally brought me to the Wajdas, and her husband.

I was pleased to see her, for before her marriage and departure to the town of Piaski, she had always shown a special affection towards me. Sometimes she would comb my hair, or wash my shirt, or give me a freshly baked cookie.

The villagers gossiped a great deal about her. They said she had, in her youth, slept with every man in the village, and later with every German soldier who would have her.

Tadek, her husband, a muscular, extremely handsome man, knew all about her past but didn't care. His right hand was that of a child; because of some disease, it had never grown. As a result, he used his left hand to perform the most difficult task, and performed it better than most could do with their right. In his brother-in-law's blacksmith shop, he would hammer away at a piece of hot steel and shape it like an artist with the greatest of ease.

I stood among all the other children who had gathered at the smith's, and gaped at their fine clothes. Maria noticed me, came over, and hugged me.

"How is everything, Zigmund?" she asked. I only blushed. "You're growing," she added, and planted a kiss on my forehead.

I noticed later how her stomach had enlarged, and realized she was going to have a baby.

Several days after her arrival, she came looking for me and we went for a walk. "How are they treating you?" she asked with concern.

"Not too well," I told her. "I would like to leave."

"If only we had more room, but I don't know where I'd put you."

"I would love to work for you, Maria," I said jubilantly.

"I would treat you like a son, but I don't know where I'd put you."

"I'd sleep on your floor," I answered.

You must get away, the voice within me said. Go! Go! To Piaski, or anywhere, but go!

"You must take me with you," I begged, and tears came to my eyes.

She held me against her protruding stomach and said, "I only hope I have as handsome a boy as you are."

"Maria," I said when she released me, "I'm afraid they will beat me if they know I'm planning to leave."

She smiled and whispered, "It's our little secret. We won't tell them. They'll wake up one morning and there will be no one to boss around. They'll think you left in a sleigh with Saint Nicholas." She laughed. "I'd like to see their faces when they find you gone." She produced a fancy handkerchief and wiped my eyes. "Don't cry," she said, and gripped my hand and now she began to cry.

The village still slept. The day was extremely cold. The holidays were over; it was now the day after the new year.

I opened the door and quietly tiptoed out of the Wajdas' house. I wore my Sunday suit, which the Wajdas had made for me out of an army blanket. Over it I wore my checkered coat, which was the only remnant I still had from home.

I walked into the stable and for the last time looked at the cows, the sheep, the horse, the pigs, the chickens, and the several dozen rabbits which I had raised with such care and pride and was now leaving behind.

For a moment I recalled fondly how that past spring the Wajdas had presented me with a female rabbit, and how I had borrowed a male from a boy in the next village, and for days on end had tried to mate them.

I now closed the stable door and quietly walked towards the blacksmith shop. Maria and Tadek were already seated on the sleigh and were waiting for me. When they saw me they waved me on, and I ran towards them. Tadek extended his left hand to me. I took it, and suddenly found myself in the back of the sleigh.

I heard a whip crack, and little bells attached to the harnesses began to ring.

The town of Piaski seemed to me to be overrun with German soldiers. Here one stood on guard duty, there another walked along the street with a young girl, further on, a truckload of them turned the corner.

It was late afternoon when our tired horses pulled into the little town, turned near a large, decorative church which stood at the entrance of the town, and then followed along a few narrow cobbled streets; a few more turns, and suddenly

Tadek pulled at the reins and we stopped in front of a small house on a side street.

"Piaski," said Maria, and now I recalled how I had been there once before.

"A town of thieves," I heard my mother say now. I remembered how, when we were escaping from Lublin on our way to Siedliszcze, we had passed through this town.

"What's the name of this town, Mommy?" I had asked.

"Piaski, Jankele," she answered. "A town full of thieves."

The man driving us turned and smiled. "Let's get out of here before we get robbed," and he whipped his tired horse.

"Is everyone here really a thief, Mommy?" I asked in astonishment.

My mother looked up at a structure. "I once had a friend living here. God only knows where she is now!"

"Was she also a thief, Mommy?" I tugged at her sleeve.

My mother laughed. "No, Jankele, not everyone here is a thief. It's only a saying. In Chelm the people are supposed to be fools, and in Piaski they are supposedly thieves."

"Zigmund! Zigmund!" the voice seemed to be coming from far away. The wagon-driver's face vanished; only his smile was left, as if hanging in the air. My mother's image disappeared and my little brother Josel's sleeping body melted into nothing. "Zigmund, we're here. Help Tadek with the horses." It was Maria pulling my arm. "You're all right?" she asked.

"Yes, only a little frozen," I answered.

Days passed, then weeks, and there was little for me to do. In the morning Tadek would leave with his two horses and not return until night. I would sit with Maria and talk. Sometimes I would help her by peeling potatoes or fetching water from the pump.

"You really don't need me, do you?" I asked one day.

"Sure we do," she replied. "Especially when the baby comes," and she patted her stomach. "You know how to diaper babies?" I nodded my head. "Wait till spring, you'll help me." She now held my face in her hands and looked into my eyes. "Tell me, heartbreaker, what do I do to have a son like you?"

I heard screaming and crying, wailing and sobbing. I awoke and saw a naphtha lamp burning on the table. Several women came out from Maria's bedroom. Later, Tadek sat silently at the table gulping one glass of vodka after another. I got dressed, but was afraid to ask anyone what had happened. I approached Tadek, but he turned from me.

"Come with me, you'd better come with me," a voice said.

I turned and saw an elderly woman who lived across the street. "Come to my house, boy, they won't need you here anymore."

Again I turned to Tadek, but once more he turned from me.

"What's happened?" I asked, half choking, but no one answered.

"Come with me son," the woman said again in a soothing voice.

"What's happened to Maria?" I demanded to know.

Tadek poured the remains of the vodka into his glass and quickly poured it down his throat.

"Come," I heard the woman say, and now her arm descended on my shoulders and she led me out.

It was still dark outside; we crossed the street and entered a small hut whose walls were covered with family photographs.

"What's happened to Maria?" I asked in a pleading voice.

She motioned me to sit down. "Maria gave birth to a boy," she said, "only it isn't a boy." She now made the sign of the cross. "The body is that of a boy, but the head, the feet . . . are that of a pig." Again she made the sign of the cross, and then fell on her knees in front of a holy picture and began to pray.

When dawn came, we drank tea and ate bread with marmalade. The old woman told me of how lonely her life was in old age. How her husband had died years ago, and how her only daughter had been killed during the bombings. She was alone, all alone.

In turn, I found myself telling my fictitious orphan tale. When I looked at her again she was sobbing. "You poor child," she was crying.

If only she knew my real story, I thought, would she cry more or would she perhaps throw me out into the street?

By noon we were walking along the streets of Piaski. Several German soldiers passed us. We now entered a building and climbed some stairs; the old woman knocked on a door, which was opened by a little girl in a blue tunic.

"Is your mother home?"

"Yes," replied the little girl, and we entered.

The room contained a piano, lace curtains, carpets on the floor, and fancy ornaments throughout. From the kitchen came the odor of cooking. In a corner of the room stood a cage with several birds in it, and sleeping on one of the chairs was a furry yellow cat.

How fortunate a girl to live like this! I thought. I glanced into the bedroom and saw a rather large bed with huge goose-feather pillows and coverings. On the walls hung family photographs and little souvenirs brought home from an excursion or holiday in some mountain region and a visit to a big city.

My eyes looked and my heart cried. I recalled our little place in Pulawy with our big bed and, above it, a wall tapestry depicting reindeer in a forest. On another wall, a painting of my mother done from a photograph by a traveling artist. Now I remembered the smell of my mother's borsht; the illustrations on the tin box of tea from China; my mother combing her long black hair; my father whistling, "Si, si, si"; and the sound coming through the earphones of my father's radio, a physical instructor calling out, "One, two, three, one, two, three, one, two, three."

The little girl's mother now came out carrying a hot plate of soup.

"Mrs. Kochanski!" she exclaimed upon seeing us.

"I brought a guest," said the old lady, pointing to me.

"Sit, you're in time for lunch," said our hostess.

We sat down, ate the hot soup and bread, and then watched the little girl depart for school.

Mrs. Kochanski went on to explain in great detail how I happened to be in Piaski, how I had been orphaned, and how I now found myself alone and without a job.

Our hostess listened with great sympathy, then looking at my worn shoes, she said, "The first thing I would suggest is that you take him for free shoes." I looked up; so did Mrs. Kochanski. "Yes," our hostess continued. "If his father is in Germany on forced labor, then you can get him a pair of free shoes with wooden soles." Addressing me now, she said, "Your father is in Germany, boy, is he?"

"Yes, he is," I answered, "but how can I prove it?"

"Just give them the name, they can look it up. I'm surprised you haven't collected before now. My husband is also in Germany and we've collected many things."

"We'll go, we'll get shoes for you," I heard Mrs. Kochanski say.

"Very well," I said.

"As for work," our hostess went on, "I'll give you the name of a friend. They could use a boy like him. Tell them I sent you."

When we left the apartment and once again found ourselves on the street, I was certain we were walking towards some German office for my shoes with the wooden soles.

If I refuse to go, Mrs. Kochanski will suspect something. I must go, I must, I reasoned.

I visualized the scene: I am questioned about my father who supposedly is working in Germany. Not being able to find him in their files, their suspicions are aroused. They examine my face, my eyes, they now pull down my pants, and laugh.

"Jew, Jew, Jew!" They laugh and give me a pair of shoes with wooden soles and then they shoot me. Mrs. Kochanski cries.

We now passed the church and turned sharply into a road leading to a village situated on top of a hill.

"What about my shoes, we forgot the shoes."

Mrs. Kochanski smiled. "Let them choke on their shoes, the swine!" She held my arm tightly as we made our way along the narrow road leading towards the village.

From both sides of the snow-covered road, little huts with straw roofs peered at us. Here and there a horse would pass pulling a sleigh; now a dog came out and barked at us as if we were thieves.

Mrs. Kochanski knocked on a crooked door and a voice from within beckoned us to enter.

The hut consisted of one large room with two small windows, two beds, a table with chairs, a stove in which now burned a welcome fire, and a religious picture hung above a dresser.

"Good day," said Mrs. Kochanski.

"Good day," I said, half murmuring.

"Good day," came the reply from several voices.

The head of the household sat at the end of the table puffing on a pipe and making a pair of slippers out of straw. He was a short, calm man with eyes that looked as if they were about to break into tears. His wife, a tall, heavyset woman with hair combed to the back and an angelic face, sat beside him. Two grown boys nodded politely and a girl, busily engaged in washing dishes, smiled and returned to her task.

"I've brought you a boy," I heard Mrs. Kochanski say.

I removed my hat and coat and sat near the stove warming my hands and watching the mysterious things which were taking place inside the fire.

What are the Wajdas doing now? I wondered. Do they miss me? Perhaps they have informed on me and the Germans are looking for me. I should have changed my name. My God! What is my real name? . . . What is it? I can't remember. Zielinski? No! That's not my real name. I've got to think. I know, I remember! If the Germans look for me they'll be looking for a Zigmund or Piotr Kuncewicz. I have to change it, but how? Mrs. Kochanski already knows me by that name. How can I change it now?"

"Where is the boy from?" Mr. Kozak was now asking.

"From the Pulawy district . . ." And as if in confidence now, she said, "The father is in Germany. The poor boy was being beaten daily by a no-good stepmother. When I heard of that, I said to myself, 'As long as I'm alive, no flesh and blood of mine will suffer like that." I sent for him immediately. He's been with me these past weeks, but the poor boy needs to be on a farm, he loves animals."

"So he's a relative of yours, Mrs. Kochanski?"

"Yes, yes, on my husband's side . . . cousins." She now smiled at Mr. Kozak, then turned and forced a smile out of me.

"What's your name, boy?" Mr. Kozak was now addressing me. My smile quickly disappeared and for a moment it seemed to me that I had no name. "Is he shy?" inquired Mr. Kozak.

"You too would be shy in a strange home," said Mrs. Kozak, and threw several logs into the fire.

"My name is Jan Kochanski!" I finally blurted out. I expected Mrs. Kochanski to react in some fashion, but the old lady simply smiled.

An hour later, the Kozaks decided to employ me. Mrs. Kochanski stood up, put on her coat and shawl, and embracing me warmly said, "Be a good boy, Jan, and be very obliging, these are good people . . . I'll write your father in Germany and tell him that you are being looked after." She now turned to the others and said, "May the good Lord Jesus Christ bless you and your little home for this good deed you're doing." She opened the door, and before departing, once again addressed me, "Jan . . ."

"Yes?" I said, and ran up to her.

"Jan, you won't forget to say your prayers and go to church every Sunday?"

"I won't forget," I promised.

She kissed me and I kissed her. "May Jesus Christ watch over you," she whispered, and shut the door behind her.

FOUR

☐ Mr. Kozak was a quiet, patient, and meticulous man. Unlike Mr. Wajda, he never ordered or even asked me to do work. Instead, he would proceed to do it himself, at which time I would jump to his aid and beg him to let me help. We worked quietly, for he wasn't one to talk. He'd puff on his pipe, sometimes cough, and occasionally throw me a glance.

In many ways he reminded me of my grandfather, the baker from Pulawy, who could walk kilometers and never say a word, but somehow communicate with me by the touch of his hand.

Mr. Kozak and I became an inseparable pair. I rose when he arose, I ate when he ate, I worked when he worked, and I went to sleep when he did.

"Go Janek, go play with the boys," he would suggest on many occasions. But I wouldn't go, for his gentle nature and kind manner drew me to him.

As time went on, little by little he told me of his life. The two boys, Zbigniew and Antek, were not his own, but his wife's from a previous marriage.

"They're lazy good-for-nothings," he confided in me one day.

Anna was his own daughter; she reminded me of Genia in appearance and was about her age, but she was distant and cool to me.

I now longed for Genia's sweet smile and joy for life. I hoped that somehow she would appear, turn me over, and tickle me.

Mr. Kozak sat at the head of the table, and unless he started eating, no one else did. Whenever meat or another specialty was served, his wife placed it in front of him and he, like a little king, would divide it according to his judgment.

Because of his poor teeth, Mr. Kozak never ate the crust of the bread, and since I was the youngest, it was understood without anyone saying so that I could have a piece of bread only if all the crust was eaten up first. I tried to do that, but the little man had an enormous appetite and as a result the bread basket was constantly filled to the rim with crust. I resented him at such moments and sometimes even secretly wished that he would become ill or go away for a lengthy period.

129

"Am I ever happy you're with us," Anna said to me one day. "At last I can have a piece of bread!"

My days were spent in the stable or the granary, and at night I would sit near the hot stove watching Mr. Kozak and an assortment of neighbors play cards, or simply talk about world events, or reminisce about youth or the good old days.

During these conversations, the talk would without fail turn to the Jews. In such instances I choked inside and was concerned that someone might notice my blushing face. Invariably I thought of excusing myself and going to sleep, but this I felt might focus suspicion on me. As a result, I would busy myself with placing logs on the fire, or simply smile, or pretend not to listen.

At other times, a villager, on his return from a large city such as Lublin or sometimes even Warsaw, would have the congregated group gape at him as he unfolded his adventures in the great city.

At one such gathering, a man held his audience spellbound as he told of what went on at Camp Maidanek.

"Jesus Christ, what has the world come to?" he was saying in a hoarse voice. "I saw Poles beating Poles, Russians beating Russians, Ukrainians beating Ukrainians, Jews beating Jews, Gypsies beating Gypsies."

The winter months came to an end. The road was dry. Butterflies fluttered in the courtyard, bluebirds were building a nest on a beam inside the stable, and I drove the cows to pasture.

In the fields I met other boys, some about my own age, but most of them older. They inquired little about me except my name and whom I was working for. We chased rabbits, we cut branches from trees and made whistles out of them, and when it rained we'd drive our cows into the forest, congregate under a tree, and talk.

On one such day, I found myself sitting on the wet grass with a potato sack covering my head, listening to stories about all the girls in the village. Some of the boys were smoking cigarettes made out of dry grass rolled in leaves; others were roasting mushrooms. We laughed as each one told of witnessing some interesting sexual contact between his father and mother, sister and boyfriend, or even strangers. One outdid the other, and each succeeding story was more interesting and revealing than the last one.

"What about you?" a voice directed the question at me. "Haven't you ever seen or done anything?" I blushed, smiled, shook my head, then turned to look for my cows.

"He's too young," I now heard someone else say.

"How old are you?"

"Twelve," I answered.

"I bet he doesn't even have hair yet," a husky voice laughed. "Do you have hair, Jan? Does it tickle you? Show us if you have hair." There was laughter all around me. "Perhaps only little hairs, just coming out!" the laughing voice said. I turned and saw a tall boy with small, half-closed eyes coming towards me. At that moment he looked like a monster.

"Let's see if he has hair." The others jumped to their feet, and the forest suddenly echoed with a loud, "Yeah, let's see!"

"No!" I yelled. A pair of firm, strong hands were attempting to undo my belt. Another pair of hands were holding my shoulders pinned to the ground. I turned and twisted. I screamed, "No! Let me go, let me go!" They were all laughing. I held onto my belt with all the strength in me, but not for long. The more I fought, the funnier they found the game. Soon my belt was gone. Someone was holding my feet, another was holding my hands, and still another was now unbuttoning my fly. I tried to shake loose, but without success.

"We won't hurt you, Jan." The laughter was now deafening.

One button, two buttons, another button, laughter . . . hysterical laughter. Someone was pulling at my pants. I now saw the rabbi at my brother's circumcision: the knife cuts the skin, my brother Josel cries, the rabbi smiles.

"Mazel tove," someone said. I see a bottle of wine and a large basin full of beans.

I scream and now cry. I've finally met death. In a few minutes they'll know I'm a Jew. Why, dear God, did I have to be circumcised?

Faces all around me looking down.

"Let's see it," someone shouted. "Take off his pants."

With all the strength within me, I somehow managed to free myself and hold on to my pants.

"Leave me alone," I said, and began to weep. "May Christ curse you for this," I shouted at them.

There was a deathly silence around me. I buttoned my fly, someone threw me my belt, I stood up, walked a short distance, then stopped under a tree, panting and still crying.

"We just wanted to see your hair," said one of them. "No reason to cry, it's just for laughs."

"Yes," said another, "we meant no harm. Just wanted to see your penis, that's all, Jan." Soon they dispersed.

"Something very peculiar about that one," I heard one of them say, and then the words echoed through the forest.

Again I saw the rabbi, but this time he was the rabbi who had circumcised me. He looked like my grandfather, the baker from Pulawy. I now hated him. I hated his beard, his name, his knife, his eyes, and . . . I did not want to be a Jew anymore.

For several days I ignored them, but soon we made up and now during the long summer evenings we ran around playing games.

At first we played ball, then hide-and-seek. Later, as the summer progressed, we tired of that and changed to "spy." One of us, chosen to play the spy, would hide and the rest had to find him. When this too became boring, someone suggested we play "Jew."

"What kind of a game is that?" asked one boy.

The one who had suggested it then explained, "We choose a Jew. He hides, we count till ten, then we search for him. When we find him we take everything away from him and then we turn him over to the Germans."

"What if he runs away?" asked another boy.

"Then we shoot him," came the reply.

In the days and nights that followed, my friends and I hunted for our made-up Jews in the barns, in the fields, near the river, behind trees, and in haystacks. The game had a real appeal to everyone, including myself. For after all it was only a game and it did offer a lot of suspense. Whenever the Jew was discovered, he immediately raised his arms. We'd surround him, remove his valuables from his pockets, and then shoot him by pointing a wooden revolver at him and yelling out, "Bang! Bang!" Invariably, whoever played the Jew would immediately fall to the ground, his arms and legs spread wide apart and his face twisted in a half-comical grimace, pretending to be dead.

To play the part of the Jew was the most interesting aspect of the game, and as a result everyone fought for the privilege, everyone that is except me. I enjoyed the role of the hunter much better. Eventually, however, so as not to throw any doubt onto myself, I too began to ask for the honor of playing the Jew.

After a lot of shouting and fighting and arguing, I became the Jew. The others turned around, closed their eyes, and began to count, "One . . . two . . . three . . ."

Where should I hide? It was dark. I had left my playmates behind in the field . . .

"Five . . . six . . . seven . . ." I ran into the courtyard

. . . "eight . . . nine . . ." I now found myself in my sleeping place and covered myself in the hay. "Ten!" My heart began to beat. I heard their voices in the courtyard, their footsteps.

"I think I know where he is," one of them was saying. It was no more a game now, the hunt was quite real.

I remembered the night when Moishe and I were discovered in Mrs. Paizak's barn. Moishe! What ever happened to my Uncle Moishe? Is he still alive? Will I ever see him again?

The door to the barn opened; I now heard whispers, footsteps. I lay still, my heart beating like a loud clock. More whispers, footsteps, and then a voice. "He's not here, let's go."

A long silence followed. I fooled them, I thought. A smile crossed my face. I stood up and shook the hay off my clothes. Quietly I walked to the open barn door and looked out into the dark night. From the distance a few voices could be heard.

Where is my Uncle Moishe on a night like tonight? Tears came to my eyes.

"We've got you!" a voice shouted from behind me. "Hands up, you dirty Jew!" I turned quickly and saw two of my companions behind me. One of them ran out and yelled, "We've got him! We caught the Jew!" The other approached me and began to search my pockets with one hand, while with the other he pointed his wooden pistol at my head.

When he turned his attention away from me, I lowered my arms, turned, and ran away.

"Bang! Bang!" I heard him shout after me, but I paid no attention. "Bang! Bang!" came the sound. My feet carried me towards the back fields. "You're dead!" he shouted after me. "I've shot you, Jan!"

I ran as fast as I could. Deep in the fields I stopped and listened. All was quiet except the crickets and the frogs in a nearby pond. The moon above was bright and round. I looked at it in wonderment.

"I wonder if my Uncle Moishe can see you now too?" I said in a low voice. I sat for a few moments, and when I stopped panting, I slowly got up and leisurely walked back towards the village.

Upon seeing me, my companions were extremely annoyed, especially the one with the wooden pistol. "I shot you three times, Jan!" he shouted. "You're dead; I shot you and you're supposed to fall dead."

"I ran away," I defended myself.

"How could you run away if I shot you three times?"

"You shot at me," I answered, "but you missed every time."

"You're crazy!" he shot back with anger. "You don't know how to play a Jew."

He turned in disgust, and pocketing his wooden revolver, he went home to sleep.

One wet, rainy day, a German soldier appeared at the small, narrow, winding river which passed through the village. He had a number of grenades around his belt. We followed him along the river's edge until finally he motioned to us to move away and lie down on the ground. He then released the pin of a grenade and threw it into the river and ducked for cover.

A small explosion followed, sending a spray of water into the air. We all stood up and ran down to the water, and there we saw fish after fish coming to the surface, floating as if dead. Several boys took off their clothes, jumped in, and threw the fish towards the soldier. A little further down the river, he threw another grenade and the same operation was repeated. When his knapsack was full of fish, he threw the rest towards us and then left on foot, towards the town of Piaski.

We fell on the remaining fish, each grabbing as many as he could, and then ran through the village yelling, "We've got fish! We've got fish!"

This happened in the early spring, but by the time summer arrived and the days were extremely hot, no one thought too much about fishing, but the boys thought very much about swimming.

On any hot summer midday, a passer-by making his way through the village would have noticed a group of boys completely naked, diving into the river's cold water, coming out, and diving in again.

"Why don't you come swimming with us today, Janek?" my friends would ask.

"Perhaps tomorrow; I have to help Mr. Kozak," I would answer, or, "I'll meet you there later," or, "I have a cold," or, "The water is too cold today."

As the days passed, my excuses became weaker and I began to fear the consequences. My companions grew suspicious.

"What's the matter with you? Perhaps you only have one ball, eh?" they laughed. "Or no balls at all!" added another.

I lay awake at night worrying about the next day and hoping it would rain or be cold so I wouldn't be invited to go swimming. I thought of adding a piece of chicken skin to my penis, but how to go about it, I didn't know. I have to find a way. I must go swimming, but how? Perhaps in my underwear! No, this is not the answer, it will make me stand out.

It was an extremely hot day when two boys came looking for me.

"Today you're coming with us, Janek," they stated, grabbing me by my arms.

"No!" I protested.

"Why not?"

"I have work to do."

"Go, Jan, go swimming," I heard Mr. Kozak say. I turned and saw him standing behind me. "Go, boy, go. It's too hot to work. I'm going to sleep and you go swimming. Enjoy yourself." I turned to my friends who were now smiling. I turned back to Mr. Kozak, but he only smiled and motioned with his hand for me to go.

On the way to the river my two friends talked without stop, but I couldn't hear them; my mind was elsewhere. "Isn't that right, Jan?" I seemed to hear them ask.

"Yes, yes," I answered, but everything was turning in front of me.

Again I saw the rabbi with his knife; he was cutting. It fell to the ground and now I realized he wasn't a rabbi, but the ritual slaughterer, the Shochet, and the object on the ground was a bleeding chicken's head. Its eyes open, staring upwards. My mother's portrait above the bed, and now Kisel was playing the mandolin and my mother was singing.

"What are you waiting for?" someone was shouting. "Come on!"

I now stood on the edge of the river. Around me my friends, all nude, were diving into the water, splashing each other, coming out, and diving in again.

"Come on, Janek!"

I began to undress. Slowly I pulled the cotton shirt over my head and threw it to the ground. I looked about me; no one was looking. I sat down on the grass, I undid my belt, then one button, then another, and another.

"Come on, Janek!"

"What's taking you so long, Jan?" screamed another.

Still sitting, I began to remove my pants with one hand, while with the other I covered my genitals. I now stood up, still holding my private parts, and with my free hand outstretched, I dived into the water.

I'm safe, I thought, and swam from one edge of the river

to the other. Someone splashed me, someone else laughed, another boy pushed my head under, and still another wanted to know if I could swim under water. My companions dived continuously, not noticing that once in the water I remained there.

An hour or so later when it was time to go, I managed to come out of the river in the same manner in which I had entered it, with one hand covering my penis.

In the following days I went swimming, and each time I gained more confidence in dressing and undressing in such a way as not to reveal my complete nakedness. I sometimes marveled at my own manipulations and at the fact that none of the others seemed to notice my rather unusual habits.

Then it happened! "Why do you cover your penis, Janek?" a boy asked curiously one day. The others immediately turned their eyes towards me, waiting for a reply. "Why, Janek, why?" I heard the boy say again. I had just removed my pants and was about to dive. A terrible fear gripped me. They may forcefully remove my hand and disclose my secret. "Why, Janek?"

"Perhaps he's a girl," and a gale of laughter echoed through the fields.

I covered my penis with both hands and held on tightly. The boys now surrounded me, their eyes focused on my hands.

"Why, Janek, why?"

I wanted to run, but was afraid.

"You see," I began, "I come from a village near Pulawy, and there we have a large river, the Vistula. People come to bathe there from Warsaw and Lublin and all over, and no one goes swimming in the nude; they wear bathing suits." I looked up and noticed that my friends were listening attentively. "My father taught me that only animals walk around in the nude, not civilized people. So if you want to be like animals, go on displaying yourselves to everyone who passes by here. I, lacking a bathing suit, intend to keep my dignity by at least covering myself with my hands."

A long silence followed during which I stood up, walked to the river's edge, and in my usual manner, dived into the water.

From then on, anyone who passed along the back road of the village on the way to Piaski would have noticed a group of noisy boys diving into the water, their right arms outstretched and their left hands covering their uncircumcised penises.

On a dark evening in late summer, a group of neighbors had congregated outside the Kozak hut and were deep in some political discussion. We suddenly heard from the sky above what seemed like the hum of a hive of bees.

As we attempted to guess how many planes there were and in which direction they were going, the sky in the distance suddenly lit up with the most beautiful lanterns I could imagine. We looked in amazement, for the lanterns were obviously far away from us, yet they were so luminous that our entire village, as if by magic, turned into day.

"It's over Lublin," someone said.

"Must be some German holiday."

"Maybe it's Hitler's birthday," said a fat woman, and burst out laughing. She was in the middle of her laughter when we suddenly heard explosions. There were more beautiful lanterns and then more explosions.

"Lublin is in flames," said Mr. Kozak. "The Russians!"

The next day it was quiet, and the days that followed were quiet also. But shortly after, while out in the pasture, I became aware of the constant sound of cannons shooting somewhere in the distance.

Perhaps the Russians are coming, I mused. Any day now I may be liberated. Perhaps my father is behind one of those cannons, dressed in a uniform, decorated with medals.

Every day I listened to the sounds and hoped they would come nearer and nearer.

One day I asked Mr. Kozak about it. He puffed on his pipe, smoothed his moustache, and without even looking at me replied, "It's the Germans. They're on maneuvers not far away."

I didn't know whether to believe him, but several days later, when the shooting came to an abrupt halt, I was sure Mr. Kozak had spoken the truth, and I even felt ashamed for having doubted him.

Weeks later, what seemed to be a whole German army invaded our village, stationing themselves in every courtyard, house, barn and stable. They were everywhere: by the river, on the road, in the fields.

Mr. Kozak's courtyard was filled with strong Belgian horses and solid wagons with huge wheels. The soldiers were moving about, washing themselves at the well, shining their shoes, cleaning their uniforms, combing their horses, and repairing their motorcycles. They played cards, sang songs, and combed the whole village for eggs.

Mr. Kozak spoke to them in German and thus found out

that they had come from the front and were stationed here
for several weeks to rest.

"The front is far, far from here, deep in Russia," Mr.
Kozak translated. "The Russians are being beaten, it's only
a matter of weeks," he continued.

We all looked up. Far, far above us we heard a hum. Off
to our right, small planes could be seen flying like wild ducks.

"They're ours," said the German officer and began to
count. "One, two, three . . ." When he had counted thirty-
two, the whole courtyard shook, and in an instant everyone
had vanished as if the earth had swallowed them up.

Several blasts followed. I found myself in the barn,
covered with straw. When I finally came out, I looked in the
direction of Piaski. Red and orange flames were to be seen,
and black smoke covered the sky above the small town.

"The cows, Janek, the cows! Save the cows!" yelled Mr.
Kozak.

I quickly unleashed the animals. "Where to?" I looked to
him for guidance.

"To the fields," he replied. "Just take them to the fields,
any fields, they'll be safer there."

I picked up my stick and with a few commands drove the
animals out of the barn and onto the main road. All about
me I saw confusion.

Villagers were running about, some towards the fields,
others almost in circles. The German soldiers were packing
their gear, and their faces, for the first time, looked frightened. The smell of gasoline was all about from their cars and
motorcycles, which were being started along the road.

Somewhere in the vicinity someone was crying, and in the
middle of the road a soldier was shouting traffic orders to his
comrades.

I hit the cows with my stick and made them move faster
and faster until at last we had left the village behind and
found ourselves in the valley through which the river flowed.
I had no idea where I was going, but decided to stay there
when I saw one of my friends with his cows.

The sky over the town of Piaski was still black when a new
group of planes appeared in the sky. One plane flew in ad-
vance, the rest followed in formation.

My friend Jerzy and I fell to the ground, but I kept my
eyes open and gazed at the planes. Through the blades of
grass I could see bombs falling from the aircraft like chicken
eggs out of a basket. Again the earth shook, black smoke
covered the sky, and the town of Piaski was once more in
flames.

"This is a town of thieves," I heard my mother say.

A terrible fear invaded my mind and I felt that at any moment a bomb would fall, tearing me into little pieces and scattering my body throughout the field and into the river.

On the horizon a circular red sun was setting when I sprang to my feet and began to run towards the village.

"Where are you going, you fool?" Jerzy called after me.

I didn't answer him. My feet carried me as if I was being pulled by a magic force.

At first the village seemed far away and then it was in front of my eyes, somewhat blurry though. The road was deserted. I turned into our courtyard . . . no one to be seen; I ran to the house . . . no one was there; I now looked into the stable . . . the horses were gone.

"Mr. Kozak!" I yelled at the top of my lungs. No one answered. "Mr. Kozak! Someone! Please answer me." Again I ran to the house, and now onto the village road, and back to the courtyard. "Mr. Kozak!" My feet carried me behind the barn and swiftly into the back fields.

The red sun was disappearing completely. "Mr. Kozak! Mr. Kozak!" The fields were deserted. I continued to run.

By the edge of the forest I saw our two horses, and when I came nearer, I saw the rest of the Kozak household and their furniture standing amongst the trees. They stared at me in silence. I wanted to say something, but only ended up staring at them in return.

"Where are our cows?" asked Mr. Kozak finally.

"I left them by the river," I answered, now realizing for the first time the reason for their stares.

"You left our cows?" his voice rose.

"I'm afraid," I blurted out. "Mr. Kozak, a bomb will kill me."

"A bomb won't kill you, Janek, but I will if anything happens to my cows. How could you leave them unattended?" I took several steps back. I could hardly recognize Mr. Kozak now, he was so unlike himself. "Go back, boy, and don't let anything happen to my cows. Watch them with your life!"

"I'm hungry," I said.

"We're all hungry," came the reply. "Go, boy, go, get moving!"

I turned and ran through the deserted fields back to the village, then along the river, and now I stood in front of my friend Jerzy.

The night descended quickly and a summer chill came with it. The cows lay down to rest and Jerzy and I cuddled ourselves in a nearby ditch.

The next morning was quiet. The grass was wet with dew and along the bank of the river a few frogs jumped and croaked. The sky too was deserted. We watched the sun rise in silence. We watched the cows rise and begin to graze. We knelt at the river's edge and washed our sleepy faces.

Bang! A shell exploded only a short distance away from where we were. Bang! Bang! Bang! Several other explosions followed immediately. Fragments were falling all about us. I quickly fell to the ground and covered my head with my hands.

"Come!" called Jerzy, and began to run towards the ditch.

"No!" I yelled back. "Fall to the ground or you'll get killed." Again another explosion. "Jerzy!" but there was no answer. "Jerzy, are you safe?" I looked about me; the cows were grazing as if the shooting did not concern them, but there was no sign of Jerzy.

I looked across the river and there on a hill stood a huge German tank, the muzzle of its cannon pointed directly at me. On top of the tank a German soldier was peering through a pair of binoculars.

What's he looking at? Perhaps at me! Maybe he knows that I'm Jewish!

I now turned, and behind me on the opposite hill I saw what must have been a Russian tank with a Russian soldier peering through a pair of binoculars.

"Jerzy! Jerzy! Where are you?" I began to tremble.

Again I fell to the ground as shells from both sides fell in the valley, exploding all around me. Now and then a shell would explode in the river and send a spray of water into the air. The cows continued to graze, completely unconcerned.

"Jerzy!" There was no answer.

What if one of the cows gets killed or wounded? What would I do? How could I explain this to Mr. Kozak?

A barrage of shells followed and small pieces of shrapnel fell all about me. I now wanted to get up and run, but I feared what the cows might do unattended. In the end I re-solved to leave them and try to save myself.

At first I thought of jumping into the river, but then in a half-crouching position I made my way to the ditch at the bottom of the hill. I jumped in and listened. Again some shells exploded nearby and then in a moment of silence I heard a faint cry. It seemed to come from close by. I crawled several meters and at a turn in the ditch I recognized Jerzy. He was kneeling, his eyes heavenward, and though he must have been praying, I couldn't hear what he was saying, for his crying made his words inaudible.

"Jerzy!" I cried with delight.

He wiped the tears with his sleeve and glanced at me. "I'm afraid." And again he turned his eyes to the open sky. I studied him for a moment and then I too fell on my knees.

"Dear Jesus," I began to pray, "please save me. Dear Jesus, please! I promise to pray to you for the rest of my life. Please, dear Jesus!" I too began to cry now. "I believe in you, Holy Mother. Please save me, but please, most of all, save my cows."

When the sun was directly above us, the shelling came to an abrupt stop. We peeked out of our ditch and quickly counted the cows. They were all there and uninjured.

"Janek, I'm going to try and make my way home," Jerzy announced.

"What about your cows?" I asked.

"To hell with the cows," came a sharp reply. "If you were smart you'd get out of here as well."

He turned from me and began to crawl along the ditch, then disappeared from my sight at one of the bends.

I sat silently watching the smouldering countryside in front of me. It was deathly quiet and the horrible thought crept into my mind that perhaps everyone had been killed and that I was the only human survivor left on the whole earth.

A murky memory of a story once told to me by my Uncle Shepsel about a man shipwrecked alone on an island now came back to me.

At first the thought almost pleased me and I momentarily saw myself as the ruler of the entire world, owning all the houses, stables, cows, horses, pigs, and roads, galloping on a white stallion across lands and forests. But horror took hold of me, and I dreaded the thought.

What would I do all alone? I climbed out of the ditch, stood up erect and yelled, "Jerzy! Jerzy!" Only silence answered me. I ran further along the bend of the hill and called out, "Is anyone around?"

A faint buzzing could be heard. I looked up, and as if diving directly from the sun, an airplane swooped down like a giant eagle coming to carry me off. I fell and shielded my head with my hands. Several bursts followed and the noise of machine-gun fire filled my ears.

When I looked up again, I saw German soldiers along a nearby road trying to jump off trucks. Some of the vehicles were on fire; others were turned over. The plane circled several times, then again dived down at the trucks, and this time attacked the convoy with its machine guns only. The running soldiers were being cut down by bullets. As soon as the aircraft disappeared, the remaining Germans got to their feet and ran to a nearby white hut.

The trucks were in flames and the whole surrounding area had an awful stench of gunpowder and smoke. Way up in the sky, the sun burned strongly, and though the plane could not be seen now, I could still hear its hum coming from far above.

Then suddenly from the white hut came shouting, laughter, a woman's scream, more shouting, again a woman's voice screaming as if addressing the heavens for help. The door opened and a man came stumbling out of the hut, walking in my direction.

When he came closer, I realized he was crying. His arms outstretched towards the sky, he was begging God for help. As he came upon me, I asked, "What is the matter?"

He laughed hysterically and wiping his nose with his shirt sleeve he said, "They're raping my wife. She's five months pregnant and they're raping her." He turned and continued to walk without any real destination. "Oh, Holy Mother, how can you allow this? The whole German Army is raping my Jadwiga!"

Some time later, a single shot rang out; the soldiers came filing out, jumped onto a truck, and drove off into the distance.

Somewhere in the sky the airplane was still humming.

Near the river's edge the man was standing half-crazed, asking for God's help, and from the white hut came the persistent cry of a young child screaming, "Mommy is dead!"

At night Mr. Kozak appeared out of the shadows, and after a long silence during which he mentally counted the cows, he simply said, "You can come home now."

I rounded up the animals and drove them into the stable.

The next day a merciless rain descended upon us, and instead of shooting and bombing, we now heard thunder and lightning. We gathered inside the hut and waited. I am not sure what it was we were waiting for. Perhaps it was for word that we were liberated, or perhaps we only waited for the rain to pass.

In silence we ate breakfast and now everyone simply sat there. It was so quiet that the ticking of the clock seemed unusually loud. I sat near the little window and studied the rain drops as they hit the pane. There was something magical about it.

What a fascinating world, all its own! I thought.

Outside the window, the village road was a mass of mud; torrents of water flowed downwards towards the river.

Beyond, the horizon was gray and hardly visible; not a man, or a cat, or a dog, or any other animal to be seen.

And then, somewhat blurred by the rain running down the window glass, two figures appeared walking along the road. The others in the room must have sensed that I was looking at something startling, for without saying a word they quickly joined me at the window.

We all stared in disbelief, for outside, completely drenched, their rifles pointing downwards, their arms up in a surrendering position, walked two young German soldiers.

A shiver ran through my spine, but this time not because I feared them; rather, because I felt sorry for them.

How different the enemy looks now!

They walked very slowly, almost as if fearing to take the next step. Their faces were soaked, their clothing drenched, and their boots caked with mud. Their faces looked so pathetic, their eyes sad, pleading, afraid. The enemy suddenly didn't look like the enemy at all. The two Germans reminded me of myself and my Uncle Moishe wandering in the fields, not knowing in which direction to move, unsure of our next step.

"Let's go out and get them," said Antek. But his voice was so unconvincing that no one moved or even replied. We simply stared and watched them disappear down the village road.

It rained for two days and when the showers came to an end, word reached us that young Russian soldiers, half drunk and riding on wild horses, had occupied the town of Piaski. Many villagers ran to the town, returning with all sorts of goods left by the departed Germans and stolen from deserted private homes.

There was great jubilation in the village, not because we had been liberated, but because of the treasures which could be taken from the half-burned town of Piaski. Here and there someone was singing. An old man, his pants almost down to his knees, was walking along the road, a bottle of vodka in his left hand. He kept taking long swigs, pouring it down his throat.

Lost cows, horses, and even pigs were still roaming the fields, and now and then a stranger would appear looking for his animals. "She has two black patches on her stomach," one would describe a cow, but no one would even listen. Everyone was too busy stealing.

While the world burned, the Germans were running, the Russians were fighting, and the villagers on the hill outside of the town of Piaski decided it was their turn to become rich.

I stood outside the Kozaks' hut and watched, afraid because I did not believe the Germans had really gone. What if it's only a trap? Perhaps it's only a trick to get me to come out into the open. I'll wait.

I waited, and before I knew it, six giants who looked more like Gypsies than Russians were sitting at our table demanding food and drinking vodka. I found out later that they were Georgians. I studied them closely, but saw no trace of my father.

Outside along the village road other soldiers, some of them Russians, some Uzbeks with very small horses, were setting up camp. Here and there an accordion was heard. Now and then a shot would still ring out in the distance, but above, the sky was clearing and the clouds dispersing and melting away into nothing.

From the next village came a story of how the Underground had caught two German soldiers and held them prisoner in a cellar. The two had pleaded that they were only ordinary soldiers who had never harmed anyone, and had produced photographs of their wives and children and begged for mercy, saying that they only wished to see their children again and live in peace. They had cried and kissed the boots of the guard and pleaded for their lives. Their captors had not been moved and had shot them.

In silence I listened to this tale, and that night in the stable, in the presence of the animals and in complete darkness, and while the sound of Russian songs could be heard, I knelt in the hay and prayed to Jesus for the souls of the two German soldiers.

Their frightened faces loomed before me that night, and many, many nights thereafter.

Soon after liberation, the town of Piaski held a carnival, and to my complete surprise, Mr. Kozak offered to look after the cattle himself, and gave me the day off.

Carefully he counted out eighty zloty and placed the bills in my palm. "You can stay the whole day," he said.

I dressed in my Sunday suit, washed my face, combed my hair, and squeezing the money tightly in my pocket, set out on my way early in the morning.

A few of the villagers greeted me along the road, others told me jokingly to bring them something back, still others warned me in jest to watch out for thieves.

In Piaski the smell of smoke, gunpowder, and rotten flesh was everywhere. Empty cannon shells lay in the streets and beside houses. Wherever I looked I saw rubble and half-destroyed homes. The roads were filled with Russian vehicles and at an intersection a beautiful blond Russian girl soldier was directing the traffic. Along the sidewalks traveled Russian soldiers, some bandaged, some limping, and others simply sauntering, as if lost.

I studied them all and searched for a face, a face I hoped to recognize.

I thought of visiting Maria and Tadek and perhaps Mrs. Kochanski, but now I wondered if they were alive, or if they had been killed by the bombs. I argued for and against going there, and in the end decided to visit the carnival first and then drop in on them with some small souvenir.

The carnival was almost deserted except for the people behind the stalls and a handful of early customers like myself. Since I had not eaten breakfast, I was pulled as if by a magnet by the aroma of steaming wieners.

How well I remembered the same smell in the old Warsaw market! Wieners with mustard. My grandfather used to buy them for me.

"How much?" I asked.

The woman behind the small stand proceeded to serve one to me and said, "Five zloty." I walked away.

It's too early to eat, I reasoned. If I spend my money now, what will I do for the rest of the day?

I walked on, and now my attention was caught by a man at a small table nimbly hiding a bean under three thimbles. I stopped and watched in amazement how cleverly he worked this game.

Further on, a lame man was playing an accordion and a young boy about my own age, a cigarette dangling from his mouth, was appealing for funds. Something within me urged me to throw a few zloty into his hat, but I resisted.

The day is young; later . . . later . . . and suddenly my eyes caught sight of a counter with a dozen or so bottles filled with different colored drinks. A small sign announced the price: two zloty a glass. It was kwas, a sweet fruit-flavored drink which I had had many times in Warsaw. Looking at the bottles I could almost recall the taste of every color. I suddenly felt thirsty, not for only one glass, not for one flavor, but for all the flavors, and while thinking of the drinks, thousands of incidents rushed through my mind, some not even related to kwas.

Later! Later! I heard the voice say again.

An old man was blowing up multicolored balloons. I

watched them and suddenly I remembered being in a shoe store in Pulawy and receiving a balloon, and when I blew it up it had the word "Bata" imprinted on it.

The man smiled at me and proceeded to try to interest me in a balloon. I held my money tightly and didn't remove my right hand from my pocket.

Here was a barrel of sour apples being sold by a fat lady with a white apron; there was a blind man selling chocolate bars; and now I saw a man and his daughter performing acrobatics. I watched with amazement, but when the man passed the tambourine around for donations, I quickly moved on to the next attraction.

In this manner I moved from one stall to another and watched and was fascinated, and allowed myself to revel in recollections and memories.

By noon my stomach ached from hunger, but still I clenched my fist and held on to my eighty zloty while I watched others bite into hot, steaming, red, juicy wieners. The thought occurred to me that the longer I delayed my spending, the more I would enjoy it and the longer my day of pleasure would last.

Again I stood in front of the stall with the brightly colored drinks and now, though my throat was dry, I resolved not to break up my even eighty zloty. At no time in my life had I ever had eighty zloty, and now that I had it, I was certainly not going to part with it so easily.

At a counter I decided to purchase a bag of candies to take home, but since it was only noon, I elected to delay this too until the end of the day.

As if he had suddenly fallen from the sky, a rather short, unshaven little man with a straw hat appeared in front of me. On a stool he placed a circular wooden disk which was divided in four equal segments of different colors.

"Place your money ladies and gentlemen!" he began to shout, and like a magnet he pulled a group of onlookers around him, me among them. "Place your bets, ladies and gentlemen!" and he rolled out a single die which was painted in the same colors as the disk.

Hands with paper bills appeared above me and quickly dropped the money onto the four different colors.

The little man shouted, "Place your bets! A winner every time!" And shaking the die in his hand, he rolled it. It came to rest with red pointing up. "Red wins!" He now paid double to those who had money on the red, and pocketed the money from the other three colors. "Place your money, ladies and gentlemen!" Again the bills appeared, covering the disk, and again the die was thrown, and again the little man shouted, "A winner every time!"

I watched with fascination and suddenly I felt a great impulse to place two zloty and try my luck.

You'll lose it, a voice within me said.

You can also win, said my other inner voice. Look at all those people doubling their money!

I had a vision of doubling my eighty zloty to one hundred and sixty.

Why only one hundred and sixty? Why indeed? And soon there was no limit to the amount I could win at this magic wheel!

Eventually I stopped counting all the money I was about to win; instead, I had a vision of myself with pockets bulging with money, my hat filled with bills, a sack of bills on my back, and then of a wagon full of money pulled by two tired horses.

I saw myself buying a new pipe for Mr. Kozak, a new dress for Mrs. Kochanski, and for Maria and Tadek, a rabbit. With the rest of the money, I planned to build a statue and dedicate it to all the people who had helped me.

I had visions of returning to the village with bagfuls of candy and throwing it into the air along the village road while the villagers jumped up catching the sweets and smiled at me saying:

"That boy is a Jew, but now we see that Jews are good after all. He has convinced us of this!"

"Place your bets!" he called again.

I obeyed. In no time at all my face was covered with perspiration, my stomach hungry, and my pockets were completely empty.

"Place your bets, ladies and gentlemen! Move on young boy, give other people a chance," and the little man with the greasy hands shoved me away. I was so deeply ashamed, so terribly ashamed. I was hurt.

I began to walk and now saw the two acrobats performing. The blind man was now wiping his brow, and at the kwas stand people were drinking the brightly colored drinks. The woman behind the counter was filling up the glasses and collecting the money as if she had ten, and not two, hands.

How dry my throat was! And now too I could smell the aroma of the steamed wieners.

What will I tell Mr. Kozak? And what will I bring home?

To my right I saw a man with a dancing bear. Someone was laughing and I felt they were laughing at me. I continued to walk and when I stopped I realized I was at the entrance of our village, and to my greater horror, judging by the sun, it was just past noon.

How can I go home so early? I sat down and watched the frogs jump in the fields. From the distance came the sounds of the carnival and very clearly it seemed that I could hear the little man's voice call:

"Place your bets, ladies and gentlemen! A winner every time!"

At sunset I stood up and walked home. No one paid any attention to me along the way. When I entered the house I found everyone at the table, about to begin supper.

"Did you have a good time, Jan?" asked one of them.

"Yes," I answered, "thank you." They waited. I knew what they were waiting for: the candy . . . the chocolate . . . or some small souvenir.

"Will you have supper with us?" asked Mrs. Kozak.

But before I could answer, someone else said, "He's probably filled himself with all sorts of delicacies at the carnival, isn't that right, Janek?"

"Yes, that's right. I'm full. Good night," I said, and left.

There will come a day yet, I told myself as I lay down to sleep, when I will go away and return a rich man and build a statue in the middle of the village and then announce to all the villagers:

"My name is not Jan Kochanski, my name is Jankele Kuperblum . . . I'm a Jew, but as you can see I'm not at all bad as you think . . . I'm good . . . I'm good . . . I'm as good as any one of you . . ."

Wild geese flew in formation above us and the wind shook the leaves off the trees. We winterized the outside walls of the hut with straw, and chained the cows in the stable for the long winter.

Thousands of soldiers had passed through our village, thousands of unfamiliar faces, faces which I had never seen, and never saw again. Generals, officers, tall Russian soldiers and short ones, dark ones and blond ones, people with slanted eyes, men with serious faces, others with smiling faces, and still others with broken arms or legs, or bandaged heads. Some played the accordion, some the harmonica, others sang or danced and then moved on and vanished like the others, only to be replaced by new ones.

Soon soldiers wearing Polish uniforms appeared. Most of them were Poles who had survived the war in Russia, others were Russians of Polish descent. To bolster their numbers, the government called up all able-bodied young men.

Mrs. Kozak cried bitterly the day her two boys, Zbigniew and Antek, received their call. She packed them each a bundle of food and then Mr. Kozak and I drove them to Piaski. They got off the wagon, patted the horses, shook hands with Mr. Kozak, winked at me, and quietly entered a building. Mr. Kozak puffed on his pipe, yelled, "Vio!" to the horses, turned them around, and we returned home.

Weeks went by without a word from either of them. The snow came, the river froze, and Mrs. Kozak cried day and night. She hardly slept, and what little sleep she got was invaded with nightmares in which she saw her two sons killed in action.

Every day Mr. Kozak and I rode to Piaski and inquired for mail at the post office. Invariably we returned empty-handed, only to find Mrs. Kozak wrapped in a shawl waiting for us in the middle of the road at the entrance to the village.

She didn't have to ask, for she could read the answer on our faces. Slowly she would climb into the wagon and in silence we'd drive home. In silence she would enter the hut, remove her shawl, boots, and coat, and only then could a faint, painful, suppressed cry be heard coming from the corner of the room.

Then quite unexpectantly, a letter arrived from Zbigniew in which he complained bitterly about the hardships he was forced to endure. He was in training in some undisclosed forest and feared he would die of hunger or freeze to death as they had to sleep in trenches.

Mrs. Kozak cried again and immediately dispatched a large parcel filled with butter, pork fat, bread, tobacco, underwear, and other assorted items.

A few days later a similar letter arrived from Antek, and again Mrs. Kozak cried, and again she packed a large parcel and Mr. Kozak and I took it to the Piaski post office.

Soon more letters came and told of even worse hardships. Mrs. Kozak shed more tears and refused to eat, sleep, or talk. She constantly busied herself with sending parcels.

One day a letter came from Zbigniew in which he told that he had completed his training and that he was being sent to the front. He wrote of his terrible fear of dying and said he didn't think he would ever see any of us again. He said something touching about everyone and even wished me a good future in a better world.

We were terribly saddened by his letter and not only did Mrs. Kozak cry this time, but so did Anna and I, and even Mr. Kozak was wiping his eyes.

We waited with great anticipation for Zbigniew's next letter, but no letter came, and when many weeks had passed and still there was no word from him, Mrs. Kozak wrote to the army office in Lublin.

Several weeks later came a reply: Zbigniew was missing in action!

About the same time, we received a letter from Antek telling us that he was now in the front lines stationed on the Vistula River fighting for Warsaw. Again he described the hunger, the bitter cold, and his fear of death.

The Kozak household now became a place of mourning. There was little conversation, and when one had to speak it was done in whispers.

Mrs. Kozak cried and read and reread all the letters from her two sons. The succeeding letters from Antek describing the unbearable state in which he found himself upset Mrs. Kozak so much that she packed several large bundles of food and clothing, and against her husband's pleas and advice, she decided to visit Antek at the front.

"How do you know how I feel?" she asked Mr. Kozak. "You didn't carry him in your belly."

We drove her to Piaski and waited with her on the highway until a Russian truck offered her a lift. She climbed into the back of the open vehicle, and although she was shivering from the bitter frost, she somehow forced a smile, the first in many months. The truck pulled away, leaving a cloud of fumes behind it.

In the days that followed, Anna cooked and looked after the household chores. We rose early, spoke little, and went early to bed.

On a snow-covered day, Mrs. Kozak appeared, walking along the village road. She hardly greeted us when she entered the house, she simply stood there as if frozen, and then slowly removed her shawl, coat, and boots, then sat down near the hot, burning stove. We stared at her and she stared at us, but said nothing. She slept for three days and nights and only then, in halting sentences interspersed with tears, did she tell us what she had seen.

"Antek has all this time been sitting in trenches near the Vistula . . . bullets whiz by overhead . . . The Germans are holding Warsaw . . . The Vistula River is frozen . . . now and then they send a few soldiers across the river . . . they usually get shot, but they keep sending others . . . Several soldiers died from frostbite . . . Mines everywhere and many soldiers get killed that way . . . Along the road you see dead German soldiers nailed to trees, their arms stretched pointing towards Germany and a sign attached to their dead bodies, 'To Berlin' . . . Antek asked about everyone . . . He's afraid . . . he's so afraid that he may be asked to go along the frozen river . . . You can see bodies lying about on the river and wherever else you go."

Neighbors came to visit and listened and asked questions and debated. Some even said it was better during the German occupation, others said that all the officers and generals in the Polish army were either Russians or Jews and they were killing off the Polish soldiers on purpose, still others offered the opinion that the Jewish officers had all deserted and left the soldiers to be slaughtered by the enemy. This led to a discussion about Jews in general and more particularly about what cowards they are and how they never wanted to fight for Poland.

"We give our lives, while they do business," said one of them.

It's not true! I wanted to shout.

Isn't it? said my other voice within me. What about your Uncle Mendel?

And now I could almost see my Uncle Mendel, one of my father's brothers. His face radiant, he was smiling and lifting me above his head.

"Jankele, you've grown!" he was saying.

"Where is your uniform, Mendel?" someone was now asking.

"It's this way," my uncle was explaining. " 'What's the point to it all?' I think to myself. 'With me or without me the war is lost,' so I buy some civilian clothing from this peasant and I wrap it in a newspaper. The next outhouse I see, I walk in and come out dressed like you see me now. The uniform, the gun, everything, I throw it where it belongs."

That's an isolated case, I reasoned with myself.

Isolated? questions the other voice, mocking me. "Didn't your grandfather Shie Chuen, the shoemaker from Warsaw, have two toes missing from his left foot?

What about it?

What about it? The voice laughed within me. Come now, fool everyone else, but not yourself. Don't you remember it told how your grandfather cut off his two toes to avoid being taken into the army in the First World War?

I now blushed with shame, for it's all true . . . all true, and this cowardice is the fear I also fear within me.

What is it that makes me so afraid? Why couldn't I kill the kittens? Why do I fear bombs, guns, and grenades? How is it that my Uncle Mendel deserted the army while Zbigniew gave his life fighting and Antek too may never return alive?

Whatever it was within me that made me like my uncle and grandfather, I had to discover and kill and then become as brave and as fearless as Zbigniew and Antek.

One day in late winter, while feeding hay to the cows, I felt the presence of some other person in the stable. I looked in all directions but couldn't see anyone.

My imagination, I consoled myself. But suddenly I saw a bearded face peering out from the pigsty. I screamed. The face looked unfamiliar and more frightened than my own; the two small eyes shifted from side to side. I screamed again. The stranger started to approach me. I backed away.

"Janek, why are you screaming?" I backed away and now found myself pressed against a wall. The stranger came nearer. "Janek, don't you recognize me?" the voice was familiar and when he was almost upon me I said: "Zbigniew!"

And then I was really frightened. Is this a ghost I see? "You're alive, Zbigniew?" I asked with chattering teeth.

"I think I'm alive," he said. "Go tell my mother I'm here."

"All right," and I began to move towards the door.

"Janek!" he called after me. I turned. "You'll keep it a secret won't you, Janek . . . my being here I mean . . . ?" He looked so aged, so much wiser somehow, and in his eyes I saw a fear which many times before had been in my own.

Weeks later on her return from one of her trips to the front, Mrs. Kozak was unusually pleased, and unlike the other times, she now smiled again and talked and even laughed. She went about her business as if the war were over and as if she were never going to take another trip to the front again. I found her sudden change of behavior extremely puzzling, but didn't give it very much thought.

That same week when I entered the barn one day, a pair of large, cold hands covered my eyes and a voice asked, "Guess who?"

"Let me go, Zbigniew," I yelled.

"Guess again," said the voice.

The hands parted now. I turned and found a Polish soldier in front of me. His head was completely shaven, but I nevertheless recognized him.

"Antek!" I yelled.

"Look how you've grown."

"Hasn't he though," added Zbigniew.

"Go, Janek, and tell my mother that I've arrived and ask her to bring me some of my own clothes." I started to go. "And, Janek, you know how to keep a secret don't you?"

I smiled and shook my head. What does he know of secrets? I asked myself.

The two brothers remained hidden in the barn and only came outside at night to smoke a cigarette or walk around the courtyard. I brought them their food, ran messages for them, and spent my free time asking about the war and their part in it.

In this manner the days and the weeks went by and when the snow had melted and bluebirds appeared again, Zbigniew and Antek left their hiding place and Mrs. Kozak announced to the neighbors that her two boys had arrived the previous night: they had been released from service.

From then on, the neighbors would fill the Kozak hut almost nightly and bombard the two brothers with questions about the front. Zbigniew and Antek answered them all and sometimes even told in great detail of certain actions against the enemy in which they had taken part. The villagers listened with great interest and showered their two heroes with words of admiration.

"As long as we have soldiers like you," said one of them, "Poland will never be suppressed."

The evening would always end with either a joke or a song about a Jewish soldier in the army, or better still, a statement by Zbigniew or Antek about how those Jewish officers had deserted the Polish army and left the simple Polish soldiers to die at the hands of the enemy.

Although I had not seen a German soldier for many months, and even though I saw many signs of the enemy's defeat, secretly I still felt that my liberation might prove to be short-lived. I never divulged my fears to anyone else, but in the dead of night I would lie awake and argue with myself.

Perhaps these soldiers aren't Russians at all!

Come now, you idiot, said my other voice.

It's possible, they could be Germans in disguise.

Why would they go to all that trouble?

To lure me out of hiding, that's why, I replied.

At other times I imagined that perhaps I was in a deep sleep and that everything around me was simply a dream. I will wake up and find the Germans still stationed in the courtyard.

Desperately I wanted to feel free and unafraid. I longed to tell someone, anyone, especially Mr. Kozak, my secret. I made plans. I even practiced for the occasion.

"Mr. Kozak, I'm a Jew!" And yet, day after day I kept delaying this moment, for not only was I afraid of the Germans' return, but also I feared the villagers themselves.

Almost daily I heard stories about Jews who had come out of hiding and were murdered. Sometimes along a deserted farm road, other times on their return to their former houses, and worse still, in broad daylight in the Piaski market. These killings were credited to the underground organization known as A.K. (Home Army).

The villagers themselves were hardly shocked by these atrocities. On the contrary. "The nerve of these Jews," I heard one say. "They come out of hiding and right away they want their houses back."

"They inform on anyone who did them the slightest injustice."

"They're all communists . . . Hitler was right."

I listened and pretended not to hear, but within me my fears grew. Several times the Russian police arrived in the village and arrested several members of the A.K. Again I heard the familiar venom against the Jews:

"Some Jew turned him in."

Perhaps they mean me, I thought. I am the only Jew here who knows the members of the A.K. in our village. Did I inform on them? Perhaps I did and don't even know it.

Ever since my arrival at the Kozaks', I had always attended church on Sundays. I understood little of what went on, but I mimicked others. When others kneeled, I knelt; when others stood, I stood; when the lady next to me turned a page in her prayer book, so did I; and when someone in front of me crossed himself, I followed his example.

Now that I was liberated I wanted to stop this act of mine, but for some reason I didn't consider it an act anymore. I found myself going to church instinctively. My daily prayers were no longer simply to fool, for I was saying them with conviction and sincerity.

These discoveries upset me, for I now realized how far removed I was from the boy Jankele Kuperblum. It was as if there were two of me: one, Jankele Kuperblum; the other, Janek Kochanski. Janek Kochanski I could see well, but Jankele Kuperblum stood on the horizon, almost a blur in front of my eyes.

A terrible guilt beset me and a voice constantly urged me to return.

Shame, Jankele! Shame! You're free to leave and yet you make no attempt to return to the fold. You're free! Don't you realize what I'm saying to you? You have survived . . . the game is over. Why are you lying there without a smile on your face even? Jankele, the war is over. The Germans have left . . . the Russians are here. They've been here for months. Any day now the whole war will be over. Jankele, don't you understand, the Germans have lost! You can come out now and return home.

Indeed I had survived, I had survived months ago and yet I had not recognized the happy moment. I wanted to shout, to dance, to laugh, to jump into the river, to swim, to run, to leap into the air and fly over the rooftops of the village huts. I wanted to do all those things. I felt I should do them, but in reality I couldn't even force a smile.

I have survived, I thought, but who has survived with me? Where are the others?

And now for the first time in many months I again remembered that I once had a mother named Edzia, a brother named Josel, and uncles named Shepsel and Moishe . . . Moishe, where could Moishe be?

I thought of my father and wondered if he was alive, or perhaps buried somewhere in a grave which I would never see.

My thoughts led me into a deep melancholy from which I could not free myself, and I went deeper and deeper into it until I found no reason to go on living. I survived for nothing! I told myself.

How did you survive? said the other voice.

What do you mean, how?

What did you do? Whom did you betray?

No one. I swear it. It was by chance . . . luck!

Was it now? Come on . . . And the voice laughed. You left your mother unprotected.

How was I to know she'd be taken away?

But you didn't even go looking for her, did you?

Where was I to look?

The voice laughed again. And your Uncle Moishe, didn't you let him go to his death?

I tried to stop him, but he wouldn't listen to me.

The voice broke into shrills of laughter. Weren't you pleased that he decided to turn himself in?

No! No! Why should that have pleased me?

Your Uncle Moishe looked a little Jewish and his Polish wasn't all that good. Without him you had a much better chance.

I loved Moishe, I defended myself.

Of course you did, but you had to sacrifice him. Now, who else did you do in?

I didn't answer.

You're guilty, Jankele. You know you must be guilty. How else could you have survived?

I felt as if a pair of enormously massive hands, hands so large and strong that they could only belong to God, were tightening around my throat and choking me.

"Holy Mother!" someone cried out.

A knife flashed in front of my eyes and I fell, as if into space, and then I heard a thud. My eyes were half open and I saw blurred faces belonging to giants looking down at me. I heard voices too, but I didn't know what they were saying. Everything seemed very far, far away.

"Why did you do it?" asked Mr. Kozak the next day.

I opened my eyes and looked at him quizzically. He held my belt, but to my astonishment, it was cut in half. I sprang to my feet.

"Who cut my belt?" I demanded.

"I did, don't you remember?" I was silent and simply stared at him. "Didn't you know what you were doing, Jan?"

"Please tell me, what did I do, Mr. Kozak?"

"You attempted to hang yourself," he replied softly. "Why did you do that, Jan?" I turned my eyes from him.

Why did I do it? How can I explain everything to him? Perhaps I should tell him my secret.

Tell him, said one of the voices. The war is over, why not tell the man the truth?

Don't tell him, said the other voice. You never know, he could kill you, knife you, shoot you, betray you, and who knows what else?

The war is over, someone has to know who I really am. I'm tired of being somebody else.

I was going to tell him. I wanted to unfold everything, but when I turned to face him, he was gone and only the cut belt lay beside me.

For days I waited for an opportunity to cleanse myself. I wanted to see whether I could exist not as someone else, but as myself. The chance never seemed to come. Whenever we were together, someone else would join us, or if we were alone I would think he was in a bad mood, or I would get frightened at the last moment and decide to delay it again.

But finally when we were working together in the barn one day, I said, "Mr. Kozak!"

He puffed on his pipe and kept turning the wheel of the chaff-cutting machine. "Yes, boy," he murmured.

"Mr. Kozak, I've been wanting to tell you something for a long time." He didn't even look at me. "Mr. Kozak," I went on, "I want you to know that since I've come here I've been keeping a secret from you." I looked at him, but he went on nonchalantly as if he wasn't listening. We continued to cut, and then brought the machine to a halt and refilled it with more straw. He gripped the handle of the wheel, about to start turning it again; then he threw me a glance and said:

"What were you saying boy?" and waited.

"Mr. Kozak," I blurted out with a trembling voice. "Mr. Kozak, I want you to know that I'm a Jew!"

His eyes turned from me and he began to turn the wheel again. I did the same, and when we had finished I expected him to question me or be angry or be happy, but to my dismay, he was silent. His silence puzzled me and then later worried me. Perhaps he intends to harm me!

During the days that followed, none of the members of the family or the villagers acted differently towards me, and since none of them asked about my well-kept secret, I deduced that Mr. Kozak for some reason had decided not to reveal it to anyone else.

Perhaps he didn't hear you well, said one of my inner voices, or maybe he heard you but thought you were joking with him, and that's why he's remained silent!

I felt unsatisfied and I waited for another opportunity to bring up the subject. In the meantime fears raged within me. He's silent because he plans to kill you.

No, he's silent because he's wise and . . .

Outside the Kozak hut, neighbors congregated in the early evening and talked. I sat amongst them hardly listening, but wondering how it was that day turned into night, and night turned into day.

My mind wandered now to other questions for which I had no answers, but suddenly I became aware of someone's presence and when I turned my head I saw Eryk approaching us.

He swayed from side to side, sometimes almost falling, and then catching his balance. His right hand was in his pocket and in his left hand was an almost empty bottle from which he was taking long gulps along the way.

"Look at him," said someone, "getting drunk, poor devil. They arrested his brother Bronek today."

"They should arrest all of them," said another. And he added, "All they ever did for Poland was rob the poor."

"Come now," said someone else. "They killed quite a few Germans."

I could see the same group of people sitting in the same place, at the same time of day, only it was still during the German occupation, and along the village road a wagon pulled by two beautiful horses would appear. We all looked up and listened to the approaching sound of voices singing a patriotic Polish song.

"It's the A.K.," someone whispered with admiration, and by this time the horses and wagon were directly in front of us.

In the wagon, dressed in half-Polish, half-German uniforms, and holding revolvers or rifles, I saw familiar figures. Eryk was there, his brother Bronek, and others, and the one I recognized immediately was their leader, Kasztan. He was a short, bow-legged man, but the Polish officer's hat which he wore made him appear much taller. He waved to me and I to him, and then the horses and wagon disappeared into the night and the song too faded into the distance.

The next day in a village stable, several strange horses would be tied to a post and Eryk, his brother Bronek, Kasztan, or one of the others would say to me, "Janek, be a good boy and get some feed for the poor animals."

In the summer I would simply help myself to some drying hay in a field, and in the winter I would do the same from some haystack.

"We can trust you," Eryk would say. "We know you wouldn't tell anyone."

I fed their horses and listened to their stories of how the horses had been taken by force from some poor farmer in a distant village who had been told it was all for the cause of Polish liberation. They drank and laughed and displayed the gold rings taken from frightened Jews whom they had killed. The horses would remain in the stable for several days and then they were sold. A few days later, new horses would appear and again I'd be summoned to feed them. Again I heard the laughter and watched them drink and listened to their heroic accounts of how they had frightened some poor farmer, of how they had killed some running Jew and robbed him of everything he had on him, including his underwear, and left him naked in a deserted field.

On some occasions they even told of killing a German soldier and taking his weapon from him, which they would display for me with great pride, and sometimes they would re-enact the whole scene of how the killing had been performed.

I was terrified of this group; I could imagine what they would do to me if they ever discovered my true identity. But because I feared them, I decided that my best protection was being close to them. Therefore, I listened, and laughed, and sometimes at their insistence, I even took a drink of vodka, and although it never happened, they even promised to take me along on one of their missions.

"When the war ends, Jan, you'll be decorated for this work," Eryk used to say at times. Momentarily I would forget who I was, who they were, and I would truly believe I was involved in a secret patriotic underground organization. I'd stand up, reach for one of their revolvers, and point it towards a target in the stable, imagining I was about to shoot a German. The target dissolved and instead I once again saw Eryk.

He was now upon us, his eyes glazed and white saliva dripping from the corner of his mouth. He stared directly at me and then hurled the empty bottle onto the roof of our hut.

"He's drunk," said one of the neighbors.

"Have you heard from your brother yet?" asked another one, trying to calm him.

Eryk didn't answer him, but continued to stare at me. A chilling fear overtook my being, and something within urged me to run. But I was paralyzed, unable to move.

"Jew!" Eryk finally shouted. "Dirty filthy Jew! You betrayed my brother, you betrayed the others, you are the one. Jew!" He pulled out a revolver from his pocket. As if moved by some power, I jumped and stormed into the hut, falling onto the floor in a corner of the room. Three successive shots followed, and the words, "Filthy informer Jew," and then a commotion.

They all know then. Mr. Kozak did hear me. The whole village must know by now.

"He's gone home," said Mr. Kozak when he entered several moments later. "He's drunk and doesn't know what he's doing or saying. Come out, Jan."

I didn't move and that night I begged them to allow me to sleep in the house. I slept little and when I did sleep my dreams were filled with shadowy figures who chased me from place to place. I now feared for my life, but at the same time I was relieved that they all knew who I really was.

Days later, a car pulled up in front of Eryk's house and two Russian soldiers were seen entering. Shortly after, they came out with Eryk, shoved him into the vehicle, and drove off.

Again there was talk in the village and this time the word spread that it was Kasztan, their leader, who had betrayed them all. He had been the first to be arrested and some villagers claimed they had seen him in Piaski riding around with the Russian Secret Police.

Then Kasztan arrived in the village wearing new leather

boots and sporting a German Luger under his belt. He stood at the gate of his father's hut and shot at little birds in the trees.

Two days after his arrival someone aimed at him and shot him through the head. His body lay like those of the birds, in the middle of the village road, his face twisted, his legs spread apart, and his eyes open, staring into the heavens.

"You have nothing to fear now," said Mr. Kozak.

"I've decided to leave, Mr. Kozak," I said, half trembling. "I think it would be better if I left."

Mr. Kozak looked at me and his eyes bulged with anger. "You will not leave!" he shouted. "You'll stay right here and work for me, do you hear?" I was surprised at his rage which I had never thought possible of him. "Do you realize I saved your life, boy? Do you realize that had we been discovered, all of us would have been killed and everything we own would have been burned to the ground? Do you realize what that means? You'll stay right here and work for us for the rest of your life."

"You can't keep me here," I retorted.

"I can and I will," he snapped back at me. And he added, "You owe me your life!"

Nonetheless, I made plans to leave the following day. But when I prepared to pack my clothes I couldn't find them. How could I leave without my clothes, my two pair of long underwear, two shirts, two pair of pants, and my coat?

I sat in the barn and meditated. Not only did I fear the whole village, but now, Mr. Kozak as well.

The next day I said, "Mr. Kozak, I've thought the whole matter over and decided to stay. The truth is that I have nowhere to go anyway, and if you want me, I'll stay with you for the rest of my life." Mr. Kozak smiled, said nothing, and that same day returned my clothes.

The rest of that week was uneventful and on Sunday all of us drove to church.

Another week went by and again it was Sunday. Although it was a warm day, I put on my two pair of underwear, two shirts, and two pair of pants. As usual, Mr. Kozak prepared the horses and everyone, dressed in their Sunday best, mounted the wagon ready for the journey to the Piaski church.

"Jan, we're waiting," called Mr. Kozak.

"Go without me," I shouted back from the barn. "I slept in, I'll go to late mass."

"Vio!" I heard the familiar order to the horses, and then their rhythmic trot, the screeching of the wheels, and then silence.

I looked about me in the barn and saw the place where I slept during the summer months; the tools which I had used were now hanging on the walls. I looked around the court-yard and touched the handle of the axe which was embedded in a large, dried-out tree stump. The chickens almost blocked my path with their familiar clucking as I made my way to the stable and looked fondly at the pigs, the cows, the now-empty horse stall, and knew that this was the last time I would ever stand there . . . the very last time.

Is anyone watching me?

I entered the house and found Anna dusting the shelves.

"I'm going to late mass," I said. She turned and smiled.

"Want something to eat before you go?"

"No, I'm not hungry," I answered, and moved towards the door.

"Take some cookies for the road," she said, and handed me several. I moved on. "Jan!" she called, "Aren't you going to say good-bye to me?"

She knows, I thought. She knows.

"Good-bye, Anna," I said.

"Good-bye, Jan," and for the first time she kissed me on my cheek.

"I'll see you later," I said.

Her smile was still on her face and she shook her head and said, "Good luck, Jan."

When I reached the village road I turned to look back. She was leaning in the doorway gently waving her arm. I waved back, then turned and walked on. I could feel her gaze behind me, but I forced myself not to look back again.

The village road was deserted and unusually quiet; every step I took seemed to create a loud noise and then echo throughout the length of the village. A dirty black dog standing at an open gate stared at me but did not bark. From behind a lace curtain I caught sight of an old woman's face, covered with creases, peering out at me.

When I approached the house where Kasztan had lived, I stopped to look at the place where he had been shot.

I looked around me but saw no one, and yet I felt I was being watched. At any moment I expected someone to point a gun from behind a window curtain or barn door and then a shot to ring out.

Turn back, said one voice.

Keep going, said the other. Don't be afraid.

Turn back or you'll be sorry, said the first. You won't get out of this village alive. They're waiting for you.

I was paralyzed, afraid to move, almost unable to move, and I would have turned back except that by now I was almost at the other end of the village. Step by step I moved on, at all times either whistling or faking a smile so as not to look frightened.

Eight more houses and I'll be out, I comforted myself . . . seven more houses . . . six more . . . I took several more steps, I looked to the left, I looked to the right . . . five more . . . four . . . three . . . two . . . I now feared the worst. Perhaps they're waiting for me in the last house! I glanced towards the house and saw the door open, and then a man came out with a rifle. The voice now laughed hysterically.

You should have listened to me. It's too late now.

"Nice day," said the man, addressing me.

"Yes it is," I answered, and looked again and saw a cane in his hand instead of a rifle.

The road led downhill. In front of me stood the town of Piaski and behind me, the village.

I'm safe, I've made it!

Not yet, cautioned my other voice. You might still get it in the back.

I'm safe, I'm safe . . . I'm safe, I convinced myself, and turned and saw the village behind me, perched on the hill.

The town of Piaski was also deserted; there was hardly a soul to be seen. The silence of the town was broken by chanting coming from the church. Quickly I moved on, my eyes staring at my feet as they trotted along the cobbled road.

Suddenly the singing stopped; I stopped. I looked up. The huge, gleaming church loomed before me and on the road in front of it stood the wagon with the two horses, and sitting erect in the wagon observing me was Mr. Kozak.

I was stunned, trapped, ashamed, afraid, but I did not move. I stared at him and he stared at me.

Will he run after me? I wondered. Perhaps he has a gun! I'll have to find out. I took a step backwards. Mr. Kozak remained stationary. I took another step, then another, and another, and he remained sitting as if frozen to his seat and simply stared at me, as if accusing me of ingratitude with his silence.

Eventually I turned and walked towards the highway. There I stopped to look back. Mr. Kozak hadn't moved but kept staring.

You're a dirty filthy Jew, accused one of my voices. The poor man saves your life, and the first opportunity you have, you run out on him. It's typical of you Jews.

I'm grateful to him; I wish I could tell him how much he has taught me and how truly I love him, I defended myself.

Don't bother, Jew boy, said the voice, and then in a mocking tone added, Once a Jew, always a Jew!

"Jump on," a voice called out. I looked up and saw a wagon with three men and a red-headed woman. "Where to?" asked the driver. I jumped on but didn't answer.

The wheels began to turn, the horses started to trot, and then to gallop. The town of Piaski, the church, and Mr. Kozak became a speck on the horizon, and then not even that.

There was talk in the wagon and there was laughter, but I hardly listened. Instead, I watched the cobbled road and looked at the trees and the houses and the fields, and eventually they dissolved into one another until sometimes the houses seemed to be on top of the trees and the earth turned and we, it seemed, were flying above everything, pulled by galloping horses.

Now and then an army truck full of soldiers would pass by and sometimes the uniformed men would shout greetings to us; at other times they just stared into space like dead bodies.

Along the side of the road a sign announced the name of a town or village, and every so often there would be a bent figure carrying firewood from the forest.

The road turned and twisted, uphill and then downhill, and by early afternoon we were in territory which seemed very familiar to me. Every house, every tree, every bend of the road brought back memories, and then my attention was drawn to a site where a farmhouse had once stood and now lay burnt to the ground, except the chimney which still stood erect like a lonely monument.

"A bomb," said the red-headed woman, as if to herself.

"No," replied the driver, "the underground did it." He took a deep breath and paused as one does to arouse curiosity in others. From the corners of his eyes he scanned our faces; then as one who knows more than he finds it wise to tell, he simply said, "He was an informer." Turning his head he spat onto the side of the road, then wiped his mouth on his sleeve. "They shot him in the dead of night while he was asleep, his wife too; then with a single match the whole village lit up for hours."

"I think I heard about this incident," said one of the passengers. "Wasn't his name Bogusz?"

"That's the one, the very one," answered the driver, and again he spat.

That's why everything looks so familiar to me, I realized now. I've been here before, of course! I now recalled how this very Mr. Bogusz had examined my penis.

"Do you by chance pass Siedliszcze?" I asked the driver.

"Is that where you're going, boy?"

"Yes," I replied. "I'd be grateful if you let me off there." He nodded his head and remained silent until about an hour later when he brought the horses to a sudden stop, turned, and stared at me.

"What are you waiting for?" he finally asked. "I thought you wanted to get off at Siedliszcze."

"Is this it?" I asked in surprise, as we were on a deserted road.

"You walk down that road for about a kilometer."

I jumped off the wagon, thanked the driver, bid them all a good day and proceeded down a muddy road leading to the town.

Soon the church tower became visible and then I heard the ringing bell. The road was familiar and yet so different and strange, as if I knew it and yet didn't. I entered the town itself and here too everything seemed strange. I had the feeling I had been there before, but not in real life, only in a dream. Except for an occasional Russian soldier or a lonely farmer driving through the town square, the town was deserted and desolate. Again I feared being shot.

Someone may recognize me, I thought, and walked slowly, unassumingly. I wanted to stop and talk to someone, but thought that my questions could betray me.

A street, another street, one turn, then another, and now to my left was the place where we had lived. I wanted to stop and go in, examine, look around, inquire, but I feared even to look in that direction.

I must look, I must, I kept saying to myself. Perhaps my mother is there; perhaps everyone is there; perhaps they've all returned and are waiting for me.

I didn't stop to look; I did not really look, but only shifted my eyes to catch a glance. Instead of the house, I saw flat ground and a few well-tended trees.

"Dear God!" I whispered. "Dear God!"

I wanted to stop and take a good look but I didn't, for my fear would not allow me to. I just walked on as if that flat ground and the young, growing trees were of no concern to me.

I walked and walked until the town was behind and wet

fields lay before me. I walked but didn't know where I was going or what I was looking for, and yet I took certain turns and jumped across brooks. As the sun was setting, I stood at the entrance of a courtyard and looked at a young cherry tree which I remembered planting once.

I was touching its fragile young branches, and I turned when I heard a voice.

"What are you doing there?" Mrs. Golombek stood at the barn door holding a bucket of milk, which she now dropped. She made the sign of the cross and exclaimed, "Oh, Holy Mother, it's Franek. It's our Franek!" She ran towards me, embraced me with all her might, and when she released me I fell like a football into Mr. Golombek's arms, and then into Ina's.

At supper they showered me with questions and kept looking at me and touching me as if perchance I were only a mirage and would soon disappear.

Their joy in seeing me again was so overwhelming that it didn't entirely surprise me when the next morning Mr. Golombek took me aside and, after clearing his throat several times, began, "Franek, chances are that your family is dead and as you know we already think of you as our own son, we always did. We would like you to stay with us, and if you agree, you can take on our name and when the time comes you and Ina would share this farm and everything on it."

He now held me by my shoulders and tried to look into my eyes, but I had turned in embarrassment and cast my eyes downwards. "You don't have to decide now, Franek, think about it," and he left me.

How wonderful it is to be wanted, to have a home! I thought. I'll accept. I'll gladly accept. Franek Golombek . . . sounds good!

My eyes turned and I looked across the wet fields in the direction of Kulik.

Moishe! My God, Moishe may be alive and if he has survived he'll be looking for me at Mrs. Paizak's.

I rushed into the house. "I have to go, I have to leave right away." Mr. Golombek turned white. "I have to look for my uncle," I said. There was a deathly silence during which time Mr. Golombek stared at his wife, and she in turn at him.

Finally he said, "If you don't find him, Franek, will you promise us you'll return?"

"I promise," I said without hesitation. "If he isn't there I'll be back tomorrow."

Once again the Golombek family stood at the gate crying and waving good-bye to me.

I waved back and then turned and ran along the path leading to the road, along the road, and then I cut across the flooded fields. My feet were soaked but I wasn't even aware of it. My heart pounded from exhaustion and my legs could hardly carry me much further, but I resolved not to rest, for I felt certain that at the end of my journey my Uncle Moishe was waiting for me, perhaps even my mother . . . perhaps . . . perhaps . . .

FIVE

☐ I stood on the road leading towards the Paizak farm. There stood the house, the familiar barn, the cherry trees behind it, and the sound of a rooster could be heard. I stopped and observed and wondered if they'd recognize me. What will they say? A smile crossed my face, a smile of victory. I have made it! Mrs. Paizak didn't think I had a chance and here I am, about to prove to her that I have outwitted the whole German army.

Young weeping willow trees grew on both sides of the road and now looked as if they stood on guard for the returning hero marching between them. A dog began to bark as I entered the courtyard, and soon a tall, lean stranger with a wrinkled face and a creased hat came out of the barn. He looked at me and I at him, and then with fear in my voice I asked:

"What has happened to the Paizaks?"

He stuck his head into the barn and shouted, "Someone for you, dear." A woman with gray hair appeared from behind the barn door and studied me intently, but it was soon obvious she was straining her eyes, so I approached her closer. Mrs. Paizak looked aged and troubled.

"You looking for me?" she asked when I stood quite near her.

"Don't you recognize me, Mrs. Paizak?" I asked in a choking voice. She came closer and studied me, and then without warning she screamed and covered her face with the palms of her hands.

"I can't believe it, you're alive!" The stranger looked perplexed and Mrs. Paizak kept uncovering and covering her face, and finally she embraced and kissed me. When she finally freed me, she pulled out a long handkerchief and began to wipe away the tears flowing from her eyes.

"We heard you had been shot by the Germans," she was now saying. "Is it really you, Kubush?" And once more she kissed me and then whispered, "My little boy."

"Where is Genia?" I asked.

"She'll be home soon. She went to visit her father's grave."

"And Stashek?"

"In the back field. Go see him, go."

I ran behind the house and saw Stashek in a garden patch at the bottom of the hill. I remembered how mean and ter-

167

rible he had been to me, but now I wanted to forgive him. I wanted to show him I didn't carry grudges.

"Stashek!" I called, and ran towards him. "Stashek!"

He glanced at me and immediately continued with his work. "What are you doing here?"

"Aren't you happy to see me?" I asked, still trying to befriend him, but he didn't answer.

I returned to the courtyard, and soon after, Genia, dressed in a beautiful coat, high leather boots, and an elegant hat, entered accompanied by a young man. She held tightly to his arm. She was laughing, but suddenly she noticed me. Her face shone like the sun and her smile almost melted my whole being. With outstretched arms she rushed to me, and I to her, and we embraced.

Later I learned that the stranger was Mrs. Paizak's new husband. The young man with Genia was her fiancé, and they were to be married shortly.

Several days later when we were alone, Genia confided that although he was good to her and quite a decent and hard-working man, she did not love him.

"Then why are you marrying him?" I asked.

She smiled and said, "Because I got tired of waiting for you, Kubush," and now we both laughed. "Remember," she said softly, almost whispering, "how we used to tickle each other?" I blushed and didn't answer. She winked and said, "I've thought about you very often, and if only you were a little older . . ." Again I blushed. "I have to marry him now, Kubush."

"But why?" I asked.

"It's my mother's idea. She thinks I'll be saved from the deportations that way."

"What deportations?" I asked.

"Didn't mother tell you? All Ukrainians are being deported from Poland and everyone thinks we will be shipped to Siberia."

"But why, Genia?"

"Because there were a lot of Ukrainians who collaborated with the Germans. My mother thinks that if I marry him, and he's Polish, that I and the farm will be saved. She wants Stashek to find himself a Polish girl too, but he won't listen."

"What about your mother?" I asked with concern.

"She'll be deported, her husband is Ukrainian too."

"When will this take place?"

"That we don't know," she replied. Then she added, "It seems, Kubush, that Jews and Ukrainians have the same bad luck." And now she smiled again and without warning began to tickle me.

Since there was no sign of Moishe, I planned to return to the Golombeks, but both Genia and Mrs. Paizak urged me to stay awhile.

"He may still show up, Kubush. Wait a few days longer."

I waited and hoped for many weeks. My eyes peered through the window, hoping that every approaching figure, every speck on the horizon would, upon coming closer, turn out to be my Uncle Moishe, but I was not so lucky.

One bright, sunny day I journeyed to my grandfather's grave. I didn't know exactly what I would do there, but I felt I should at least look at his grave, perhaps stand there or sit beside it for a short time, or even talk to him, and perhaps ask for advice.

From the distance I recognized the huge dried-out tree, but when I came closer I could not find the grave, nor the stone which used to mark it. Instead, all I saw was an elderly farmer planting tomatoes.

I wanted to question him but I was apprehensive about showing interest in a Jewish grave. I paced back and forth along the road, looking this way and that.

Perhaps I have the wrong place, or the wrong road, I eventually thought.

Let him harm me if he wants to, I said to myself firmly, but I must know!

I approached the elderly farmer. "Excuse me for disturbing your work, sir, but perhaps you can tell me if there was ever a grave around here?"

The farmer stood up from his kneeling position and approached me.

"That Jewish grave used to be right here," and he pointed to a spot where several tomato plants were growing. "Why are you asking?" and he looked at me with suspicion.

"Just wanted to know what happened to that dirty Jew's grave," I said, and casually walked away. When I had gone a short distance I turned to look back, and saw the farmer still standing and watching me. Suddenly I broke into a run.

I fell on the roadside from exhaustion and closed my eyes. Perhaps I am lying on someone's grave now, I thought. Perhaps all the fields are really cemeteries.

I looked around and it seemed for a moment that not only the surrounding fields, but in fact the whole world was one large cemetery with no markings and no survivors to mourn for the dead.

Summer came and there was still no sign of Moishe. I lost all hope and decided to return to the Golombeks.

On the day of my departure, Genia cried and Mrs. Paizak reminded me that she had a few of my mother's belongings which I was welcome to have.

I refused them and set out on my way, but instead of crossing the fields towards the Golombeks, I headed towards the river, crossed it, and by sunset stood once more at the entrance to the smithy in the village of Malinowka.

Upon seeing me, Mr. Sidlo the blacksmith nodded and continued with his work as if I had never been away from the village.

"Aren't you surprised to see me?" I asked him. He hammered at a piece of red-hot steel and turned and shaped it, hitting it with all his power.

"I was rather hoping you'd show up," he finally said and threw me a friendly smile. Again he hit the piece of steel, then stopped, threw the hammer down, turned to me, and said, "I'm married now and wait until you see the farm I have." He slapped me on the back. "Want to work for me?" He waited for an immediate answer.

"I just came to look around and see how everybody is faring."

"I thought perhaps you came back to get a few more beatings from that bitch Wajda!" A smile appeared at the corner of his mouth, and then we both broke out laughing. "Come, you look hungry."

He closed the shop, locking it with a huge key; then getting onto his bicycle, he pointed for me to jump onto the back. As we drove through the village, Mr. Sidlo waved to people who passed by, and they looked on with envy at his treasured bicycle.

At a farmyard fenced in by beautiful shrubs, he turned in, and now I saw a large cherry orchard, and through it, an elegant white house, a stable, and a barn. The courtyard was large and extremely clean. Mr. Sidlo watched me with satisfaction as I scanned the surroundings. He led me into the house.

He introduced me to his wife, "This is Zigmund, he's going to work for us." And he playfully patted her pregnant belly. "We'll treat you well, not like those pigs the Wajdas. We'll buy you some clothes, pay you a monthly salary, and you'll sleep in the house, right here, not in the stable like an animal."

"I can't accept," I said apologetically, and then went on to explain that I had to return to the Golombeks.

Mr. Sidlo was troubled. "That's a great shame, Zigmund, you can't imagine how much you would mean to us."

"I'm sorry," I said, "but I've already promised."

"I understand," said the blacksmith. "It's a pity, I could have really used your help, especially now with the baby coming." He suddenly looked so pathetic that I felt sorry for him. "If you could at least stay for two or three months, you'd be saving my life." His hand descended on my shoulders. "Well, can you give me at least a couple of months? By that time the baby will be here."

I now felt a warmth, an attachment to him. It was he who had welcomed me to Malinowka when I had come looking for shelter. How could I refuse him?

"I'll stay for several months," I said.

What about the Golombeks? a voice gnawed within me. Is that how you repay kindness? Is that how you keep your word?

I'll write them, I'll explain everything, defended the other voice.

When will you write?

Tomorrow, answered the other, and I went to bed.

The cot was comfortable but sleep would not come. I had visions of the Golombeks standing at the gate waiting for me to return, looking towards the horizon, hoping and waiting and crying and never knowing where I was or what had happened to me.

Mr. Golombek's face would now dissolve to become another face that looked very much like my father's. Moishe suddenly made an appearance, his arms outstretched like a bird's; he was flying above me and shouting, "Jankele, where are you?" And the echo from his voice almost deafened me.

Far away on the horizon, against a bright, setting sun, stood a wagon with two horses and on the wagon sat Mr. Kozak in the same position as when I had last seen him.

"Jankele, where are you?" my Uncle Moishe's voice could still be heard.

The cows grazed in a field adjoining the village road. The grass was green, thick, and tall. Barefoot I'd sit in this rich pasture, keep watch on my flock, follow the flight of a multi-colored butterfly, and I'd sing a Russian or Polish song.

Passers-by would very often stop to listen, and on days when I didn't sing they would shout to me, "Sing something!"

"It's a gift from God," some told me, and others predicted that I'd without a doubt become a singer of great renown.

Weeks had gone by and I had not communicated with the Golombeks, and now I felt it was almost too late.

How could I explain this long silence? I therefore resolved to stay on beyond the two months. Perhaps forever, I mused.

You'll have to tell them your secret, my voice kept urging me.

I'll tell them, I'll tell them.

I waited for an opportunity and it almost came one evening at supper, but somehow Mr. and Mrs. Sidlo became involved in a bitter quarrel which led Mr. Sidlo to hit his pregnant wife, and storm out and lock himself in the stable.

He emerged several hours later with a childish smile on his face and so drunk that he tried to enter the house through a window. In his right hand he held a small revolver, which he tried without success to point at his wife's protruding belly.

"I'll shoot it out of you!" he shouted at her.

Perhaps it's just as good I didn't tell him, I now thought. Who knows what he might do to me if he knew.

For several days there was deathly silence in the household, but just as suddenly as it had begun, the quarrel ended, and again there was peace.

"Mr. Sidlo," I began, "what would you say if I told you that my real name isn't Zigmund?"

"What is your real name then?" he asked without interrupting his work.

"My real name is Jankele Kuperblum."

The blacksmith stopped hoeing the potato patch, looked up at me, and broke out laughing. "What kind of a name is that?"

"I'm sorry for having lied to you all these years." His expression now changed and he looked quite seriously at me. "I'm a Jew!" I added and felt tremendously relieved.

"Is that a fact? That's good, very good," and he studied me intently. "Do you know Goldman?"

I shook my head. "Who's Goldman?"

"He's a Jew. Several months ago he came out of hiding and had himself and his daughter baptized, and changed his name, but everyone still calls him Goldman. Before the war he owned the place the Wajdas live in, now he has a farm about as nice as this one, though not as much land."

I must find out what Goldman looks like, I thought. That very same evening I made my way to his farm, and from behind an apple tree I peeked into his house.

At the table sat a girl combing and braiding her long black hair, and beside her sat an elderly man drinking a glass of milk. I expected him to resemble my grandfather the baker, with a beard and hat, but instead, he looked very much like any other farmer in the village of Malinowka.

How I envied them! How much I would like to have been a part of them, but I didn't even dare enter their house. What would I say to them? And so I watched their every move until the naphtha lamp was blown out and they went to sleep for the night. Slowly I walked home, and as I had done in Pulawy as a child, now too I played a game with the moon. I ran and the moon followed me, I suddenly stopped and so did the moon.

For several nights in succession I observed the Goldsmans and even once saw them during the day walking along the road, but I only looked and never made contact with them.

At night I lay awake and thought of them walking peacefully along the village road, as equals, without fear, without having to lie, free to do as they wished. And now my thoughts led me to my survival and again an accusing voice within me seemed to thunder:

How is it that you, and only you, survived?

I don't know, I answered.

Think hard, advised the voice again. Think of the promises you made.

I thought, and now a huge cross seemed to appear before my eyes and on it the figure of Jesus Christ. He came off the cross slowly, very slowly, walked towards me, and then he seemed to melt into thin air.

Jesus Christ saved me! I closed my eyes. I'll remain here forever, but first I have to get everything settled properly.

The very next day, in a halting voice I asked Mr. Sidlo to make arrangements for my baptism. I assumed that my decision would please him, but to my surprise, he showed no sign of great jubilation.

"I'll speak to the priest about it," he answered coldly.

When Sunday finally came, Mr. Sidlo and his pregnant wife dressed in their very best, hitched the horse to the wagon, and as on every other Sabbath, departed for church, which was not far from the town of Chelm.

Impatiently I waited for their return and began to imagine how everything would soon change for me.

Late in the afternoon I heard the sound of the wagon in the courtyard, and quickly ran out and waited for the good news. To my dismay, Mr. Sidlo smiled, unhitched the horse, but said nothing about my baptism.

"What did the priest say?" I finally asked.

Mr. Sidlo struck his forehead with the palm of his right hand and said, "I forgot, I completely forgot." He now put an arm around my shoulder and tried to console me. "Next Sunday for sure."

I was terribly disappointed, but tried to hide it. Instead, I began to study the catechism and to memorize all the prayers.

The following Sunday seemed like a lifetime away, but in time it came, and again the Sidlos went to church, and again came back. This time it seemed the priest had been too pre-occupied.

In the weeks that followed, he gave me other excuses and once even questioned the wisdom of my becoming a Christian. I argued, persisted, and eventually broke out crying one Sunday evening, and begged him on bended knees.

"I'll tell you what, Zigmund," he said. "Let's wait until the baby comes, and then we'll have a double ceremony." And he added, "I promise."

I counted the days and prayed nightly for the baby's birth. Mrs. Sidlo's stomach seemed enormous now, and yet there was still no baby. It was only when I had given up all hope and had stopped praying for its delivery that I was awakened one dark night by a shrill cry coming from the next room.

"It's a boy, a boy!" shouted Mr. Sidlo. "Are you ready, Zigmund? This Sunday I'll make the arrangements," and he gulped down a large glass of homemade vodka.

I counted the days, the nights, the hours. I waited impatiently, and even during my sleep, the words of the catechism seemed to come off the printed pages and dance in my head.

At long last, the appointed day finally came. I rose early and watched a warm sun appear. I looked at the tranquil sky and listened to the birds chirping in the trees. I prepared the wagon, harnessed the horse, and packed some feed for his lunch.

There was jubilation in the courtyard. Neighboring children stood at the gate and gaped as Mrs. Sidlo came out of the house carrying the baby. Someone now decorated the horse with beautiful flowers, and soon the guests arrived and waited in the assembled wagons.

"Vio!" someone yelled, and the first wagon pulled out for the long drive.

I shut the barn door and quickly jumped onto the end of our wagon.

Mr. Sidlo turned and stared at me. "Where do you think you're going?"

I looked at him in disbelief. "You promised," and I held back the tears.

"Not today, Zigmund," he shot back sharply.

"But you promised," I repeated.

"I don't remember, perhaps I did and perhaps I didn't. Someone has to stay behind. We can't leave this place unattended."

"Please!" I pleaded. "I want to get baptized."

"Let him come," said Mrs. Sidlo.

Her husband looked at her coldly. "You just hold onto the baby and let me handle this." She lowered her head. "Perhaps next Sunday. I'll speak to the priest."

I slid off the wagon and watched them pull out. Mrs. Sidlo waved to me. The assembled children ran after the wagon screaming and shouting and I sat down in the middle of the courtyard and cried.

Dressed in my Sunday best, with my shoes dangling over my shoulder, I left the village of Malinowka in the early dawn the next day. With a pounding heart, I headed across fields, across brooks, along dusty roads. Closer and closer to the church in the village near Chelm, to the priest, to be baptized, to be a Christian, to be free, to be good, to live.

The day was extremely hot and the journey was long. In the late afternoon the church came into view. It was a massive structure built of large gray stones and surrounded by a shrubbery fence.

Panting like a little dog, hungry, and thirsty, with sweat pouring down my entire body, I stood at the little wooden gate leading into the garden. Among the well-kept trees and rosebushes, I saw the bent figure of the priest.

I stood motionless, somewhat afraid of what was about to happen. The priest's back was turned to me, but then, as if he had sensed my being there, he turned without warning, straightened up, observed me for a moment, and slowly came towards me.

He studied me sympathetically, and without saying a word, extended his hand, which I gladly took, and in this manner he led me into the interior of the rectory.

In the dining room he pointed to a chair for me to sit down on; then he disappeared behind a curtain. I sat in silence and studied the objects on the walls. Soon he returned carrying a tray with bread, cabbage and meat, and a glass of milk.

"Please eat," and he sat down to watch me devour the food. Between spoonfuls I studied his kind, smiling face and now I recalled seeing him when I had lived with the Wajdas. He had come to bless their house, I remembered, and had given me money.

I wonder if he remembers me?

When I had finished eating, he cleared the table and then

once more sat down opposite me and very simply said, "I know why you're here."

How is it possible for him to know? I wondered. Do priests speak to God?

I looked at him closely and now wondered whether indeed he was a priest at all, or perhaps some divine being, like an angel or a messenger, or perhaps, perhaps Jesus Christ himself wishing to test my belief.

"How do you know why I'm here?" I asked.

Momentarily he closed his eyes, took my hands into his, and said, "There are certain things one senses, my child. You've come to be baptized." I nodded my head. "Why?" he asked.

"I want to be a Christian and believe in Jesus Christ."

"But why my child? You are Jewish, why not remain a Jew?"

"No . . . no!" I protested. "You must baptize me . . . Please!"

"Why?" he asked again, forcing me to look straight at him.

"Jesus Christ saved my life," I answered, "and now I must repay him for this."

Again he closed his eyes, and when he opened them he smiled. He reached for my face and stroked my cheek. "How young you are!" he exclaimed. "How old are you?"

"Thirteen," I answered.

"How much you must have suffered at so young an age! Don't feel obligated. You don't have to convert or repay anyone for your life."

"Please, please, Father, you must. You can't refuse me. Please listen to me. I know the whole catechism by heart. I used to go to church every Sunday and I want so much to be normal, like everyone else. Please, I beg you."

"No, my son, you're too young. You don't know what you're asking me to do. I cannot do it." I began to cry. He looked at me with sorrow in his eyes, and then said, "If you want to believe in God, you don't have to convert, for if there is a God, then there is only one God." He moved very close to me, and as if transmitting a secret he whispered, "But after what you and I have seen, I wonder if there is a God." He handed me a clean handkerchief, one like I hadn't seen in many years, and he motioned for me to wipe my tears. "I'll tell you what," he said. "I'll baptize you if your parents agree to it."

"I have no parents," I answered.

"I thought not," he replied. Then he added, "In that case, come back to me when you're twenty-one years of age," and he smiled broadly. "But, chances are that when you reach that age, you'll have changed your mind and will be most certainly far away from here. Perhaps in a distant country."

He gave me food for my return journey, blessed me, and sent me on my way back to Malinowka.

The road seemed very long and difficult; my heart was sad and heavy, and I felt terribly disappointed in him. Perhaps he's not a priest at all, but the devil in disguise! I thought. He can't prevent me from becoming a Catholic, I'll try another priest, I promised myself.

Night fell and I was still a distance away from home. The road was illuminated only by naphtha lamps burning in village huts, and out of the darkness, dogs could be heard barking as if they wanted to devour me. I looked up at the dark sky and wished I could don wings and fly away into the heavens and be lost among the stars.

It was very late when I finally arrived home; Mrs. Sidlo was still up breast-feeding the baby.

"We were worried about you," she said.

I undressed and went to sleep and dreamed that a priest baptized me, and at the same time, using a needle and thread, he sewed a piece of skin onto my penis. I was flying above the village and below me all the villagers were kneeling and praying to me. Their prayer suddenly turned into shouting, and with clenched fists they threatened me and told me to go away. The shouting became louder. I covered my ears. Then I awoke in a sweat. I cleared my eyes and shook my head, hoping to free myself of the dream, but the shouting would not stop. It was coming from somewhere in the village.

I opened the door, looked out, and saw an orange fire dancing in the air somewhere in the distance.

The next day the story spread very quickly that a group of drunks had broken the windows and doors to the Goldman house and had shouted, "Go to Palestine, you dirty Jews!" Goldman and his daughter had run into the fields like wild rabbits, and the drunks had burned their farm and reduced everything on it to ashes.

No one went looking for the Goldmans and they were never seen again.

Leave at once! urged the voice within me. But for some reason I wanted to stay. I wanted to prove to myself that I did not fear anyone, but fear I did.

Every passer-by seemed like a potential enemy, a surprise attacker, a killer.

Mr. Sidlo, too, I didn't fully trust, for he was now constantly shouting orders at me. Soon even that ceased, and instead he began to ignore me altogether. It was as if I was a ghost and couldn't be seen or didn't exist, except in my own imagination.

Mrs. Sidlo was kinder and spoke to me in whispers, but only when her husband was away at the smithy or in the fields.

One evening when I was left to look after the baby, I poured myself a glass of milk. Mr. Sidlo entered and angrily grabbed the jug and glass from my hands, and shouted at me, "Stop drinking up all the milk, there's a baby who needs some too."

Within me an anger raged, but I suppressed it and said nothing. I remained silent till the following Sunday when he asked me to run an errand for him.

"It's Sunday," I answered. "It's a rest day."

He looked stunned. Once more he repeated his request, and again I informed him what day it was and added that from now on I intended to be treated like a human being, with respect and certain rights and privileges.

"I'll ask you once more," said Mr. Sidlo.

"No!" I replied, and turning from him I went into the orchard, climbed into a tree, and began picking cherries and dropping them into my mouth.

"I'll ask you for the last time."

I looked down, and framed between two branches, stood Mr. Sidlo, his revolver pointed directly at me. A sadistic smile crossed his face. I jumped down and stood against the cherry tree. He came closer, his gun almost touching my chest.

"Now tell me again," he went on. "Tell me if you will run an errand for me."

"I would do it," I said, "but since you denied me a glass of milk . . ."

"You dirty Jew," he cut in. "When I give you an order, you run."

"I won't," I said firmly. "And I'm not a dirty Jew."

"You're a dirty, lice-infested son of a dirty bitch of a Jew. If you don't obey me I'll kill you, God is my witness that I'll kill you right here, right now!" A chill went through my body. "I'll shoot you, you filthy dung," he said, raging.

"Go on, shoot me," I answered him. "It doesn't matter to me anyway. I have no one and there's little reason left for me to live. Go on, kill me, pull the trigger and be done with it."

He took a few steps backwards, and closing one eye, began to aim the revolver at my head. "I'll count to ten; if you

don't change your mind by then I'll let you have it . . .
One . . ."

"I told you to shoot me," I said, holding my head up high.
"I have nothing to live for, but you have a wife and child. If
you shoot me now, be certain that the police will find out
about it and you'll be arrested and made to pay for it."

"Are you threatening me, Jew boy?"

"Shoot me, go on," I shouted.

He dropped the gun to his side and broke out laughing.
"I'll spare you this time, but you'd better leave while it's still
safe. If I see you here again, I swear by Jesus I'll shoot you
like one shoots a mad dog."

"I'll leave," I replied, "only if you pay me like you promised you would."

"Thank your God I've spared your life; now go and don't
let me see you in these parts again."

"I've worked for you and you owe me pay," I shouted, but
by this time he had turned and walked into the courtyard.

I leaned against the tree, embraced it, and now began to
sob. "Dear Mother," I cried, "Why was I chosen to remain?
Why didn't I die with you? Dear Mother, where am I to go
now? Where is there for me to turn to? Oh, Mommy, if only
you were alive! Without you, what good is my life?"

Soon I cried myself out. As if waking from a deep sleep, I
now heard the baby's cries coming from inside the house. I
looked around and realized that night had descended and
that the wind was chilling my scantily dressed body. I began
to shiver and tried to cover myself with my arms.

I'll ask for my clothing, I thought, and began to move towards the house, but soon stopped.

"Where shall I go then?" I whispered. And although I
knew there was no one to hear me, for some reason I expected an answer. Since none came, I began to walk, passing
the cherry trees which now in the dark looked like monstrous
creatures about to consume me.

I stood on the village road and looked back towards the
house. It was dark and even the baby's crying could not be
heard. I looked along one side of the road and then along
the other side: no one to be seen. My eyes scanned the field,
and there too, deathly silence except for the wind bending
the tall wheat.

My feet led me across the road and I lay down in the
wheat. The sky was very dark; I tried to see faces in it, but
failed. Then I concentrated on the wind, and the longer I
listened, the more I began to recognize the melodies it was
playing. Now the song was very clear, very clear . . . It

was my mother's song about the wagon driver. Again I looked up at the sky and now I could make out my mother's smiling face in it, singing as I remembered her singing, and beside her stood Kisel, strumming on his mandolin.

Vio, Vio, little horses,
Vio, Vio, my dear ones.

Now the driver of the song appeared as well, sitting on the wagon and pulled by six galloping horses. He hit them across their backs and lightning appeared in the skies, and then the driver and horses became smaller and smaller as they vanished into the great distance and disappeared behind the clouds. Again there was lightning, this time followed by thunder, and suddenly the singing came to a halt. Kisel vanished and my mother's face, too, dissolved into darkness, and from the heavens came rain.

Turning my face towards the ground, I pulled my shivering body together. Let it rain, I thought. Perhaps it will make me grow like the wheat.

Like a fox I peered through the wheat, watching the Sidlo house across the road. My clothes were drenched, but the sun was now making an appearance from behind the horizon, and casting warm rays of sunshine. The faint cries of the baby could be heard, several people passed along the road on the way to Chelm, a dog was barking, a door opened, a cow mooed, and now Mr. Sidlo appeared on his bicycle on the way to his daily work at the smithy. A smug smile was glued to his face and he peddled with an assurance and satisfaction which I could hardly bear.

I closed my left eye, and imagining that I had a rifle or a revolver, I now aimed at his head, and pretending to pull the trigger, I whispered, "Bang!" In my imagination I could see Mr. Sidlo fall onto the road, his face deep in the mud. When I opened my eye he was still on his bicycle, disappearing around the bend.

A moment later, my body bent like a rabbit, I ran towards the house, and now stood erect, facing a frightened Mrs. Sidlo.

"I want my clothing," I said with authority, like a partisan.

"Take whatever is yours," she answered in a trembling voice. "I'm sorry," she said, "I'm truly sorry for you, but what can I do? I too am afraid of him."

"I'm not afraid of him," I shot back. "He doesn't frighten me with that toy pistol of his."

"He isn't just fooling, Zigmund. Please take my advice and leave. Why don't you go back to your own people?"

"I'm not afraid of your husband, Mrs. Sidlo, and I won't leave this village until I get paid what's coming to me. You did promise to pay me."

"If I had money, I'd give it to you."

"Tell your husband to leave the money with you, I'll be back!"

"When?" she asked when I was already in the doorway.

"That I can't tell you, but I'll be back and money had better be here or I'll inform the authorities about everything."

She ran after me and began to cry. "Please, Zigmund, don't do anything foolish. I'll get the money for you."

"I'll be back," I said, and left. When I reached the road I realized that I had no destination, but I felt good. For the first time I did not fear, but others feared me. I felt strong, dangerous, unafraid.

For the moment I imagined I had two revolvers, one in each pocket, several grenades around my belt, and my other pockets were filled with ammunition. I fancied that the whole world feared me. With assurance, I began walking, taking firm, long steps like a soldier. At a familiar pond by the roadside I stopped to wash my body. The sun was now very warm and the air smelled good. I looked about me and it felt wonderful to be alive. Somehow it did not matter that I had nowhere to go. Why worry about tomorrow, I told myself.

I sat at the edge of the pond throwing little stones into the water and watching the continuous circles these pebbles created. Here and there a huge frog would stick its head out, as if wondering who I was.

"Catching fish?" asked an unfamiliar voice. When I turned, I saw a lean, barefoot boy much older than myself. He was so old in fact that he had hair growing on his face. He wore dirty white linen trousers and a torn shirt. His hair was very long and one of his eyes looked as if it had been damaged.

"Just resting," I answered.

"Good, I was afraid perhaps someone else had discovered my fishing place." I now noticed a basket made of twigs in his hands and my eyes rested on his right hand. "What's the matter? What are you staring at?"

"Nothing, really, I was only looking at your basket."

"That's all right, boy," he said gently. "I don't mind you

looking. Here, take a good look," and he shoved his right hand in front of my eyes. Two of his fingers were completely missing. I looked up at him and smiled. "My name is Bronek," he said, and extended the mutilated hand.

"Zigmund is my name," I said, and we shook hands.

"Want to know how I lost my fingers?"

"If you want to tell me," I answered nonchalantly, but secretly I was very interested.

"It was a mine, one of our own, an accident."

"Were you in the army?" I asked.

"No," he replied, "I was in the partisans in the Ukraine." My eyes opened wide. "Were you really?" I asked.

"Yes," he replied, "for two years."

"Did you ever shoot any of them?"

"As many as I could."

"How many?" I asked.

"Who knows? I never counted. I used to blow them up by the dozens. I was the mine expert," and he laughed.

"Didn't you use a gun?" I asked.

"That too," he replied, reaching into his pocket and withdrawing a large German Luger. "One like this one," he said, and threw it towards me. "Be careful, it's loaded," he added when he saw me picking it up.

That same afternoon my new friend taught me how to take apart, clean, and use his Luger. With this knowledge and having him as my friend, my confidence grew even more and I feared nobody, least of all Mr. Sidlo.

With the basket, we caught little fish, and in a nearby field we dug some new potatoes. Bronek led me to a house in which he occupied the smaller of two rooms.

We threw the fish and the potatoes into a pot on a stove and boiled them together. By the time they were cooked, night had fallen and so we ate in darkness.

In the adjoining room lived about ten men, all much older. Their room was illuminated by a single candle, but no one was visible as the room was filled with smoke from pipes and cigarettes.

"All refugees passing through," said Bronek pointing to them. "One hardly knows the other, just like you and me. Tell me about yourself."

I hesitated at first, but then I told him of my troubles with Mr. Sidlo.

"You can stay with me. We'll bring in some extra straw from the barn and you can sleep in the other corner. Don't worry, Zigmund, we'll help each other. As for that Sidlo, I think we can fix him with this," and I could hear him undo the safety catch on the Luger.

"You mean shoot him?" I asked with fear.

"If necessary," came a calm reply from the dark.

From the next room, the sound of a musical instrument could be heard.

"Isn't it beautiful?" I remarked.

"Come, you'll meet the others." He opened the door and we entered.

On a bed by the window sat a man with hollow cheeks and large, bony fingers, playing a concertina. Near the candle, four men were playing twenty-one; others were already sleeping, someone coughed, another snored. The room stank with human odors.

"This is Zigmund," announced Bronek, but no one even looked at me.

"May I try your concertina?" I asked the man when he stopped playing.

"Can you play?"

"I've never played," I answered, "but I'm sure I could play something if you let me." He shook his head, turned from me, and began to play a new melody.

We returned to our room and lay down for the night.

Through the window I saw the stars above. I'm lucky, I thought to myself, to have someone like Bronek. God keeps an eye on me.

I tried to sleep, but my eyes would not close. I suddenly felt ashamed for not having told Bronek the complete truth about myself.

Perhaps he could help you, you fool, said one of my voices. He's a partisan, and partisans are for the Jews. Tell him everything, don't be afraid.

What if he doesn't like Jews? Perhaps he was in the A.K., cautioned my other voice.

So you're afraid again! said the first voice taunting me.

I'm not afraid! shouted the other voice in my defense. I'm not afraid of anyone anymore!

"Bronek!" I was now shaking him. "Bronek, wake up!" I suddenly felt the muzzle of the Luger pressed against my chest. "Bronek, it's me, Zigmund."

"What do you want?" he asked in a tired voice.

"I just wanted to tell you the truth about myself. To begin with, my real name is not Zigmund, and I'm a Jew . . ."

"That's all right," he mumbled, "my real name is Adolf and I'm a German," and he began to snore.

The following night, Bronek began to tell about his days with the partisans in the Ukrainian forests. He talked with great zest and seemed to relish every incident he recalled. I sat up in the darkness, and from his descriptions, I could almost imagine the real happenings. Every attack, every shot, every action became ingrained in my memory, so that soon I almost believed it was I and not Bronek who had partaken in all these adventures.

How exciting it all seemed, and how I envied my friend for having gone through such events! I began to yawn, but Bronek continued; his voice became faint and very distant.

"Zigmund." I felt someone shaking me and opened my eyes.

"What is it?" I asked, sitting up.

"I asked you if you're really a Jew," I seemed to hear Bronek say.

"I told you that last night," I answered, and went back to sleep.

"No fooling?" said my friend. "How did you manage to survive?"

"I'll tell you tomorrow," I said, half asleep.

"Tell me now, I'm very interested," and he shook me once more and made me sit up. He asked questions and I supplied the answers. He listened with great interest, and when the sun rose that morning he knew everything there was to know about me. Rubbing his tired eyes, he now let out a laugh. "Why do you remain here?"

"Where should I go?" I asked.

"To Lublin, the big city," he replied firmly.

"I don't know anyone there, and no one knows me."

"But you're Jewish and there are other Jews there."

"Why don't you go to Lublin?" I inquired.

"I will," he said, "as soon as I get hold of some money for train fare. I'll tell you what . . ." He became quite excited. "We'll both go to Lublin. We'll do well there . . . I'll pretend to be Jewish too and we'll be helped by rich Jews . . . Better still, you'll tell them that I saved your life and they'll treat me like a king."

He's right, he's absolutely right, I thought. I should go to Lublin. I turned to him and said: "Let's go to Lublin right now."

He laughed. "No, no, my friend, you can't go to the big city dressed like we are, no shoes, no money in our pockets. How would we eat there? We couldn't very well steal potatoes or go fishing in the streets."

"But you told me other Jews would help us."

"Yes," he answered, "but it may take some time before we make contact. We need a little money, Zigmund, and as soon as we get it, we'll go." He paused, lowered his eyes, then casually asked, "Didn't your parents leave you their gold and silver?"

"We were very poor," I answered.

There was a long pause. Bronek stood up and looked out the window. "That Mrs. Paizak you told me about, she has it all. But of course!"

"You're wrong, Bronek."

"I have the whole thing figured out." He turned and jumped into the air. "Sure, your mother gave all her possessions to this Paizak woman for safe keeping. Now, once your mother is taken away, what does this whore do? She tells you to give yourself up, right? When you refuse, her son threatens you. They don't want you alive."

"You're wrong," I pleaded with him. "All Mrs. Paizak got were a few pots and pans."

"That's all you know about. It's all yours, and I'll see to it that we get it all back. Tonight we attack Mrs. Paizak!" He pulled out his revolver, ran outside, and burst back into the room pointing the gun at me. "All right, Paizak, let's have it or I'll blow your head off." I began to tremble. Bronek jumped into the air, touched the ceiling, and then fell to the floor convulsed with laughter. "You're frightened," he said. "Look at you, you're frightened."

"Very well," I said, "just to satisfy you I'll go to the Paizaks and ask them."

"Are you ever a dope!" he shouted. "What will you ask? 'Mrs. Paizak, may I please have my mother's gold and silver and fine silks back?' And she'll say, 'Certainly, my dear boy,' and hand it to you just like that!" He hit me on the side of my head. "I know," he went on. "The only thing people understand and respect is this," and he held up the Luger. "Tonight we attack and tomorrow we'll be in Lublin smoking real cigarettes."

The moon lit our way as we cut across the fields in the direction of Kulik. Bronek had spent several hours taking the revolver apart, cleaning it, and then assembling it again. He had taken aim several times, loaded it, shoved it behind his belt, and ordered me to lead the way. I felt I was about to take part in a most dangerous and heroic mission and I had visions of being decorated for my bravery.

It was good having Bronek by my side with a gun with real bullets in it, a gun that could shoot and kill. I'm a partisan, I told myself, and what we're about to do is for the cause!

It was close to midnight when we crossed the river. A little further and we now stood on a low hill from which the Paizak farm was visible. It was the same place where I had parted with my Uncle Moishe.

Moishe! I thought. Perhaps he's waiting for me at the Paizaks!

A terrible guilt, fear, and shame all wrapped up in one, now overtook me, and suddenly I didn't feel like a brave partisan at all. Instead of feeling protected by Bronek, I now feared him, and somehow hoped the night would pass without my getting shot by him.

As we approached the house, he pulled out the revolver. His tongue was hanging out like a hungry dog's, and he tiptoed like a sly fox about to attack a chicken.

"Wait!" I shouted, and we both fell to the ground.

"What's the matter with you?" he whispered in an angry tone. "Someone might hear you."

"I can't allow you to do this."

"Don't tell me what I can do. Nobody tells me, least of all *you*." He was very angry.

"Bronek, she's a good woman. I can't allow you to frighten her like this. Besides, you might do something. Accidents do happen."

"Nothing will happen if she co-operates," he answered through his clenched teeth.

"But I told you, she hardly has a thing of ours."

"We'll soon find out, let's not waste time."

"I'm not going," I said, and sat down. "You don't know what you're doing. You've picked the wrong person."

"Very well," he laughed, "I'll go myself and tell them you sent me to collect the treasure."

"No!" I yelled, and leaped at him and held him by his legs. "Please, Bronek, I beg you, don't. You stay here, I'll go myself."

There was a long pause; then Bronek took a few steps away from me, looked up at the round moon, and in a forlorn tone said, "And I thought we would have some action tonight. Oh God how dull life has been lately!" He removed the bullets from his revolver and shook them in the palm of his left hand. "As you wish," he finally muttered. "You go and see how you manage without me."

"I won't be long," I said.

"If you need me, just whistle," he whispered, and I now heard him reloading the Luger.

The distance to the house was short, but on that occasion it seemed extremely long. A dog began to bark and when I turned to look back, I saw Bronek in the distance, his gun pointing at me.

Perhaps he's planning to shoot me! What a terrible way to die. God, why am I being punished? Dear Jesus, where did I go wrong? I'm sorry, perhaps I was unkind to Mr. Sidlo; if so, then I repent.

A small naphtha lamp burned inside the Paizak house, the dog barked louder, I heard someone's voice in the courtyard. I looked back and saw the immobile figure holding the gun, and now I saw the gun alone. It was huge, and now I saw Bronek's bad eye, his right hand with two missing fingers; the dog was barking, I could imagine his eyes and sharp teeth, and then the thought struck me, What if Bronek is right? What if my mother did leave a fortune in Mrs. Paizak's care?

My other voice now laughed, where did your mother get such a fortune, wise one?

Perhaps she had it without my knowledge, it's possible, perhaps.

Diamonds sparkled in front of my eyes, gold candlesticks shone in the dark, and fine laces touched my body. I looked at the sparkling diamonds again and saw Mrs. Paizak's crying eyes.

"My dear boy, my dear boy," she was saying and kissed my cheeks.

Bronek was standing in the same place, his gun still on the ready.

"Well?" he asked when I approached him.

"I've got it," I said, and pointed to the bundle under my jacket.

A satisfying smile crossed his face. He lowered the revolver and silently, like a pair of field mice, we returned to Malinowka, seen by no one except the moon above.

It was dawn when we reached there, and now, sheltered in our little room, Bronek waited to see the spoils. Reluctantly I unbuttoned my jacket and unfolded a creased bed sheet with a large hole in the middle.

"What's this?" he shouted, his bad eye almost popping from its socket.

"This is all that's left. The pots were used up long ago," I answered.

He fell into a deathly silence and simply stared at me; then he opened the window and let out an animal-like scream. A stray black cat suddenly appeared on the ledge of our window and looked at us with frightened eyes.

Bronek aimed the gun and fired the bullets into the cat's body. The animal twisted and fell limply to the ground.

I was determined to go to Lublin, but in order to do so I had to have enough money for the journey. Bronek mentioned a holdup, but I rejected it immediately and instead offered to sell my mother's bed sheet.

Bronek laughed and said, "It would hardly be enough for train fare."

"We'll see," I said optimistically.

"Good luck to you," he said, showing little faith in my plan.

Early in the morning, with the bed sheet under my arm, I set out to visit the market in the city of Chelm. By noon I had arrived, and standing in the midst of bombed houses, overturned trucks, and burned-out tanks, I found a very busy market place, alive with shouting and bartering.

A lady was selling a man's suit, another one was selling bread; here an old farmer was displaying eggs, and there a young boy no older than myself was selling a bird in a wooden cage. Further on, a circle of people had gathered; I pushed my way through. A blind man was playing a large accordion, and beside him stood a slender boy with blond hair, singing a Russian song.

I watched with admiration and envy. If I could do that! I thought. If I would be allowed to sing and have people gather around to listen!

Some of the spectators cried, all applauded, and some threw money into the hat which lay on the ground. If only I could play an accordion, then I could play and sing all by myself, and perhaps I could earn my living like that in Lublin!

I moved away, but the boy's voice and the music followed me throughout the market. Someone was feeding a horse, and here stood a peasant woman holding several chickens under her arms. An old man leaning against the wall was vomiting, and from the distance came a shout, "Thief!" And now a young barefoot boy was pursued by a bald, heavy-set man with a long moustache.

There were all sorts of odors here. It smelled of manure, of freshly baked bread, of new potatoes and fruits, and also of burned flesh and bombs.

"Shoes! Shoes! Shoes!" I heard a voice. I turned and followed the call, thinking I would perhaps see a shoe dealer like my grandfather. "Shoes!" shouted the voice. My eyes caught sight of him. "Shoes!" He was a tall, lean man with a hungry look on his face. His eyes were large and his hair was long and disheveled. He wore a gray farm suit and from the corner of his mouth hung a long cigarette rolled with newspaper. "Shoes! Shoes!" In his hands, in front of his chest, he displayed a pair of brown shoes. They had obviously been worn, but were now repaired and shined. "Shoes!"

I came very close to him and gaped at the shoes, then looked down at my bare feet and tried to figure if they would fit me. At first the man ignored me, but now he cast a glance towards me and said, "They're your size."

Immediately I moved away and a little further on began shouting, "Bed sheet! Bed sheet!" And I unfolded the sheet for everyone to see. "Bed sheet for sale!" People milled about me, but no one threw so much as a glance in my direction. I studied their faces and tried to guess if any of them were possibly Jews. "Bed sheet!" I looked at their eyes, I watched their walk, and in the end gave up guessing.

Where are the Chelm fools then? How often in the past had I heard stories about the Chelm fools? In those times I had assumed Chelm was only an imaginary place, but now I stood in its market.

Chelm had changed. The Chelm fools, as they were described in the stories, could not be seen. The little Jews with the black caftans and white and blue phylacteries were gone. The ones with the long beards and sidelocks were not here. A smile appeared on my face as I vaguely recalled a story of how the Chelmites once pushed a mountain, and another about the Chelmite who was asked what he would do if he found a million rubles in the market place and knew who lost them. The Chelm fool replied without hesitation, "If I knew that the money belonged to Rothschild, I would keep it, but if I knew that the million rubles belonged to the poor rabbi of the old synagogue, I'd return it to the last coin."

Faces paraded in front of me and from the distance came the sound of the accordion and with it the haunting voice, *"The night is dark; only the bullets are wailing in the Steppe . . ."* He was now singing in Russian.

"Bed sheet! Bed sheet for sale!" I called out again and again and began to move about. A woman with a shriveled face stopped for a moment, examined the sheet with her scarred hands, and without comment moved on to something else.

"Shoes! Shoes for sale!" I looked up and once more saw the tall man. "Shoes! Shoes!"

"How much do you want for them?" I asked.

He studied me for a moment and said, "You can't afford them." Then he shouted the same refrain, "Shoes! Shoes!" When I began to go he called after me, "You!" I turned. "I'll let you have them for five hundred zloty."

I walked away. Perhaps some day I'll be able to afford them, I mused.

"Bed sheet! Bed sheet for sale!" Again I studied the faces and looked this time not for the Chelm fools, but for my Uncle Moishe.

He did go to Chelm, I reasoned. Wouldn't it be something if I ran into him here quite by accident? It's possible, why not? Everything is possible. One only has to believe and have faith.

"How much for the sheet?" asked a young woman, her head wrapped in a multicolored kerchief.

"I don't know," I answered. Her question had caught me by surprise.

"How do you expect to sell it," she asked, "if you don't know how much you want for it?" And she waited for a reply.

"Five hundred zloty," I said quickly.

She looked at me and burst out laughing; then stroking my cheek she said, "You're so very good looking," and walked away.

The blood rushed to my face and I blushed, not so much because of what she had said, but because she had laughed at the price. If only it was possible to get five hundred zloty for the bed sheet, I thought, then I would return to Malinowka with shiny brown shoes. Suddenly a thought came to my head and I ran to find the tall man.

"Mister, you want five hundred zloty for your shoes, and I want five hundred for my bed sheet, why don't we trade them?" I proposed, smiling at him.

The man growled, "Go away, boy!"

He frightened me and so I moved away. "Bed sheet for sale! Bed sheet for sale!" A Russian soldier passed by playing a harmonica. "Bed sheet for sale!"

"Shoes!"

"Bed sheet!"

"Shoes!"

"Bed sheet!"

"Shoes!"

"Cigarette holders!" This was a new voice and the voice was my own. It was a much smaller and weaker voice than I had now, and as in a dream in which the images are not too clearly defined, I saw myself on the corner of Pawia and Smocza streets in Warsaw.

"Cigarette holders! Cigarette holders!" cried my voice pleadingly.

People rushed by me aimlessly. In the distance someone

screamed and a little later one passer-by asked another, "What's the commotion?"

"A girl committed suicide." The first one shrugged his shoulders and walked on.

"Cigarette holders!" called my voice again, and a woman carrying several parcels stopped in front of me. "How many, madam?" I asked. "They're very fine and made of glass."

"If you help me carry these parcels to my apartment I'll give you something." Without hesitation I grabbed the parcels and followed her. We walked along Smocza and then turned at Gęsia Street.

We turned into a courtyard, entered one of the buildings, and walked up four stories. Outside her door she offered me ten groszy. I bowed and thanked her and quickly returned to the corner of Pawia and Smocza, and there I bought a piece of sweet cake from a vendor.

I ate the cake slowly, making it last, and every bite and turn of the tongue could not last long enough. The cake finally devoured, a terrible guilt set in.

I'm eating cake and what will I bring home for my mother and Josel? I'm selfish. I had no right to enjoy it so much. I won't tell them. They don't have to know about it. Perhaps I'll make some more money today and buy cake to take home. I moved across the street.

"Cigarette holders made of glass!"

I now thought of my father in Russia. I wondered when the war would end and I tried to imagine what it would be like to kiss Esther, the girl who lived on the same courtyard on Pawia Street.

The day passed and a bright red sun set behind the drab buildings. The noise of vendors and buyers subsided and the corner looked almost deserted. The statue of the Holy Mary could be seen in the middle of the road enclosed by an iron fence. An elderly man knelt in front of it reciting a prayer.

How odd those Gentiles are! I thought. And how they can eat pork, I'll never understand.

An evening wind appeared and I began to shiver from the cold, but I still refused to go home. I resisted because I was ashamed to return empty-handed and also because I hoped and believed a miracle would happen, and it did.

"How much are they?" asked a young man.

"One for five groszy, three for ten," I answered him.

He examined the merchandise and then said, "A kid down the street sells the same ones for three groszy apiece."

"He probably got them from a different supplier," I answered quickly.

"Don't fool me," said the man. "I know where you all get them. In the ruins of the bombed factory. You pay nothing for them, so why not sell them cheaper?" I remained silent. "I'll tell you what, I'll make a deal with you. How many do you have here?"

"Several hundred," I answered.

"Good," replied the man, "I'll take them all from you at three groszy each."

I could hardly believe my ears. Indeed it was a miracle.

"It's a deal," I said jubilantly.

"The only thing," said the stranger, "I don't have any money on me, so if you don't mind walking me home, I'll pay you there." I agreed and we began to walk. "Just a little further," said the man. I didn't mind the walk at all. For this kind of miracle, I would have walked to the other end of Warsaw. "Just a little further," and we turned into this street and went up that street and at long last we entered a court-yard. "Here we are," said the man. "Wait here and I'll be down in two minutes with the money."

I leaned against the gate of the courtyard and tried to fig-ure how much money I would make. I got confused and the figures swam in my head. I could almost see my mother's face shining with pride as I handed her the money to buy bread. Perhaps she'll write my father about it. He too will be proud!

The guilt for eating the cake vanished completely and I knew that God had sent me an angel in disguise. "Perhaps it's an act of God," I whispered.

I waited and waited and heard doors opening and closing, but no sign of the stranger. The courtyard turned dark and here and there a small light appeared in a window. I shivered from the cold, and although I was worried, I didn't lose hope.

At long last, the man appeared in the dark. "I'm very sorry to have been so long, but I had trouble finding my money. I don't know where I hid it. Just so it won't be a complete waste for you, here's three groszy and I'll take one." And he helped himself to a cigarette holder and disappeared into the night. I put the three coins into my pocket and walked out into the street.

"How much?" asked a voice.

"What?"

"How much do you want for it?" repeated the voice.

"Five hundred," I said.

"It has a hole in it," said the voice. It was a young girl with long blond hair. Beside her, silently looking on, stood her husband, barefoot and carrying a chicken under his arm.

"Did you steal it?" asked the girl, smiling at me.

"No," I replied.

"I'll give you two hundred zloty; that's all it's worth."

I hesitated for a moment but then said, "Very well, it's yours," and handed her the sheet. Out of her stocking she pulled a bundle of money, counted off two hundred, and handed it to me.

I held the money tightly. "Shoes! Shoes!" The voice seemed to beckon me.

Once again I faced the tall man, "I'll give you two hundred for them," I said and showed him the money in my hands.

He threw me a vicious look and said, "Not enough. I'll tell you what, because I like you, I'll let you have them for four hundred."

"Two hundred is all I have," I pleaded with him.

"You don't want to buy them, you want to steal them. Get away boy and don't let me see you again, you make me so mad."

I moved away and strolled between the wares.

A man was quarreling with his wife and here a Russian soldier with a disfigured face that looked like a shapeless football was examining a decorative plate. A billy goat got loose and ran through the market, pursued by his owner.

I walked and walked, and without meaning to, I somehow ended up at the shoes again. This time I stood at a distance and watched. Oh, how I wanted those shoes! But how could I possibly afford them? The man beckoned me with his finger. I ran over to him.

"Look," he began, "it's getting late and I've been here since early morning. I'm tired and hungry, give me three hundred and let me go home." And he extended the shoes to me. I held them and could now smell the fresh shoe polish on them.

"I only have two hundred," I said again.

"I'll kill you!" he shouted, and grabbed the shoes from me.

Again I walked away, but this time the man followed me. "Two hundred and fifty," he shouted. I shook my head and left him standing shaking his fist at me.

The crowds began to disperse as the sun fell to the rooftops of Chelm. The few stalls were being dismantled; the goats were moved away; the horses were harnessed and driven off; even the blind accordionist packed his instrument, and I saw the young boy counting the money. Soon they too were gone. The place was littered with garbage.

I turned up my collar. My hands in my pockets, I set out for the journey back to Malinowka. I had only taken a few steps when I heard the voice calling, "Wait! Wait!" I turned and immediately recognized the tall man. He was running towards me. "All right," he said, breathing hard, "it's like stealing I tell you, there you are, let's have the two hundred." The shoes were now in my hands once more. "Let's have the money, boy!" he shouted. "What are you waiting for?"

"I want to try them on," I answered. "What if they don't fit me?"

"For two hundred they have to fit yet?" he growled like a dog. I put the shoes on, tied up the laces and now paraded in front of him. He waited impatiently and looked at me with distaste. "Well?" he said, "May I have the money now?" Slowly I took off the shoes and began to examine them. "What are you doing now?" he inquired, gritting his teeth.

"Are the soles made of leather?" I inquired.

"Of course!" he shouted. "Please, boy, let me have the money, I have a long way home."

There must be something wrong with the shoes, I reasoned. Why else would he be selling me a five-hundred-zloty pair of shoes for only two hundred?

"There's nothing wrong with the shoes, boy, don't waste any more of my time," he begged now.

I handed the shoes back to him and said, "I don't want them." And I began to run.

He pursued and caught up with me. Gripping my arm and in a pleading voice he said,

"Please, boy, please, I swear by Jesus the shoes are good."

"I don't want them."

"Please, I need the money. Make it one hundred and fifty then."

"No!" I replied. "I don't want your shoes." He loosened his grip, freeing me.

The sun had already set when I left him standing in the deserted market place of Chelm, his head bent, the shoes hanging limply in his hands, and his voice still to be heard calling, "Shoes! Shoes! shoes for sale!"

Many hours later on the road back to Malinowka, a strange thought occurred to me: perhaps I had met a Chelm fool after all. Perhaps that's what they really look like!

Hearing about my money, the collection of strangers from the next room became extremely friendly towards me and began asking for handouts. One needed medicine, another vodka, a third cigarettes.

Bronek suggested I give him the money for safekeeping, but I declined, fearing I would never see it again. He laughed menacingly and asked, "Don't you trust me?"

I kept the bills in my trouser pocket, and repeatedly during the day my hand would reach automatically to make sure they were still there. At night I lay awake and held the money tightly in the grip of my fist.

Every sound, every movement coming from the next room would send shivers through my body, and I began to imagine they were coming to do away with me and steal my money.

One man wanted to sell me a few letters, another a torn wallet, and still another a soiled hat. I listened to their offers, and though I feared them, I still refused to part with my money.

They now appealed to my sympathies by pointing out that we were all lost, drifters, looking for a home, for a normal life, destitute, and all should help one another.

I did not intend to see my money vanish on smoking, drinking, or gambling. I have to get to Lublin, I kept thinking.

Repeatedly I asked Bronek about leaving for Lublin, but he kept delaying it. "We don't have enough money yet," or, "Next week," or, "We'll talk about it."

The days and weeks came and went and still Bronek made no move. The atmosphere became very tense now and the old men refused to talk to me, but whispered derogatory remarks about me to each other. They stared at me with cold expressions as if wishing to devour me. Even Bronek hardly talked, and once accused me of being a "stingy Jew." I protested and tried to explain, but he would have none of it. I began to fear for my life, and knew that if I didn't part with the money I would fall victim to this collection of strangers.

One afternoon I offered my two hundred zloty to the man with the hollow cheeks and bony fingers, for his concertina. He accepted, and that very evening, while in the next room they were celebrating with vodka, I sat in the dark and tried to play like the blind accordionist in Chelm.

You must leave for Lublin, the voice rang in my head. Go, escape! Don't wait for Bronek, he'll never take you.

Again I lay in the field of wheat and watched the Sidlo house, and once more I saw my former employer leave for work, and again, like a cat, I made my way to the house and now stood facing Mrs. Sidlo.

"I've been waiting for you," she said, and now went to a vase and took out some bills and handed them to me. "You see, Zigmund, my word is good, but please don't tell anyone. If my husband knew, he'd probably kill me."

"I'll never forget you for this," I said.

"Go, Zigmund, go! And don't judge us too harshly."

On the road I stopped, and making sure no one was watching me, I began counting the money. She had given me three hundred zloty. Quickly I removed my hat, tore an opening in the lining, and hid the money there.

That afternoon I said to Bronek, "Tomorrow I'm going to Lublin whether you come or not."

"Go if you like," was his answer. "Next week I'm going for sure."

"I'm leaving tomorrow," I said firmly. "I'm not going to listen to any more of your promises." And I began to gather my belongings.

"How do you plan to get there?" he asked. "By foot perhaps?"

I wanted to tell him of my new wealth but I thought better of it, so I said, "I'll get on the train somehow."

He laughed and then asked, "And what are you going to do with your concertina now?"

I was puzzled by his question. "Take it to Lublin," I answered.

Bronek laughed again and this time could not stop. Still laughing, he ran into the other room, and a moment later they were all staring at me and peals of laughter emanated from their bellies.

"What's the matter?" I asked, not understanding the reason for their merriment.

The man with the hollow cheeks approached me and said, "They're laughing because you plan to take the concertina to Lublin."

"What's so funny about that?" I asked innocently.

"It's the Russians," he answered. "They'll take it away from you the moment they see it."

"Why?" I asked.

"No reason except that they take away all musical instruments and watches."

"That's right," shouted the others like a chorus. I studied their faces and now turned to the hollow-cheeked one.

"What shall I do then?"

The man was silent for a moment, then said, "You'd better sell it before you leave." And he paused and looked at me intently. "I'll give you fifty zloty for it."

"Fifty zloty!" I shouted. "Why, the other day I gave you two hundred for it!"

"That's right," answered the man, "but fifty is all I have left." And again like a chorus the others rolled with laughter.

"Take fifty," advised one, "or you'll get nothing."

"I won't sell it for less than two hundred zloty," I announced, and taking the instrument, I walked out and headed straight for the house where a widow lived with eight children.

When I explained my dilemma to her, she agreed that she too had heard that the Russians confiscated musical instruments, and offered to buy the concertina.

"But as Good Jesus is my witness, I have no money." She now waited for me to say something, and indeed I was about to donate the instrument to one of her fatherless children when she added, "Perhaps you would accept this coat in exchange." And she now produced a long army coat of a greenish color with decorated brass buttons.

I had never seen such a coat and so I asked her what sort of coat it was.

"Belgian Army," she answered. How it came into her possession, I didn't bother to ask. The coat looked as if it had never been worn and the fabric was sturdy. "It will make a good suit for you," she said. I left the concertina and came out carrying the coat over my shoulder.

"You had no right to do that!" shouted the man with the hollow cheeks. "You had no right selling my concertina! Bastard Jewish swindler." And he returned to his room and lay down on his bed and stared at the ceiling.

That night I used the coat as a pillow, and when I rose early the next morning I quickly washed my face, combed my hair, and gathered my few belongings.

"What are you doing?" asked Bronek.

"I'm going to Lublin right now," I answered bravely, and waited for a reaction from him. He stared at me. "Do you want to come along?"

"Not today," he answered. "Why don't you wait a few days, then we'll go together?"

"I'm not waiting one more minute even," I said, and now extended my hand to him. "Good-bye, Bronek."

"Good-bye," he answered, and instead of giving me his hand he pulled out the Luger. I turned and began to walk towards the road. I passed the window and saw the hollow-cheeked man looking out at me, a bitter expression on his face.

"If you take one more step, I'll shoot you." The voice was Bronek's. I froze to the ground and turned my head. Bronek was pointing the gun at me. "I thought we were going to help each other, Jew," he now yelled.

I turned and walked. My urge was to run, but I could not allow myself that. I felt compelled to leave without fear and with dignity. I walked on, taking normal steps, and didn't look back even once. Soon Bronek was but a memory, his mutilated hand on a German trigger, his laughter pursuing me for many kilometers from the village of Malinowka.

SIX

□ "Which way is it to the train?" I asked an aged farmer working by the roadside.

"Follow that road; make a turn to the right at the next one."

In front of me was an open horizon, a bright sun shone above, and the sky was friendly and wide. Now and then I would stop to rest, and taking my hat off, I would feel under its lining to be sure I still had the money. Once I even counted it. "Three hundred zloty," I whispered.

Fields of wheat swayed gently and potato and cabbage patches lay restfully by the roadside. Here and there someone was working, but the road was almost deserted. "Which way to the train?"

A young girl studied me, then answered, "Straight ahead, about two kilometers."

The sun had become larger now and very red as it prepared to disappear for another day. How strange, I thought, that the sun rises from one side and sets on another and yet the next day appears again from the first side! How is that possible?

"Which way to the train?"

"Over there." I looked and in the distance a small train station came into view. The sun was about to disappear completely; the road in front of me was clear. I was overjoyed at seeing the railway tracks and from the distance came a familiar train whistle. I began to run and as I ran I noticed a group of boys moving towards the road to block my way.

I slowed down and silently prayed that they wouldn't pick on me. To show them I wasn't afraid, I began to whistle, and though I feared what might happen, I walked with assurance, smiling and holding my head up high.

The little station was almost in front of me, the sun was not to be seen, and the boys, all barefoot like myself, holding sticks in their hands, now joined hands and encircled me. I pretended not to be concerned.

"Where are you going?" asked one of them.

"To the train," I answered.

"What you got there?" asked another, pointing to the Belgian coat.

"It's just a coat."

"Let's see it."

"What for?"

"We would like to see it," and he now moved to snatch it from me.

"Leave me alone," I shouted, "or I'll take on the whole bunch of you." An unbelievable laughter arose all around me.

"Try me first," said the roughest-looking one, and now moved to face me.

My legs began to tremble. "Let me go. Please let me go," I said in a pleading voice. Again there was a peal of laughter.

"Come on, hit me," said the boy in front of me.

"I don't want to hit you," I answered. "I just want to get to the train."

"You'll have to hit me," he was insisting, and suddenly, to provoke me, he snatched my hat from my head.

"Give it back," I shouted. Quickly he hid it behind his back, and when I tried to get it he threw it to one of his friends. I leaped there and now saw my hat flying through the air and falling into the grasp of another boy. Again I tried to catch it and failed. The hat went from one to the other and I, like a frightened animal, ran in a circle, my face and body now covered with sweat, my heart pounding.

"Please give it to me!" I begged, but my pleas did not help. They continued to laugh and shout, and the more frightened I appeared, the more they seemed to enjoy it. When for a moment I stopped, the one holding the hat held it out to me and tauntingly, as if to a kitten, said: "Here, here, come and get it."

When I was about to reach, the hat took off like a bird, and now another voice said behind me, "Here, I'll give it to you, come and get it."

But this time I did not move; I could not move any more. As if this was more than I could bear, or as if I had come close to surviving and yet was going to perish at this last moment, I simply sat down and cried.

"Here, here," said the voice, "come and get it."

"I'm not strong enough to fight all of you," I began. "In fact I'm probably not strong enough to fight any of you, but there is a power that watches and judges, and He will make sure that you're damned for this."

The laughter now turned into stony silence and when I turned to look at them they were not staring at me but had their eyes cast downwards. A small boy with scarred legs and crossed eyes came forward and handed me my cap. I took it and made sure the money was still there; then with my sleeve

I wiped my eyes. When I finally stood up and once more tried to look at their faces, they had dispersed and were in the adjoining fields herding their cattle together.

The small train station now stood before me, and except for a well-dressed lad about my own age, there was no one to be seen. The boy wore short pants, long socks, and sandals. His hair was blond and neatly trimmed. Beside him stood a large suitcase and in his right hand he held a leather leash, at the end of which was a huge brown boxer dog with a muzzle on its face.

When the dog made a move to jump me, the boy pulled the leash and ordered, "Sit down, Adolf."

How I envied that boy! For, looking at him, I remembered of how I had looked at one time. My mother used to dress me up, and then we would go visiting, or walk in the park and watch people fly kites.

"Where can I buy a ticket?" I asked.

"Inside at the window," he answered, pointing to the interior.

Behind the little window sat an old man in a uniform and glasses which seemed to be falling off his nose.

"One ticket to Lublin."

"That will be two hundred and thirty zloty," announced the man, and waited for the money. I took off my cap and embarrassingly counted the required amount and handed him the bills. He produced a ticket, punched and stamped it, then wrote something in a book and finally handed it to me saying, "Don't lose it, now."

"When does the train come," I inquired.

He looked at the clock on the wall, and as if addressing himself, he said, "Shortly, very shortly. Should be here any minute."

The well-dressed boy with the boxer dog was still there when I came out. "Are you waiting for the train as well?" I asked.

"Yes," was his reply.

"You going to Lublin?"

"Yes."

"Are you alone too?" I inquired, hoping to have his company for the journey.

"My mommy is over there," and he pointed to an outhouse a short distance away.

"You live here?" I went on.

"No, in Lublin," he answered. "We've been visiting my grandmother."

"You live in Lublin then?" I asked.

"Yes."

Again a familiar fear invaded my thoughts. What if Bronek lied to me? What if there are no Jews in Lublin? Perhaps the war isn't over and the Germans are still in Lublin waiting for me at the station!

"I guess the Germans have left Lublin, eh?" I asked nonchalantly.

"Where have you been?" asked the boy. "The war is over, the Germans are kaput or don't you know that either?"

I remained silent and swallowed the insult. "What about the Jews?" I began, the word getting stuck in my throat.

"What about them?" asked the boy looking at me.

"Well, are there any of those dirty Jews back in Lublin?"

The boy twisted his face, making himself look like a monkey, and said, "The place is crawling with the lice carriers."

A shiver went through my body.

"My father says," he went on, "that Hitler made one mistake . . . in not killing all of them."

"You can say that again!" I agreed.

"Don't worry though," he continued, "the A.K. will finish them off."

"What makes you say that?" I inquired.

"My father told me," he replied with assurance. Then he added, "He knows, he's an officer in the army."

His mother now appeared and about the same time a train whistle was heard in the distance. The woman combed the boy's hair, straightened his jacket, and picked up the suitcase.

It was almost dark when we boarded the train. I watched the boy, his mother, and the boxer dog enter a coach, and then made sure not to enter the same one. I ran towards the back as far as I could go, and then jumped into a car filled with Russian soldiers.

Beside a window I found a seat and suspiciously eyed everyone around me. Some of the soldiers were sleeping, others were playing cards or eating, and some were writing letters. I held on tightly to my few belongings, especially my Belgian coat. Nobody paid attention to me, no one was concerned. They didn't even notice me.

The train began to move; outside it was dark. Through the window I could see little lights shining in the distance. I reclined and closed my eyes.

Thousands upon thousands of images flashed through my mind about as quickly as the speed of the train. My whole life was now before me, but only in fragments, and what stood out most was the ugly face of the brown boxer dog, staring at me, waiting for me, devouring me.

"Lublin, everybody off!" someone shouted.

When I opened my eyes, half the coach was already cleared; the remaining people were pushing towards the exit. Through the window, I could see silhouettes of people with baggage moving by swiftly. Sounds of engines, of hissing, of turning wheels, and sounds of whistles came from all directions.

"Lublin, everybody off!" A man in a blue uniform was now looking at me.

"Are we in Lublin?" I asked, wiping my sleepy eyes.

"Yes, everybody off," and he disappeared into the next car.

Quickly I grabbed my belongings, adjusted the hat on my head, and moved towards the door. I stepped out into a cold and extremely dark night, and found myself standing on railway tracks.

"Get out from there!" someone shouted at me. I could hear the voice but couldn't see the face. I moved away onto another track, but now saw an engine coming towards me. I jumped out of its way and into the arms of a railway repairman with a dirty face and a lamp in his right hand.

"Watch where you're going, sonny," he growled angrily.

A short distance away an engine was puffing and smoke emanated from its pipes. Nearby, flames twisted and turned, and lights seemed to be hanging in midair. Strange shouts could be heard all about, but there were no faces to be seen. I was petrified.

Is this really Lublin? I wondered. Or perhaps the train I was on had an accident and I was killed and this is hell!

"Somebody help me!" I shouted in panic. "Where do I go? Please show me the way to the city!"

"Follow me," said a voice beside me. A short man in a long coat, carrying two heavy suitcases, was now in front of me. "It's easy to get lost here," he was mumbling. I could hardly keep up with his pace for he moved very swiftly, and after crossing many rails and making several turns this way and that, we were now mounting steps leading to a huge building. All about were people rushing, yelling, screaming, crying, hurrying with their baggage. The whole scene seemed most unusual and frightening.

I looked in front of me, but the little man had now been lost among the many other onrushing bodies.

Dear God, I now thought, if only I had Bronek with me! He would know where to go. Here I am all alone, lost. I don't

even know whre I am to spend this very night. What about
the next night? And the night after that? If only, dear God,
you would take mercy upon me and guide me. Please help
me, I'm lost.

As if coming from a great distance, a faint voice was now
calling, "Beds for the night! Nice clean beds for the night!"
I turned in the direction of the voice and soon I saw a small
woman wrapped in a winter coat. "Beds for the night! Clean
beds! No bedbugs!"

A smile appeared on my face as I thought, People are kind.
God looks after everyone. He heard my plea!

I moved closer to her and asked, "You have beds for the
night?"

"Yes, nice clean beds. Would you like one?"

"Yes," I answered jubilantly. "How kind of you to be doing this!"

The woman looked puzzled. "You have it all wrong, boy.
It has nothing to do with kindness, it's a hundred zloty a
bed."

I took a few steps back. How is it possible, I thought, that
someone would charge for sleeping?

"No money, boy?" she inquired.

"Where do people sleep who have no money?"

"Over there," she answered, "in the waiting room."

"Thank you," I said, and followed the mass of people moving in that direction.

A voice was coming through loudspeakers announcing
the departures and arrivals. A soldier with a bandaged face
was searching for someone; a little girl with a brace on her
left leg was crying for her mommy.

At last I entered the waiting room, and once inside I
stopped to look in amazement. The room was enormous and
was illuminated by several large lamps hanging from a very
high ceiling. The stench here was almost unbearable, and
although the room was huge, there was not enough room to
walk through, for every bit of space was occupied by sleeping bodies curled up on the floor. Some of the newcomers
rushed about looking for an empty space, a corner, anything. Just a place to sit down even.

Carefully, so as not to step on anyone, I made my way to
the other side of the room. The sounds of snoring and groaning seemed to create a kind of music which echoed throughout the enclosure. I looked here, I looked there, but hardly
anyone looked at me.

With luck, at long last, I found enough standing room
against a wall. I deposited my belongings on the floor and

held them tightly between my feet. I shut my eyes and began to sleep. Soon, however, I lost my balance and fell onto a fat, sleeping woman. I stood up, looked across the room, and caught sight of the young blond boy, now in the arms of a Polish officer dressed in a fancy uniform with shiny medals. His mother walked beside them leading the boxer dog. The father was showering the boy with kisses and the boy beamed with happiness.

"Over here," a voice called. "Over here," repeated the voice in Russian. When I turned to my right I saw the smiling face of a Russian soldier who was motioning for me to join him. I hesitated for a moment; then picking up my things, I approached him. "There's enough room here for both of us," he said cheerfully. "Make yourself comfortable," and he removed his small suitcase to the other side.

"Thank you," I said shyly, and sat down beside him. We said nothing for the longest time, but simply looked at each other.

The soldier smiled, eventually forcing a smile out of me. "That's much better," he said. "You look much better when you smile." Both of us laughed now.

I studied his face closely and looked for signs of recognition. Perhaps he's my father, I mused. Wouldn't this be a miracle? He looks a lot like my father. What about the scar? I see no scar on his face.

He's not your father, dismissed one of my voices. Everyone you see you think is your father. Are you sure you remember what your father looked like?

Of course I remember, I answered myself.

Again I examined his face in detail. The soldier was neatly shaven, his hair was trimmed, and the top part of his uniform was freshly pressed. His trousers and boots I could not see, for an army blanket covered that part of his body. His teeth were of uniform size, and his eyes were dark and sad and seemed to penetrate my soul. He now reached for his little suitcase, unlocked it, and turning to me asked, "Perhaps you're hungry?"

"No, thank you," I said, although I was weak from hunger.

"Don't be shy," he said smiling. "We can share everything that's here." And he pushed the suitcase in front of me so I could see its contents. A large piece of sausage, a loaf of bread, and several large German chocolates were inside. He produced a knife from his pocket, opened the blade, and began cutting the sausage. He divided the bread with his hands. "Eat, no reason to be shy with me." I took the sausage and bread and bit into them, never turning my eyes from him. "Where are your parents?" he asked between bites. When I didn't answer, he quickly added, "I'm sorry for asking, please forgive me."

"I'm Jewish," I suddenly blurted out. "My father is in Russia, his name is Kuperblum, perhaps you know him?"

The soldier took another bite and shook his head. "Here, have some chocolate. Those criminals make good chocolates."

"Were you in Germany?" I inquired.

"Yes," he answered, "I fought in Berlin."

"Did you by any chance fight in Pulawy?"

"No, where's that?"

"That's my town," I answered. "I'm surprised you've never heard of it."

"I'm sorry," was his answer.

You see, said my mocking voice, not only is he not your father, he doesn't even know your town.

He could be pretending, I answered in anger.

I lay back, using my army coat for a pillow. "Go to sleep, boy," said the soldier and now covered me with his own coat. The lights high above on the ceiling shone brightly, someone nearby was crying, and the clock on the wall above the doorway read two o'clock. Through all the snoring, groaning, crying, and general tumult, a very clear whistling sound reached my ears. Someone was whistling Schubert's Serenade in exactly the same way as I remembered my father whistling it.

When I opened my eyes the next morning, the first thing I saw was a one-legged man moving about on a crutch. Judging by his trousers, I surmised he was a soldier. My eyes traveled upwards to the rest of his body and rested on the face. The face looked down at me. It was the same face from the previous night.

"Did you sleep well?" he asked, smiling at me.

"Yes," I answered. Then I asked, "Where are you going?"

"Someone is supposed to pick me up here." I stood up and gathered my belongings. "What about you, boy? Where are you going?"

"I don't know yet," I said. "I don't really know where to go. If I had an accordion I'd go on the street and play."

His eyes lit up. "Can you play?"

I lowered my head. "Not really, but I'd love to learn."

"Why don't you come with me?"

"What would I do with you?" I inquired.

"You'll join the army. We'll give you a uniform and you'll run messages, or better still, you'll join the band and be the drummer."

"Is that possible?" I asked with enthusiasm.

"Sure," he answered. "Come, perhaps they'll even teach you how to play the accordion." He now noticed someone and began to wave and shout, "Over here! Over here!"

Out of the moving masses of people, a beautiful young Russian girl soldier appeared and now stood saluting him. She immediately picked up his coat and suitcase, and he whispered something into her ear. Her attention now shifted to me and she put her arm around my shoulders.

"Come with us," she begged in a most soothing voice. We began to walk, and finally after great difficulty, made our exit out of the waiting room, and soon we were descending the steps of the train depot.

In front of me I saw the streets of Lublin covered in early morning mist. Hardly a soul to be seen. It was deathly quiet and unfamiliar. An army car was waiting at the curb.

"Come, boy," said my soldier friend as he entered the car. "Come with us."

I smiled to him and answered, "I want to look for my people."

"Good luck then," he said, and shook my hand. The girl embraced and kissed me, then also entered the car. I began to move away when I heard the soldier's voice shouting, "Wait boy! Wait!" I ran back to him. "Take this with you," and he gave me the remaining chocolates.

"Remember me," I pleaded with him, "and if you see my father, tell him I'm looking for him. His name is Zelik Kuperblum." He nodded his head, smiled, and the car drove off.

The day was just beginning and the mist, which set upon the city like a fog, made visibility impossible. I began to walk, seeing only a few meters in front of me. I saw no one, but echoes of footsteps and motor vehicles came from all directions. I walked slowly, uncertain and very afraid.

I kept walking and soon a glowing sun made its appearance from behind the buildings on the horizon, and now a street came into view. I suddenly stopped and looked about me and felt like an animal lured out of the woods into an open field. How uncertain I was, and so afraid! If only I could, I would have gladly returned to Malinowka.

In a street mirror I saw an image: it was the image of a young boy with closely cropped hair, torn cotton pants, and dirty bare feet. The face was serious, almost too serious, and on his shoulders was a small bundle and a green Belgian

Army coat with brass buttons.

Is it really me? I asked myself. I wonder if my father would recognize me now?

Other people were now seen walking to and fro, and as the sun rose higher, the streets became busier. Many trucks and horse-drawn carriages moved along the cobbled road. Soldiers, civilians, hungry looking individuals, and cripples all moved about, some with no more certainty on their faces than there was on my own.

Where shall I go? The streets looked so unfamiliar and the faces that passed me did not remind me of the people I once knew. I moved towards a passing stranger about to utter the question, but before I could open my mouth, I turned and walked on. If I ask him about Jews he'll immediately suspect who I am, and might kill me.

Such thoughts and many similar ones crossed and recrossed my troubled mind. In the end I chose an individual who was walking in my direction and I asked him very casually, as if the question carried no importance:

"I hear there are Jews in Lublin again. Where do they live?"

The man was dressed like a peasant, and although it was quite warm, he wore a fur hat, a heavy three-quarter coat, and boots. "You're a Jew?" he demanded.

"No!" I protested quickly. "I'm just asking," and I began to walk faster so as to lose him.

"Wait!" he called after me. "Come with me, I'll show you where they are." We walked in silence. We turned one street, then another, crossed a market place, then along a boulevard. "Look over there!" said the stranger finally, and pointed to a moving carriage with an elderly driver and two well-dressed passengers. "They're Jews."

My heart pounded. "How do you know?" I asked.

"I can tell," came the reply.

I looked closely at the two passengers and noticed their long hooked noses, their black, shifty eyes, the immaculate suits they wore; and what disturbed me most was that they were being driven by a Gentile driver while they sat in comfort.

Why don't they walk like everyone else? I wondered. A horrible shame came over me and now more than before I felt I had made the wrong decision in coming to Lublin. I had nothing in common with these people. I didn't want to be a merchant or usurer, I didn't want to do business, sell herring or shoes, or be driven in carriages by Gentile drivers. I wanted none of those things. I wanted to farm the soil and live by the labor of my own hands, but most of all I didn't want to be a Jew.

"Come! Come!" called the stranger. I looked up and saw him a short distance from me. "I'm in a hurry," he said when I caught up with him. We crossed a bombed section and soon were walking up a street on a hill.

Perhaps I should turn and run back to Malinowka, or why not to the Paizaks? I should have remained with the Golombeks. What a fool I was not to have stayed there. I wonder what Mr. Kozak is doing at this moment? Perhaps I should make my way to the highway and try to get a ride to Piaski?

"There!" said the stranger, and shoved me towards a short, stocky man with a broad nose and short, fuzzy black hair who was leaning against a courtyard gate. "One of yours," he added, and walked down the street.

The stocky man took a puff on a cigarette which he had just lit, and turning his face from one side to the other, observed me with suspicion. "What do you want?" he finally asked.

"Are you a Jew?" I asked, my eyes focused directly on him, as if he was some rare animal.

"What do you want?" he asked again, and began to move into the courtyard.

"I too am a Jew," I said.

"Be on your way, boy!" he shouted angrily. "We've had enough trouble." He moved towards a door, opened it, and began to enter. I ran after him and held on to his jacket.

"Please, you must believe me," I pleaded. "I'm Jewish. You must help me." The man turned and said something to me in Jewish. "I'm sorry," I answered, "I've forgotten how to speak Jewish." Again he eyed me with suspicion and his face was filled with doubt and indecision.

"Wait a moment," he said. And then he called, "Esther! Come here a minute." A beautiful woman with long black hair and shiny eyes that sparkled with life came out of the doorway.

"What is it?" she asked.

"He says he's Jewish."

The woman stared at me and then slowly began to smile and then laugh, and soon she was rocking with laughter. Her husband joined her in the laughter, and before I knew it, they had both disappeared into the apartment and bolted the door behind them. In desperation I knocked on the door with all my might. "Go away, we don't want trouble!" they shouted. But I continued to knock. "We'll call the police," they threatened.

"You have to believe me," I shouted back, and once again pounded on the door. The door finally opened. "Please," I begged, "let me take off my pants and prove to you that I'm a Jew."

The man looked at his wife and she at him and then both at me. "Where are you from?" asked the man.

"Pulawy," I answered quickly.

"What's your name?"

"Kuperblum," I answered. "Jankele Kuperblum."

"What was your father?"

"A shoemaker."

"And his father?"

"A baker . . ."

"Very well," said the man. "Come with me. There's a man here from Pulawy, he'll know if you're telling the truth."

The woman shook her head and kept repeating, "He looks like a Gentile peasant . . . he looks like a Gentile peasant . . . he . . ."

The man led me down a dark hallway and knocked on a door.

"Come in," said a guttural voice from inside, and we entered into a small single room whose only source of light was one small window which was covered with a blanket.

On a huge iron bed which occupied most of the room, lay an enormously heavy man with curly red hair. Jumping on top of him and all around him were about eight or ten children of various ages who looked like little cubs playing with a big bear. The man in the bed growled, cleared his throat, coughed, spat, and finally looking at me, said, "What's this?"

"He says he's a Jew from Pulawy."

The bear sat up and motioned for me to come closer. "Who was your father?" he inquired.

"Zelik Kuperblum," I answered, somewhat afraid of him.

"Zelik's son," said the bear. "You're Zelik's son? You're then Chaya-Eta's grandson?"

"Yes," I said.

"You have family in Lublin," he shouted. "He lives down the street."

A chill went through my body and I wondered who it was that survived. "Follow me," said the man who had brought me there, and shortly we were on the street.

Perhaps my Uncle Mendel is alive, I thought, or perhaps it's Moishe or even Shepsel, or even . . ."

The man led me into a barbershop and now introduced me to the owner, a short, balding man with sparkling eyes. He was busily engaged shaving someone. The barber listened to the introduction, and then in disbelief said, "You couldn't be Zelik's son . . . You don't even look like a Jew." He immediately caught himself and I could see he regretted making the remark. "This is wonderful!" he now shouted. "Zelik's son has survived!" He ran out of the shop and in a loud voice shouted towards an apartment window above, "Fela! Fela!" A young woman stuck her head out and looked down. "Come down quickly!"

The woman came running down the stairs and now stood in the barbershop panting. "What's the trouble?" she inquired with concern.

"Who do you think he is?" and he pointed to me.

"I don't know," she answered.

"Take a guess," urged the barber. "Who does he look like?"

She scanned me up and down, smiled pleasantly, then said, "What's to guess, he's a peasant boy, that's all there is to it."

Over lunch the barber and his wife shot questions at me as to how I survived. What happened to my parents? When did I last see my grandfather the baker? They in turn explained how we were related.

It seemed to me that the relation was very distant, but I didn't want to point that out. On the contrary, I was very pleased to have someone insist that I call him cousin.

"I remember you," the barber said, "when you were still in your mother's belly. Ah . . . your mother, let me tell you, she was a most beautiful woman with a voice like a canary. And your father too was nobody's fool. He played the mandolin, taught dancing, and always had more girls on the string than he could handle."

"Chaim, shame on you," said Cousin Fela.

"That was when he was still single," Cousin Chaim corrected himself quickly.

The apartment was extremely small, two miniature rooms, one a kitchen, the other the bedroom. A vase with a bouquet of fresh flowers stood on the dining table, several framed photographs of elderly people decorated the dresser, while on the wall hung an old drawing of a cat playing with a ball of wool. The floors had been freshly washed and scrubbed and were now covered with newspapers. From the stove came a long-forgotten aroma which brought back memories of my life in Pulawy. On a wooden board near the stove, Cousin Fela began to chop fish, and this chopping sound conjured so many images for me, and suddenly I recalled how my own mother used to chop fish every Friday.

The smell of chicken soup now filled my nostrils, and this

too resulted in a multitude of images awakening in my mind. I sat and watched, and said little. I offered to help and Cousin Fela allowed me to peel a carrot and cut up an onion; otherwise, we just smiled at each other.

Late in the day she covered the table with a white linen tablecloth, placed two silver candlesticks on top of it, and when the sun had set and my Cousin Chaim had locked up the shop, we all sat down to eat. She lit two candles, covered her head with a white shawl, and closing her eyes and making motions with her hands, she blessed the candles. I looked at her face and now thought that she looked so much like my mother.

Perhaps she is my mother, I thought. Perhaps he is my father. Is it possible?

First we ate gefilte fish with horseradish and chalah, and then in a large bowl, she served the chicken soup with noodles and lima beans. The taste was so familiar and yet so distant, so very distant. I looked at the burning candles, glanced at their faces, and noticed them watching me.

Perhaps I'm not eating properly, I thought.

"What's the matter, Jankele, don't you like it?" asked Cousin Fela when I stopped for a moment.

Quickly I picked up the spoon and began to eat again, and now tears fell from my eyes directly into the soup. I did not wipe the tears, I did not want them to see me crying, and so I kept my head lowered, eating the soup and the tears.

"You'll stay with us as long as you want," said my Cousin Chaim.

"You'll be like our own son," added his wife. She prepared a basin of hot water for me and I washed my hands, face, and made an attempt to cleanse my feet, but the dirt refused to budge.

"We'll have to buy you a pair of shoes," commented Chaim. And now Fela handed me a pair of her husband's pajamas and asked me to put them on. I looked at myself in the mirror and upon seeing my image I burst out laughing: I looked like a clown. The two of them joined in the laughter, and on this jovial note, I was shown into the bedroom, and for the first time since I had lost my mother, I lay my head on a real pillow and covered my body with real bedding.

The room was in darkness and from the kitchen came the sounds of conversation, but my cousins were speaking in what must have been Jewish.

What are they saying? I wondered. They're probably talking about me.

My eyes closed and sleep came quickly, and when I awoke

early the next morning I found the two of them sleeping on either side of me.

I felt ashamed, deeply ashamed, for beneath me everything was wet with urine.

I wanted to run, to escape, not to face them, but I could hardly move without waking them. If only I had wings, I now thought, I would fly out the window.

Slowly, meticulously, I managed to leave the bed and quietly got dressed. On tiptoe I made my way down the stairs and then to the street. I turned and ran until I came to an open-air market where merchants were assembling their stalls.

On the horizon the sun was rising, and all about me the city was waking and beginning its day's work. I stared at the people and the buildings; I recognized one of the streets:

Suddenly it was winter and the city lay covered in snow. My mother, carrying a few bundles, kept repeating to me, "Hold on to me, Jankele." At the intersection were German soldiers with machine guns.

"Move on!" they yelled at us.

"Hold on to me, Jankele," pleaded my mother again.

A large building in front of me seemed to rotate now, the sun glared and moved in front of my eyes. The people seemed to be walking backwards, but instead of features they had blank faces like potatoes.

"Where is my mother?" I called out in a loud voice. "I held on to her, where is she now?"

People gathered around me and stared. I wanted to escape, I wanted to run, but a pain in my knees prevented me, and although I tried, I couldn't even walk. A fever rushed through my body and without warning I vomited and splattered the clean sidewalk with pieces of gefilte fish and fragments of the once sweet chicken soup with lima beans.

For several days I stayed in bed. A doctor with large bulging eyes hovered above me. Endless glasses filled with tea and lemon, whispers from the other room, all in that strange language, Jewish, and the room itself seemed to be turning this way and that way, as if the building was floating on a stormy sea.

As soon as I was well again, Cousin Fela led me to register. We climbed countless steps and on the third floor of a shabby structure, partly destroyed by bombs, we entered a room. An assortment of people of various ages was there. Some sat patiently waiting, others paced the floor back and forth. Some talked to others, some stared into space. They were all Jews.

How sickly they look, I thought. An old woman smiled at me, disclosing her rotten teeth. I stared coldly at her. Her smile broadened and she now held up a candy for me to take. I turned my head from her and thought, Jewish swindler, I wonder what she wants?

We sat and waited and now and then a young girl would open the door and call, "Next!"

The walls of this outer office were covered with names and sometimes greetings or messages. Some were in Jewish, and those I could not read.

"Moishe Zigleboim was here," read one; "Ania Meilman," was another; "Szmil Zaifman was here and left for Lodz."

My eyes scanned the four walls until I became dizzy, but I could not find the name Kuperblum, or Moishe Chuen.

"Why don't you write your name?" asked Fela.

"No!" I replied sharply.

"Next!" called the girl, and Fela pulled me by the sleeve. We entered a very small office where a short man wearing glasses told us to sit down.

A conversation followed between this man and Fela, but since they spoke in Jewish I couldn't understand what was being said. They're talking about me, I thought.

Licking his pen, the man began by asking, "What is your name? Where were you born? When were you born? Your father's name . . ."

He shot one question after the other, stopping only to ink the pen. When I had finished recounting my entire experience, giving dates, names, and places, the inquirer behind the desk sighed and then showed particular interest in Mr. Sidlo.

"You say he threatened you with a gun?" and he looked at me through his thick glasses. "We can have him arrested for that," he said, and began making a note on another piece of paper.

I jumped up and screamed, "No! I don't want harm to come to him."

The man took off his glasses, and wiping them with his handkerchief, said, "But that peasant threatened to kill you! Why do you object to his arrest?" He put the glasses on again and leaned towards me. "We could have him in jail," and now he smiled.

"No!" I shouted again. "You must not harm him."

"Why not?" he asked, his face serious now.

"Because," I began, "I don't want him to think I informed on him."

The man threw a glance in Fela's direction, then once again turned to me. "Why are you concerned what he thinks?"

"I don't want him to think badly of me."

Again the two of them spoke in Jewish and soon we were on our way out. As we entered the outer office, Cousin Fela once more suggested I write my name on the wall.

"You never know," she said, "someone might find you this way."

"Let's go!" I said, and pulling her towards the door, I ran down the three sets of stairs, leaving her behind calling after me.

"Jankele, wait, wait for me!"

I heard her but I didn't stop or slow down. I wanted to be far away from the man with the thick glasses, the strange faces of the people waiting, and the white wall with the assortment of unfamiliar names.

My days were now spent going shopping with Fela or sitting in the barber shop watching Cousin Chaim cut hair and amuse his clients with stories and jokes, and sometimes I would walk the streets and study faces, hoping and praying that one of them, any one of them, would eventually turn out to be my mother, my father, my Uncle Moishe, or anyone at all from my family.

When I met with no success, a new thought presented itself: I will be the one to capture Hitler. For several days I walked the streets looking for a monstrous little man with a small moustache. The idea was most appealing. It's possible that he's hiding here in Lublin, I told myself. Everything is possible.

At night I lay awake and began to imagine the attention I would receive should I succeed in capturing him. I followed several suspects, but they turned out to be ordinary people who couldn't even speak German. However, I did not give up hope. I'll find him, I thought. I'll be the one to recognize him!

One morning I went to the old market and sold the Belgian Army coat. That same evening my cousins, in rather halting sentences, their eyes staring at the floor, attempted to tell me that perhaps it would be better if they placed me in an orphanage.

"Don't think we don't want you, Jankele," said Cousin Chaim. "You can stay here if you wish, but we're thinking of you. It's going to be very lonely without you. We'll miss you terribly but at least we'll know we've done the best for you."

"There'll be other boys and girls just like you," said Cousin Fela, trying to force a smile. "They'll send you to school. You'll have a bed of your own. Here the place is so small, so crowded."

"You'll come to visit us often, Jankele," consoled Chaim.

"And we'll come visit you too," added his wife. "Believe us, we love you as if you were our own, but we know it will be better for you there."

The next day, Cousin Fela led me to a structure situated on a rather elegant-looking street, and there, on the second floor in an office, we were told to wait. Behind a desk sat a girl with long black hair. She wore a white blouse and around her neck was a dainty gold chain at the end of which hung a small Star of David.

I stared at the little star and now saw my mother in Warsaw sewing armbands with blue Stars of David upon them.

"He'll not do," I heard a woman say. My Cousin Fela was now being addressed by a huge woman with short-cropped hair, dressed in a white smock and white shoes. As she talked she swayed from side to side.

"What can I do?" I heard Fela plead.

"We cannot admit this boy in this condition." She now approached me closer and looked at me with disdain. "Look at him," she shouted. "He needs a good bath, a change of clothes, and his feet, they're caked with dirt, and no shoes . . ." She touched my hair. "He's probably infested with lice."

"That's why I'm bringing him here to you, so you can take good care of him. I have no facilities."

"My good woman, we cannot allow someone who is a carrier of lice and dirt to mix with the many other children we have here."

Fela became angry. "Are you telling me that the children you have here came out of the forests, the attics, and the death camps all dressed in white shirts with clean fingernails? This boy is an orphan like the others, he needs your help."

The big woman hardly blinked. "The others have no one, this boy has you!"

That evening while Fela scrubbed my body with a stiff brush trying to loosen the dirt, I kept crying, "Please don't send me there."

"Don't worry, they'll be kind to you," consoled my cousin, and submerged my head in the basin of hot water.

In the morning I said good-bye to Cousin Chaim and once again Fela led me to the office of The House for Children. Once again we waited, and again the same huge woman dressed in white appeared and now examined my hair, asked to see my hands, and looked disapprovingly at my bare feet.

"Still dirty," she commented.

"I tried my best," Fela defended herself.

The woman touched the white shirt I was wearing. "Isn't it too large for him?" she asked acidly.

"It's my husband's, but it's clean," replied Fela.

"Very well," said the woman, "he'll do." Then directing herself to me, she ordered, "Say good-bye and follow me."

I looked up to Cousin Fela. "Jankele," she began, "believe me, we're doing this for you. You don't know how much we'll miss having you with us, but it's really best for you." I tried to smile and nodded my head. She embraced me. "You'll come to visit us, won't you?" And releasing me, she turned towards the steps to walk home.

"Come!" ordered the woman. I obeyed.

From the other end of the hallway came an onrushing group of well-dressed boys and girls, yelling, laughing, and shouting. I was afraid of them. Quickly I turned, wishing I could run back to Fela, but she was not to be seen.

On the street below, a colorful parade was passing. Soldiers carrying flags, horsemen with swords, soldiers in tanks, and others on foot, marching in unison, their heads high, their uniforms gleaming and reflecting in the sunlight. A large brass band came into view playing. A young boy about my own age dressed in a soldier's uniform walked behind drumming. The sidewalks were lined with people cheering and some even threw flowers, and from the balconies and windows came applause. Streamers, flags, and huge pictures decorated the street and buildings. Most of the pictures I did not recognize, but one was well known to me: that of Joseph Stalin. A gigantic portrait of him hung on a wall opposite the window from which I was looking out. His face stared directly at me, his eyes so full of understanding, so honest, his face smiling.

The dormitory was deserted, for the others had decided to watch the parade from the streets. I alone stayed behind.

Although by that time I had been there for several days, I still felt shy, distant, and afraid of the other boys and girls. They seemed to look at me with suspicion and as time passed it seemed to worsen rather than improve. The other boys were constantly playing football, and because I didn't know how to play, I declined the first few invitations; and soon I was never asked again. Instead, I would go wondering through the streets of Lublin looking at faces. Looking, always looking.

They sang songs, laughed, played games, and could speak Jewish at will, while I sat at the corner of my bunk bed and simply observed and felt I didn't belong.

Perhaps I should escape, I thought.

Where will you go? asked one of my voices.

If only I had an accordion, I'd go into the streets and play and sing and make my way somehow.

In a moment of fantasy I would imagine myself playing an accordion in the street, and in a loud voice singing, "The night is dark . . ." People would line the streets and balconies, and as at the parade, throw flowers and applaud.

In store windows I saw accordions, and some days I would stand looking at them for hours and dream.

In the evening while the others congregated to play ping-pong or chess or tell stories, I sat at the window and looked out at the portrait of Stalin facing me from across the street.

One evening a voice within me said softly, He won the war, he loves Jews. If only he knew your torment, he would send you an accordion.

I'll write him a letter, I answered. I'll write Stalin a letter!

Armed with paper and pencil, I wrote a long and detailed letter to Stalin explaining to him who I was and why I wanted an accordion. The next day I dropped it into a mailbox, then returned to the window in the dormitory to wait for my accordion.

While I sat and waited, the others went on excursions, played football, and played practical jokes on each other, especially at night. The boys' long dormitory with two rows of double bunk beds would come to life when the huge woman dressed in white, who turned out to be the Mother, called, "Lights out!"

Using flashlights, several boys would approach a sleeping victim, and while others watched from the distance, they would place pieces of paper between his toes and fingers, and then with a match light the papers. This was called "Bicycle" because, once the flames reached the flesh, the victim would move his arms and legs as if he was bicycling.

On another night, parts of a victim's body would be painted with bright colors. The practice was usually to paint the penis and face. One night the painting group invaded the girls' dormitory and painted all the girls' faces. The next day when the girls awoke, upon seeing each other, they laughed and squealed.

The following night, some of the girls entered our room, and when the bell rang the next morning and we tried to jump into our trousers, we found the pant legs had been sewn up.

In turn, the boys invaded the girls' room again, and this time tied strings to their bed blankets. All these strings were tied to one master cord, and then at an appointed time the cord was pulled, yanking off all the blankets and leaving the girls exposed and screaming with fright.

One boy was known as the "horse," and was older than many of us. He constantly talked about his penis, and at night we could hear his bed screeching as he masturbated. Once, a thin but strong string was tied to his penis, and the other end to the dormitory door. When early the next morning the Mother opened the door to wake us, the "horse" jumped and screamed in agony, while the plotters broke out in peals of laughter. However, the best-planned and most visually interesting practical joke was called, "The Destruction of Stalingrad," and this was accomplished by removing the bedboards from under the mattresses. When the victims jumped into bed for the night, they fell through onto the floor, or into a sleeping victim below.

On one particular evening, the whole dormitory was destroyed in this manner, with pillows and blankets flying through the room. "The Destruction of Stalingrad," someone shouted, and now the beds themselves fell apart. Someone tore a pillow and feathers began to fly around the room. Soon other pillows were torn and feathers clouded our vision like a mist or fog in the early morning. I could see no one, but heard a voice shouting, "The Destruction of Stalingrad!"

Days and weeks went by and every night another prank was played on someone. I was afraid of falling asleep because something might be done to me, and as a result I resisted sleep for as long as I could. But to my surprise I was completely ignored at night, as much as during the day.

I felt like an island, worse, a shadow, a ghost, or perhaps even less than that. Perhaps I don't exist! I once thought. Perhaps I'm only a memory in someone's mind. In time, however, I realized they were aware of me.

"How come you can't speak Jewish?" asked a dark-haired boy with sturdy bow-legs. His name was Motel, and I had heard he had survived as a partisan in the Lithuanian forests, and that he had killed several Germans.

"I forgot it," I answered honestly.

Motel eyed me sharply with his very black, piercing eyes, and said, "Perhaps you never knew how to speak it."

"But I did speak it once," I pleaded.

"Tell that story to your grandmother," shot back Motel. The others, too, began asking questions. "Are you sure you're a Jew?" asked a tall boy with glasses. He had a large stamp collection.

"Of course I'm Jewish," I answered. "Don't you believe me?"

"Well, you're different. You don't act like the rest of us."

At night I could hear them whispering about me, and during the day they would point at me from the distance. A small boy nicknamed me Christ, and in no time at all, everyone called me by that name.

"You're a spy!" accused one emaciated boy with almond-shaped eyes. "You're a Polish spy!"

While sitting at the window and looking out at the picture of Stalin, a thought presented itself to me. Perhaps they're right. Perhaps I'm not Jewish. Perhaps the reason I survived was that I am in reality a Christian!

Almost daily I remained alone at the window, and then one day I noticed another boy looking out a second window. We looked at each other without saying a word, but finally I walked over to him and asked, "You're new here?"

"I was brought here yesterday," he replied in a Polish similar to my own.

"Why didn't you go to play football?" I asked. The boy looked out the window and then simply shrugged his shoulders.

His name was Mietek and the story of how he survived was very similar to my own, except for the fact that his parents had paid a large sum of money to the farmers who kept him as their son.

Mietek and I became close friends, and soon I discovered that we had many things in common, one of which was that Mietek, like myself, could not speak one word of Jewish. The others were suspicious of him as well, and nicknamed him The Holy Ghost.

"There goes Christ and The Holy Ghost," they would say when they saw us together.

For hours we would stand looking at movie posters, examining every photo on display. We looked at monuments and sat in the parks and exchanged experiences.

"I'll tell you a secret," said Mietek one day. I listened with interest. "I don't like the orphanage," he began. "I don't like the others, all those Jews!"

"Neither do I," I confessed. I was jubilant, for now I had someone who could share my feelings.

"You know something else?" remarked Mietek, and now looked around to make sure no one was about. "I still believe in Jesus Christ."

"So do I," I whispered. And then I added, "When the lights go out I still pray to Jesus and make the sign of the cross."

"Me too," he said, sounding very pleased.

One day he went off by himself, and in the evening when he returned, he took me aside, "It's all arranged, we can escape from here."

"Where to?" I inquired.

"I went to church today and talked to this priest. I told him about you and he wants to meet you too. He said he can baptize us and then arrange to have us sent to some farm where no one will ever find us."

I was excited and asked, "When do we go?"

"Whenever you like," answered my friend.

"Let's go tonight then," I said.

Mietek hesitated, "The church is probably closed by now, why not first thing tomorrow morning, after breakfast? When the others leave to play football, we'll pack our things and sneak out."

I agreed to the plan, and when the lights went out and the "horse's" bed began to squeak, I kneeled in my bed and thanked Jesus Christ for not abandoning me. At first I couldn't sleep, for I was too excited, and also, I waited for the night's practical joke to take place. However, except for a few whispers and isolated chuckles, it was unusually quiet. My eyes closed and sleep came easily and I began to dream.

The priest was now baptizing me, and as he sprinkled the holy water upon me, the congregated people began to laugh. I turned, and to my surprise, now saw my grandfather the baker, Moishe, my mother, Shepsel, and even my little brother Josel.

Why are they here in a church? I wondered in my dream. And why are they laughing?

I now looked down and saw the cause for their laughter. From the waist down I was naked. My face twisted with shame, I now turned towards the kindly priest.

"Nothing to worry about, my son," he said, patting my head. "Even that can be corrected." And from a gold bowl he brought out a piece of skin, and bending down he slipped it onto my penis, making it look uncircumcised. "Now he's a Christian," whispered the priest to the congregation.

"He's a Jew," whispered another voice.

I opened my eyes and saw flashlights shining at me from the dark. My body was uncovered and dozens of faces peered at my exposed penis.

"He's a Jew!" repeated the voice, and now I recognized it as being Motel's, the partisan.

Those sneaky lice-ridden Jews! I thought. I'll show them that they can't do this to me. With their own they can get away with it, but not with a Christian.

I jumped up and began swinging my arms. They ran, I followed in the dark and stumbled. The flashlights were now out and everything was quiet, but inside me an anger raged. I went to the door and flicked on the electric light, then I walked over to Motel's bed.

"It was you." Motel's eyes were shut, feigning sleep. "Don't pretend to be asleep." Motel began to snore. "I know you're not asleep, you dirty J . . ." and I caught myself, but it was too late. Motel's eyes opened wide; a smile crossed his face and he sat up, then got up facing me.

I'll beat him up, I thought. In a flash I remembered running home from school, chased by a Christian boy. Now Motel was the running Jew, and I, the strong, fearless Pole.

"What did you say?" asked Motel, his eyes cutting through me like sharp knives.

I didn't answer him. I don't want to kill him, I thought, just frighten him.

"You called me a name," Motel continued. I looked about me and now the whole dormitory was gathered around us, watching.

"I'll call you anything I like," I said firmly.

Motel smiled a sinister smile, and then said, "No! No one will ever call me names like that again. No one!" And suddenly I felt a blow in my stomach, another in the head. I was now on the floor. There was yelling and screaming.

"Enough!" someone ordered.

My head turned and again I was being chased by the same Christian boy. I now fell and hit the floor and quietly prayed, "Jesus Christ, help me."

When I awoke the next morning, the entire dormitory was deserted. My pillow was covered with blood. I sat up and studied my bruised face in a small mirror. The right eye was half closed and swellings covered most of my face. My entire body ached, especially my stomach. I began to dress. The door opened and Mietek entered.

He came over to the bed and stared at me, then finally said, "I'm all ready to go, are you?" I nodded my head. He reached under the bed and held up a small bundle of his belongings. "Aren't you taking your things with you?" he asked.

"No," I answered, and using the back stairs, we quietly walked out onto the street. The day was warm and sunny.

"Does it hurt?" asked my friend when we had walked some

distance.

"No!"

Again we were silent for a while and then he said, "I'm sorry I couldn't help you." Once again we fell into a silence, but continued to walk. We crossed a street, turned a corner, passed a statue, and now Mietek stopped to tie one of his shoelaces.

I looked about and recognized the building in front of us. It was the same building where Fela had taken me to register. People were coming out, others were entering. Some greeted each other and exchanged words in Jewish. I studied their faces and tried to understand what they were saying.

"Come," said Mietek, and we continued to walk, and soon a beautiful large church with many steps stood in front of us. Mietek winked at me and we began ascending the stairs. From above came the sound of the bells, and as we came closer to the door, the bells seemed to get louder, but when they were very loud, they suddenly stopped, and so did I. "Come," said Mietek, pulling me by my sleeve. I remained standing and silent. "What's the matter?" asked Mietek. "You haven't changed your mind, have you?"

"It's too sudden," I finally said. "Let's go back and talk it over."

"We did talk it over," his voice was rising in anger. "Are you sure you know what you want?" He waited for me to say something. But I simply stood motionless. "I'm going in," he threatened. "If you want to come, you can follow me."

He picked up his bundle, turned from me, and quietly walked up to the open door. There he stopped, turned, and looked at me. He waited for a moment, then motioned for me to follow. I remained standing. He turned, and in no time at all, disappeared through the dark doorway. I waited for him to come out, but my wait was in vain.

Slowly I walked down the steps and for a while waited again on the sidewalk. "Mietek!" I yelled several times. I started to walk, turning back often in the hope that Mietek would be running behind me, but soon the church and the street faded from view. I continued to walk, and now saw a man with a beard coming toward me.

Could it be my grandfather? I asked myself.

The man was wearing a turban. Instead of a suit, he was wrapped in what seemed to be a bed sheet. His arms outstretched towards passers-by, he kept repeating the same phrase in a strange language. His eyes looked frightened, his body frail and undernourished, and the expression on his face was that of a desperate man. Hardly anyone looked at him except for a few children who were following and laughing at him.

"Who is he?" I asked one of them.

"An Indian," answered a boy.

"What is he saying?" I asked.

"No one knows," answered the same boy. "He's been walking around like this for weeks. He's lost and nobody understands what he's saying."

I turned and began to run. I didn't know where I was going but I was afraid I'd be late. I ran across the street, into a building and then along steps, higher and higher. Panting, I fell into a room. The room was filled with waiting people and they looked up at me and smiled as if they had been expecting me.

It was the same waiting room on the third floor whose walls were covered with names. In the corner of the room sat a young woman with a crying baby in her arms. She tried to pacify the child with a nipple, but the infant continued to cry. Softly the woman began to hum a lullaby. The melody was familiar, it was the same song my mother sang to me, "Vio, Vio, little horses."

Perhaps she knows where my mother is. Perhaps my mother taught her the song! I'll have to find my mother, my father.

But where? laughed one of my teasing voices. Everyone is dead, they're all dead. You have to face that.

In a small space on the wall a man was writing his name, and when he finished, I asked to borrow his pencil. I searched for a clear spot, and when I found it, and before I began to write, I turned and saw a room full of people staring at me. Blushing I turned back and carefully wrote the following: "Jankele Kuperblum is alive."

Perhaps someone will find me now, I thought on the way back to the orphanage. Perhaps my mother is alive, perhaps she escaped and hid somewhere . . . and Moishe, he's probably looking for me . . . and my father, he's no doubt in the army still too busy . . . but soon they'll release him and he'll find my name on the wall. I began to skip and now looked up at the bright, shining sun.

It's possible, I told myself. Everything is possible.